More than Conquerors

The Churches and the Early Christians in the Roman Empire from Jerusalem to Chalcedon

— NIGEL SCOTLAND —

Sacristy
Press

Sacristy Press
PO Box 612, Durham, DH1 9HT

www.sacristy.co.uk

First published in 2026 by Sacristy Press, Durham

Copyright © Nigel Scotland 2026
The moral rights of the author have been asserted.

All rights reserved, no part of this publication may be reproduced or transmitted in any form or by any means, electronic, mechanical photocopying, documentary, film or in any other format without prior written permission of the publisher.

Scripture quotations, unless otherwise stated, are from the New Revised Standard Version Bible: Anglicized Edition, copyright © 1989, 1995 National Council of the Churches of Christ in the United States of America. Used by permission. All rights reserved worldwide.

Every reasonable effort has been made to trace the copyright holders of material reproduced in this book, but if any have been inadvertently overlooked the publisher would be glad to hear from them.

Sacristy Limited, registered in England & Wales, number 7565667

British Library Cataloguing-in-Publication Data
A catalogue record for the book is available from the British Library

ISBN 978-1-78959-391-4

"I wish I had had this 'vade mecum' when I was studying Early Church history years ago! Brimming with interest and insight, Dr Scotland's latest book is a joy to read and a wonderful tool for those starting out in Christian ministry."

George, Lord Carey of Clifton
Archbishop of Canterbury, 1991–2002

"In engagingly accessible prose, Nigel Scotland brings the thinking of the early Church to life, and helps us to understand better this vital period of the Church's change and growth."

Peter Scott
University of Manchester

"Many Christians know very little about the important stages in the early development of the Church's faith. Nigel Scotland helps to address this deficit, as he draws on his many years as a popular teacher of church history in a variety of contexts to provide this accessible account of the first four and a half centuries of Christianity in the Roman Empire. Taking the source documents at face value, he builds a comprehensive narrative that highlights the Church's practices, internal struggles and mission activities in various periods and settings and includes helpful timelines. Scotland ensures readers will know the essentials about and have a solid basis for further exploration of events, dates, key figures, controversies, councils and creeds in the remarkable expansion of the Christian movement in its most formative stage."

Andrew T. Lincoln
Emeritus Professor of New Testament, University of Gloucestershire

"Nigel Scotland's books are a great gift for the church – for leaders, students, ordinands and anyone who is keen to discover more of the rich tapestry of Christian thought. He manages to distil enormous amounts of history and debate into thoughtful and readable summaries which are both illuminating and encouraging. Written by someone who is both an academic and an active minister, Nigel's work is not just informative but brings compassion and perspective to many contemporary issues the Church faces today."

Tom Yacomeni
Rector of All Saints Weston Bath with North Stoke and Langridge

Contents

Preface... v

Chapter 1. Born of the Holy Spirit: The beginnings of the
  Christian Church 1
Chapter 2. Into all the world: Compassionate evangelism and the
  expansion of early Christianity in the Roman Empire 17
Chapter 3. The blood of the martyrs: Triumphant Christians in
  times of persecution 34
Chapter 4. Uniting a divided house: Persuading Novatians and
  Donatists to be more lenient with those who denied the Faith ... 51
Chapter 5. Deliverance from evil within: Overcoming
  Gnosticism within the Church 70
Chapter 6. On solid ground: A faith founded on apostolic
  teaching and the formation of the New Testament 87
Chapter 7. Faith in a tri-personal God: Monarchianism and
  explanations of God as a Trinity 102
Chapter 8. Guided by biblical scholars and theologians:
  Tertullian, Cyprian, Clement and Origen 116
Chapter 9. The Emperor is converted! Constantine and the
  Christianization of the Empire 148
Chapter 10. Athanasius versus the world: The defeat of Arianism
  and the establishment of the Nicaean faith that Jesus is fully
  God 160
Chapter 11. Wise men from the East: The Cappadocian Fathers
  and their caring Trinitarian faith and spirituality 174
Chapter 12. From Constantinople to Chalcedon: The struggle to
  assert that Jesus is both fully God and fully human 190
Chapter 13. The call of the desert: Monastic communities,
  hospitality, faith and scholarship 200

Chapter 14. The furthest corner of the Empire: Christianity in
 Britain and Ireland..216
Chapter 15. More than conquerors: Churches and the Christians
 in the mid-fifth century....................................232

Bibliography 255
Timelines 260
Index 263

To my lovely wife Anne

Preface

This is a book which is important for anyone who is serious about their Christian faith. Beginning with the birth of the Church on the Day of Pentecost, it carries the story through to the hugely important Council of Chalcedon. Taking place in 451, it decided that the New Testament Gospels and letters teach that Jesus was and is both fully God and fully human. Since that time this has been a core doctrine endorsed and upheld by all mainline Christian denominations and orthodox churches. The Church in the days of the apostles could perhaps be compared to a small seed but which by 451 had become a fully developed tree. During this period the Church had established a basic organizational structure and developed a pattern of leadership. Successive Church councils decided which books should be included in the New Testament, on the grounds that they could be traced back to the circle of the apostles and were in widespread use in the Church. Worship also became progressively formalized. Jesus' two commandments to make and baptize disciples and share Communion with the bread and wine as a means of remembering his presence remained its essential focus. Over time both sacraments developed with rituals, instructions and music. This process was intensified after Christianity was made the privileged religion of the Roman Empire following the conversion of the Emperor Constantine in 312 and further established when it became the official religion under the Emperor Theodosius in 381. From the second to the fourth century, Christians gradually came to understand that God is one tri-personal being and the Father and the Son are not two separate individuals. From this basis, the Church came to articulate the doctrine of the Trinity. eventually expressing it in three great statements of faith—the *Apostles' Creed*, the *Nicene Creed* and the *Athanasian Creed*.

Throughout the first five centuries, Christians and their churches faced severe threats from without in the form of brutal torture and persecution at the hands of the pagan Roman Empire and from within by false teaching, most notably from the Gnostics. After the Emperor Constantine's conversion, persecution was brought to an end, but new challenges began. In particular, the Church became a privileged institution and instead of continuing to offer a servant ministry, as Jesus had instructed, it became in many places a powerful, wealthy and dominant institution. The challenge the early Christians faced throughout the first five centuries was not only how to stand by the teaching of the apostolic faith but also how to live it out in a changing world.

Nigel Scotland

1

Born of the Holy Spirit: The beginnings of the Christian Church

The birth of the Christian Church took place in the city of Jerusalem during the Jewish Feast of Passover. On the morning of the day of Pentecost, the disciples and other followers of Jesus were sitting together in a house.[1] Suddenly they experienced what seemed like a rushing wind and they spoke in new languages and saw what looked like tongues of fire resting on each of them. The outburst of praise was evidently very loud since large numbers of "God-fearing Jews" who had come from all over the Roman Empire for the week-long feast were captivated by it.[2] Puzzlingly they heard them speaking in their own languages! Was the miracle that the disciples were speaking new languages that they had never learned or was it that the Passover visitors were hearing what was being said in their mother tongues? Elsewhere in the New Testament, speaking in tongues appears to have been in unknown languages[3] but was always expected to be under the speakers' control.

There followed what seemed like an overdose of partying with many in the crowd overwhelmed with joy and the presence of God. Peter stood up and, with the eleven other disciples alongside, addressed the crowd in what was the first ever Christian sermon. His message was sharply focused on Jesus, his death on the cross, repentance and forgiveness.[4]

---

[1] Acts 2:2.
[2] Acts 2:5.
[3] 1 Corinthians 13:1; 14:13.
[4] Acts 2:14-36.

Peter reminded the crowd that he and the disciples were witnesses of Jesus' resurrection and ascension into heaven. When the people recognized the truth of what they were hearing, they were cut to the heart. Peter seized the moment and called out to them to repent, get baptized and receive the Holy Spirit. And so began the first day of the first Christian Church with about 3,000 men and women coming to faith.[5]

Significantly this first Christian Church was a multi-cultural gathering formed of people from across the Roman Empire and beyond. Their number included men and women from Parthia, Mesopotamia, Cappadocia, Pontus and Asia. Much further afield, there were people from Egypt, parts of Libya, Cretans, Arabs and visitors from Rome, both Jews and converts to Judaism. It was this fact, many centuries later, that caused Nelson Mandela (1918–2013), the first Black President of South Africa, to remark that "the good news was born by our risen Messiah who chose not one race, who chose not one country, who chose not one language, who chose not one tribe, who chose all mankind".[6]

Models of the Church

As the apostles and early followers of Jesus carried the gospel across the Roman Empire, they quickly realized the vital need to establish local communities of believers with basic beliefs and a minimal organizational structure. Being Jews, the apostles were very familiar with two basic models of religious organization: the temple and the synagogue. The Jerusalem temple was a place of hierarchy, priesthood, sacrifices, liturgy and ceremonial. In contrast, the synagogues were devoid of priesthood, sacrifice and ritual. Their buildings were plain and worship was participatory in that any man over the age of 13 was able to open one of the scrolls containing the Law and the Prophets, read a passage and interpret it.

---

[5] Acts 2:41.

[6] Nelson Mandela, *Nelson Mandela and His Faith*, 10 December 2013, cited *Church Times*, 13 December 2013.

In the early days in Jerusalem, the followers of Jesus met every day in the courts of the Jerusalem temple.[7] The early-second-century church historian Hegesippus gives a brief description of Christian worship taking place in the inner court of the temple, led by James the Lord's brother.[8] On other days in the week, the Christians would have been worshipping in their homes.[9] Those Jews who lived outside the city also worshipped in their homes and possibly in their local synagogues. Some very early churches were patterned on the Jerusalem temple rather than the synagogue. Such seems to have been the case in Ethiopia, early tradition recording that Christianity was established there by Queen Candace's financial official who came to faith in Christ on his homeward journey following the Jerusalem Passover.[10]

The synagogue

As the apostles carried the gospel message away from Jerusalem and into the gentile provinces of the Empire, the synagogues became the preferred model for church organization. This was because it was the one they knew best as in almost every city and town in the Empire there were Jewish communities and synagogue worship. The origin of the synagogues is not altogether clear, but they appear to have emerged during the years when the Jews were exiled in Babylon and therefore unable to participate in the temple services. Synagogues, the word literally meaning "to come together", were places without priests, altars or sacrifices. There, people simply gathered together for praise, prayer and preaching.

Synagogues appointed elders in the plural and larger assemblies often had a presiding elder. Elders were responsible for public worship and pastoral care. It is clear from the New Testament that both women and men were entrusted with leadership roles in the churches, obvious examples being Euodia and Syntyche who "contended" for the gospel

---

[7] Acts 2:46.
[8] In Eusebius, *History of the Church* II.23.
[9] Acts 2:46; 12:12.
[10] Eusebius, *History of the Church* II.1.

with Paul,[11] and Lydia and Phoebe, the latter a deacon, both of whom led churches in their own homes.[12] Paul also mentions Chloe and Nympha with congregations in Corinth and Laodicea respectively[13] and lists seven female co-workers in Rome.[14] Women prophets played an important role[15] and were prominent in the movement started by Montanus which flourished in the later years of the second century and was still active in the fourth century.[16] Montanus shared the leadership of his first followers with two women prophets, Priscilla and Maximilla. All this indicates that women played a significant role in the leadership of the early Christian churches. Wealthier communities sometimes had full-time paid teachers who were known as Rabbis. Synagogues were self-governing and none had any authority over another. Each was answerable only to God for the way in which they handled their affairs. Synagogues also appointed deacons who took on responsibility for the money, buildings and pastoral care.

After the Jerusalem temple was destroyed by Roman armies under Titus in AD 70, its impact as a pattern for newly formed Christian churches was further diminished. Later, however, in 312, the Roman Emperor Constantine came to faith in Christ and made Christianity the privileged religion of the Empire. This included the right to construct buildings for public worship. Many of those erected tended to be more in keeping with the larger Roman public buildings rather than the plain smaller format of the synagogues.

---

[11] Philippians 4:2-3.
[12] Romans 16:1; Acts 16:14,40.
[13] See 1 Corinthians 1:11 and Colossians 4:15.
[14] Romans 16:3; 16:12; 16:13 and 16:15.
[15] Acts 21:9; 1 Corinthians 11:5.
[16] Nigel Scotland, *Christianity Outside the Box* (Eugene, OR: Wipf & Stock, 2012), Chapter 1.

Early Christian worship

The English word "worship" derives from the Anglo-Saxon word "worthship". Hence it means "to acknowledge the worth of something". So, as Ralph P. Martin put it, "to worship God is to ascribe to Him [Christ] supreme worth, for he alone is worthy".[17] In the early churches, "worship" embraced the whole of life,[18] but its central focus was the weekly gathering to honour, praise and worship God with heart, mind, soul and body. This latter understanding was indicated by the use of the Greek word *proskuneo* which can also mean to "bow down" or to "fall on one's knees".

At the beginning of the Book of Acts, Luke records that the early Christians "devoted themselves to the apostles' teaching and to fellowship, to the breaking of bread and to prayer".[19] The newly formed churches were communities that were focused and based on these activities.

The apostles' teaching
Jesus had been with his disciples for three years, instructing them from the Old Testament and teaching them from life and in parables, discussions and demonstrations about the Kingdom of God and its values. He summed up his teaching in his Sermon on the Mount, the Golden Rule "do to others as you would have them do to you", and great Commandment "to love God and neighbour". At the time of leaving his disciples, Jesus assured them that the Holy Spirit would come and call to their minds everything he had taught them.[20]

The apostles' teaching was the foundation stone of the life and worship of the early churches. They taught by word of mouth as they travelled and preached and also through their many letters. The most important of these were copied many times over, circulated and read in the early

---

[17] Ralph P. Martin, *Worship in the Early Church* (London: Marshall, Morgan & Scott, 1964), p. 10.
[18] See Romans 12:1.
[19] Acts 2:42–7.
[20] John 14:26.

churches.[21] We catch a glimpse of these two aspects in the Second Letter to the Thessalonians where the writer urged the church to hold fast to what they had been taught by "word of mouth" (oral tradition) or by "letter" (written tradition).[22] First-century Jews greatly valued tradition and anything of importance was quickly set down in writing. The four Gospels which later became an accepted part of the New Testament were based on earlier sources some of which may have been in Aramaic, the language spoken by Jesus and his disciples. By the middle of the second century, they were widely accepted as genuine apostolic writings and copied and read in all the churches.

Fellowship
The word "fellowship" (Greek *koinonia*) means "to share" or "join in". Fellowship in the early churches was focused on the relationship between Jesus and his people. The apostle John wrote at the beginning of his First Letter: "We proclaim to you what we have seen and heard, so that you also may have fellowship with us. And our fellowship is with the Father and with his Son, Jesus Christ."[23] This fellowship was often worked out in very practical and caring ways which can be seen in the early chapters of the Book of Acts and John's First Letter. In Jerusalem the believers "had everything in common" and sold property and possessions in order to give money to those in need.[24] This communal aspect may have been an experiment, since there is little evidence of anything similar in other town or city churches. Fellowship was necessarily most often home-based since there was persecution in many parts of the Roman Empire and Christians needed to keep a low profile.

The breaking of bread or Eucharist
Just as the structure and organization of the New Testament Church was strongly influenced and deeply rooted in Judaism so too was its worship. This is immediately apparent in the origin and development

---

[21] See for example Romans 1:7; Galatians 1:2; 1 Peter 1:1.
[22] 2 Thessalonians 2:15.
[23] 1 John 1:3.
[24] Acts 2:44–7; 4:32–7; 5:1–10; 1 John 3:17.

of the Eucharist or Lord's Supper. Despite the fact that Jesus called the Last Supper a "Passover", Maxwell was of the view that the Last Supper was based, at least partly, on the Kiddush.[25] This was a simple weekly meal shared by groups of men in preparation for the sabbath or a major festival. Maxwell pointed out several parallels between the Last Supper and the Kiddush. The Kiddush was always observed by a group of male friends as opposed to the Passover, which was a family occasion with women and children present. At the Passover, roasted lamb was shared and unleavened bread eaten. There is no explicit mention of either at the Last Supper. In fact, the narratives speak of ordinary bread. Several cups were used at the Passover while the Last Supper and the Kiddush both used only one cup. It should be noted, however, that Luke in his Gospel actually mentions two cups. The Kiddush was observed weekly, but the Passover was held only once a year. That said, it is clear that the early Christians broke bread frequently.[26]

Notwithstanding some of Maxwell's suggestions, the majority of New Testament scholars have come to accept the views of Joachim Jeremias that the Last Supper was indeed a Passover meal. He put forward ten reasons in support of this. First, Jesus called the Last Supper "a Passover".[27] Second, the Last Supper meal took place in Jerusalem. In the first century, Jewish law required that the Passover had to be eaten within the gates of Jerusalem.[28] Third, the Passover was required to be held at night because the Passover in Egypt took place at night.[29] Fourth, the Passover was celebrated in small groups, no larger than could feast on one lamb. Matthew and Mark both state that Jesus celebrated the Last Supper with the twelve disciples.[30] This, according to the *Mishnah*, represented the ideal number. Fifth, the Passover took place on the evening of the

---

[25] William D. Maxwell, *An Outline of Christian Worship* (Oxford: Oxford University Press, 1936), p. 6.

[26] Acts 2:46.

[27] Matthew 26:17; Mark 14:12 and Luke 22:8,15.

[28] Joachim Jeremias, *The Eucharistic Words of Jesus* (London: SCM Press, 1966), pp. 48–50.

[29] John 13:30.

[30] Matthew 26:20; Mark 14:17.

day the lambs were slaughtered in the temple. This accords well with the accounts of Matthew and Mark.[31] Sixth, the Passover required that four cups of red wine should be drunk. The *Mishnah* explicitly stated that only red wine should be used and always mixed with water. Seventh, all those who took part in the Passover were required to be ritually clean.[32] John's Gospel records that Peter and the disciples had bathed and were ritually clean.[33] Eighth, Jesus and his disciples "reclined" at the table at the Last Supper.[34] Rabbi Levi (*c*.300) said that people should recline to eat the Passover "to signify they have passed from slavery to freedom". Ninth, it is clear that Jesus and his disciples were *already* eating a meal when he took the bread and broke it. It was a supper. Tenth, the bread and wine fitted into the Passover liturgy. In particular, the words of interpretation which Jesus spoke over the bread and wine precisely followed those of the Passover ritual.

Very early on Christians began to keep the "first day of the week" or "Lord's Day" as their principal time for worship because it was then that Jesus rose from the dead[35] and shared a meal with the disciples.[36] The Eucharist or Lord's Supper became the focus of the early Christians' Sunday meetings. The atmosphere of their worship was one of joy and celebration as they "ate together with glad and sincere hearts, praising God".[37] Paul, in his First Letter to the Corinthians, written about 54, shows that Sunday had become established as the main day of worship in that city. "On the first day of every week", he wrote, "each one of you should set aside a sum of money in keeping with your income."[38] Significantly there doesn't appear to have been any requirement on the

---

[31] Matthew 26:17; Mark 14:12; Luke 22:7–8.
[32] Numbers 19:19; John 11:55; John 13:9–10.
[33] John 13:8–11.
[34] Matthew 26:20; Mark 14:18; Luke 22:14.
[35] Matthew 28:1.
[36] Mark 16:14.
[37] Acts 2:46–7.
[38] 1 Corinthians 16:2.

part of worshippers to tithe a tenth of their income.[39] The only instruction was to give generously and cheerfully.[40]

There are four accounts of the institution of the Last Supper in the New Testament. These are Matthew 26:20–30; Mark 14:22–26; Luke 22:14–23; 1 Corinthians 11:17–33. The Corinthian passage, which is the oldest, and the Lucan both seem to be working from an earlier source since both mention that there was a supper meal between the reception of the bread and the drinking of the wine. Indeed the Corinthian passage makes it clear that their Eucharists took place with a shared agape meal. On some of these occasions the behaviour was below expected standards with participants going ahead and eating some of the food they had brought to share before everyone had arrived.[41] It was often the case that the more prosperous members brought extra food to the meal so that there was plenty for the poorer people who by virtue of their longer working hours were sometimes delayed and missed out. The Eucharist or Lord's Supper as we find it in the New Testament has four main actions. These are taking and thanking; breaking and distributing; sharing and eating and drinking; and remembering and proclaiming.[42]

The action of *taking and thanking* which is found in all four accounts of the Last Supper is closely linked with blessing. In fact, Jesus' simple prayer of thanksgiving at the Last Supper[43] reflected the Jewish *berakoth* or prayer of blessing frequently said before a meal. It was a grace with which Jesus and all Jews would have been familiar: "Blessed are You, O Lord our God, King of the Universe, who brought forth bread from the earth." In a similar way, Paul reminded the Corinthians that the Communion cup also draws on the Jewish tradition; in this case the Passover. It is, he wrote, "the Cup of Blessing".[44] This was, and is, the third cup of wine which is shared at a Passover meal. Significantly it is also

---

[39] The tithe was originally a tax paid to the temple. The Jews ceased to pay after the destruction of AD 70.
[40] 2 Corinthians 9:7.
[41] 1 Corinthians 11:21–2.
[42] 1 Corinthians 11:23–6.
[43] Luke 22:19 and 1 Corinthians 11:24.
[44] 1 Corinthians 10:16 (NRSV). My emphasis.

called "the cup of redemption". It was this cup of which Jesus said, "This is my blood of the new testament [covenant]."[45] Although Paul writes of this being a cup "which we bless", there is no suggestion that this was an "epiclesis" or calling on the Holy Spirit to impact or change the substance of the bread and wine.

The *distributing and sharing* bread and drinking wine after the supper was eaten was a characteristic of the early Christian Lord's Supper.[46] It stands out clearly in Chapter 10 of Paul's First Letter to the Corinthians where he writes of "The bread that *we* break" and "the cup of blessing which we share".[47] The action of breaking linked the meal with the Last Supper where Jesus took the bread, broke it, gave it to the disciples and instructed them to do as he had done whenever they shared the Supper. The breaking of the bread symbolized the body of the Lord broken on the cross for the sins of the world. For the greater part of the first three centuries, Christian worship was in homes, and it is likely that each person present broke a piece from the loaf. This was a vivid demonstrable way for each person to make the forgiveness which comes from Jesus' death their own.

The *sharing* of bread and wine took place with each person present *eating* and then later *drinking* at the same time. It is from these two communal acts of sharing that the term "Communion" derives. Indeed it is intended to be a "*Holy* Communion" in which a spiritual bond is forged between the worshippers and the risen Christ. Since the Last Supper was a Passover meal, everyone would have had their own cups and partaken of the wine together. In the first and second centuries, there are references to the early believers taking their Passover cups to fellowship meals. The later practice of all communicants drinking from the one same cup was very probably a misunderstanding which derived from Jesus following the practice of the host at the Passover meal. This was passing his own cup to each person present who then in turn poured a little of his wine

---

[45] Ceil and Moishe Rosen, *Christ in the Passover* (Chicago, IL: Moody Press, 1978), p. 59. See also Matthew 26:28.
[46] Acts 2:42 and 46 and 20:7.
[47] 1 Corinthians 10:16.

into their own cups. Following this they would all have drunk from their own cups at the same time.[48]

The final act of *remembering and proclaiming* follows the act of distribution and sharing. While eating and drinking each of those present were invited to reflect on the meaning of the bread and wine. Just as the unleavened bread and cups of wine in the Passover meal carried the guests back to remember their predecessors' redemption from slavery in the land of Egypt, so the followers of Jesus are called to remember their redemption through the broken body and shed blood of the spotless lamb of God. In addition, just as the Passover looked forward to and proclaimed the coming of the Messiah and the end of the age so the Lord's Supper proclaims the Lord's death till he comes.

As Bradshaw and others have reminded us, the Lord's Supper continued to be in the context of a shared evening meal at least until the end of the second century.[49] It would have begun Passover style with the breaking of bread which was then followed by a shared meal and concluded, as in the Passover, with the drinking of wine. There are glimpses of this in the correspondence of Pliny the Younger (61–*c*.113), the governor of Bithynia, with the Emperor, Trajan (53–117). Pliny wrote that the Christians in his province were meeting together and eating "ordinary, harmless food".[50] Tertullian (*c*.160–*c*.220) also wrote of Christians taking the sacrament at mealtimes.[51]

Baptism
The Greek word *baptizo* can mean to plunge, wash, dip or sprinkle. The act of washing signifies the cleansing away of the guilt and sins of the believer's former ways of living. Various suggestions as to the origins of Christian baptism have been put forward. One of these was proselyte baptism which took place when those who were gentiles were received

---

[48] 1 Corinthians 11:23–5.
[49] Paul E. Bradshaw, *Eucharistic Origins* (London: SPCK, 2004), p. 22. See also Nigel Scotland, *The New Passover* (Eugene, OR: Wipf & Stock, 2016), pp. 20–7.
[50] Pliny the Younger, *Letter to the Emperor Trajan*. The Letter is generally dated *c*.AD 112.
[51] Tertullian, *Of the Crown (De Corona)* 33:3–4.

into a Jewish synagogue community. Another theory is that Christian baptism was derived from John the Baptist.

John, who was Jesus' cousin, was baptizing those wanting to repent of their past sins. It may well be that he in turn had derived his practice from the Essenes, a rigorous ascetic community of about 4,000, living close to the Dead Sea. Those wishing to join had a demanding waiting period of three years.[52] John's baptism had two main functions: it was to express repentance [53] and to prepare for the ministry of the "coming one", Jesus, who would baptize with the Holy Spirit and with fire.[54] Significantly, John's baptism also appears to have been sufficient for Jesus' disciples. Certainly there is no record of any of them receiving a baptism in Jesus' name.

The basic requirement for early Christian baptism was a penitent heart and a declaration of faith in Jesus' sacrificial death for the forgiveness of sins. In Acts 2, for example, Peter urged those in the Pentecost day crowd at Jerusalem who were "cut to the heart" by his message to "Repent and be baptized every one of you, in the name of Jesus Christ for the forgiveness of sins. And you will receive the gift of the Holy Spirit."[55] The case of the Philippian jailer was very similar in form. When he asked what he should do Paul replied, "Believe in the Lord Jesus Christ and you will be saved."[56]

Early baptisms were "in the name of Jesus Christ"[57] or "in the name of the Lord Jesus",[58] both indicating that baptism was an act of commitment to Christ. Later baptisms appear to have been administered in the name of the Trinity, following Jesus' great commission to "go and make disciples of all nations, baptizing them in the name of the Father and of the Son and of the Holy Spirit".[59] Baptism was by immersion and preferably in running water.[60] Both the Letter to the Romans and the Letter to the

---

[52] See Josephus, *Jewish Antiquities* 13:5–9; 10:4f.; 18:1.
[53] Mark 1:4.
[54] Luke 3:16.
[55] Acts 2:38.
[56] Acts 16:31.
[57] Acts 2:38; 10:48.
[58] Acts 8:16; 19:5.
[59] Matthew 28:19.
[60] Oscar Cullmann, *Early Christian Worship* (London: SCM Press, 1953), p. 31.

Colossians speak of being buried in baptism.[61] The baptism of the Ethiopian official by Philip appears to have been by immersion since it speaks of his going "down into the water" and coming "up out of the water".[62]

Baptism was held to be the way of entry into the Christian community. Together with the Lord's Supper, it stressed the union of the believer with the crucified and risen Christ. Paul made this clear in his Letter to the Romans, reminding them "that all of us who were baptized into Christ Jesus were baptized into his death" and that "just as Christ was raised from the dead through the glory of the Father, we too may live a new life".[63] Early Christians saw baptism as symbolizing the death, burial and resurrection of Jesus. Going down into the water depicted Jesus' death, the immersion under the water his burial and the coming up out of the water his resurrection. In a parallel way, the person going down into the waters of baptism was pledging to put to death their old life. Their burial under the water was their commitment to bury their old way of life altogether. Their coming up out of the water was their pledge to rise up and live the new resurrection life. For this reason, baptism in the early centuries was by full immersion under the water.

Baptism and the Holy Spirit
From a very early point, baptism in water was associated with baptism in the Holy Spirit. This was seen on the Day of Pentecost when Peter urged those who had been convicted by his message to "repent and be baptized every one of you in the name of Jesus Christ for the forgiveness of your sins. And you will receive the gift of the Holy Spirit."[64] In the early days of the first century, when a person committed their life to Christ, they were baptized very shortly afterwards. Then when they came up out of the water, those who baptized them laid their hands upon them and prayed for the gift of the Holy Spirit to fill them.

---

[61] Romans 6:4; Colossians 2:12.
[62] Acts 8:38–9.
[63] Romans 6:3–4.
[64] Acts 2:38.

Creeds, prayers and prophecy

At an early point in the first century, it is clear that the apostles made use of "brief confessions".[65] These were straightforward statements that expressed Jesus' relationship with God the Father and his work of redemption. One such example is found in the first chapter of Romans:

> His son, who was descended from David according to the flesh and was declared to be Son of God with power according to the Spirit of Holiness by resurrection from the dead, Jesus Christ our Lord.[66]

The earliest Christian declaration of faith was "Jesus is Lord", applying to Jesus a form of address normally reserved for the Emperor and thus highly subversive. It was a requirement on the part of anyone requesting baptism. Creeds served as a forcible reminder to believers of what God had done for them and were a means of expressing their praise and thanksgiving. There are no fully developed creeds embedded in the text of the New Testament, but it seems likely that early churches would have produced them as a means of clarifying the core tenets of their faith.

In the first century, as we have already noted, Christian worship was largely home-based on account of threats from both the Jewish and Roman authorities. Household worship included prayers, singing, speaking in tongues and prophecy.[67] Prayers were obviously at the heart of the early Christians' daily living. In Jerusalem the first believers prayed both in their homes[68] and in the temple.[69] Their prayers were both informal and liturgical, the most obvious example of the latter being the Lord's Prayer.

Early Christian worship sometimes concluded with a liturgical blessing such as the prayer known as the Grace, "The grace of the Lord Jesus Christ, and the love of God, and the fellowship of the Holy

---

[65] Floyd V. Filson, *A New Testament History* (London: SCM Press, 1964), p. 340.
[66] Romans 1:3–4 (NRSV).
[67] 1 Corinthians 14:26–39.
[68] Acts 12:12.
[69] Acts 2:46.

Spirit be with you all."[70] Another frequent prayer was "O Lord Come", which is the Greek translation of two Aramaic words, *marana* and *tha*, meaning "Our Lord, come".[71] Another common expression indicating a close personal relationship with the Lord was "Abba", an intimate word meaning "Father" but more akin to the English word "Dad".[72] *Amen*, meaning "yes" or "surely", was frequently spoken together by believers to signal their agreement or endorsement of spoken prayers.[73] *Amen* was also used at the end of doxologies as an ascription of praise to God.[74] Three phrases which may well have been used at the conclusion of fellowship and worship gatherings were, "The God of Peace be with you all";[75] "Greet one another with a holy kiss";[76] and "The grace of our Lord Jesus Christ be with you".[77]

At some of the churches, most notably at Ephesus, Corinth and Thessalonica, there is mention of people praying in tongues or prophesying. The emphasis was always on understanding and edification. Paul reminded the church at Corinth that to prophesy was to speak words that brought strength, courage and comfort.[78] He also urged the Christians at Thessalonica not to despise prophecies but to test them against these criteria.[79]

Singing
Singing was clearly a vital ingredient in early Christian worship. Paul commended the churches at Corinth for beginning their meetings with

---

[70] 2 Corinthians 13:14.
[71] 1 Corinthians 16:22.
[72] Romans 8:15.
[73] 1 Corinthians 14:16.
[74] See also Romans 1:25; 9:5; 11:36; 16:27; Galatians 1:5; Ephesians 3:21; Philippians 4:20.
[75] Romans 15:33.
[76] 2 Corinthians 13:12; 1 Thessalonians 5:26; 1 Peter 5:14.
[77] Revelation 22:21.
[78] 1 Corinthians 14:3.
[79] 1 Thessalonians 5:21.

a hymn.[80] He regarded singing as a means of experiencing the presence of Christ and affirming the message of the gospel. He urged the Christians at Colossae "to let the message of Christ dwell among you richly . . . through psalms, hymns and songs from the Spirit".[81] The mention here of "psalms" indicates the early links between Christian and Jewish worship, because psalms would have been sung in the synagogues and the Jerusalem temple. Paul also made reference to Jewish hymns in his letter to his friend and colleague Timothy and to the Romans.[82] Specifically Christian hymns were marked out by the fact that they were focused on Jesus and his oneness with the Father.

There are no references to any musical instruments being used in the worship of the early churches. That said, their gatherings appear to have been marked by joy and praise. Clearly, musical instruments were an accepted part of Jewish worship, and it is difficult to imagine they would not have been a significant feature in the newly forming Christian congregations.

There seems to be almost no reference in the New Testament to prepared homilies or sermons in the sense that they are understood in contemporary churches. The closest we come to this is in Paul's extended discourse to the Christian community in an upper room in Troas.[83] On that occasion, he appears to have been somewhat lacking in time-awareness as one poor unfortunate individual named Eutychus went to sleep, fell from a window ledge and was taken up for dead! Thankfully he proved to be unharmed.[84]

It was from these small worshipping groups of early Christians in Jerusalem and Judaea that the message of the gospel quickly began to spread across the Roman Empire. It is this rapid expansion that is recounted in the following chapter.

---

[80] 1 Corinthians 14:26.
[81] Colossians 3:16.
[82] 2 Timothy 2:11–13; Romans 11:33–6.
[83] Acts 20:7–12.
[84] Acts 20:12.

2

Into all the world: Compassionate evangelism and the expansion of early Christianity in the Roman Empire

The extent of the expansion

Following the birth of the church in Jerusalem, the apostles elected James the Lord's brother as their leader,[1] and the new believers who lived in the city began to form themselves into small home-based communities. Others who had come from many different countries to share in the Passover celebrations returned home spreading the news of what had happened and sharing their new-found faith in Christ. In this way, the gospel was carried into distant lands and local churches came into being.

In his record of the early Church, Luke focused on the life and worship of the Jerusalem Christians, the first gentile church at Caesarea in the home of Cornelius and more importantly the conversion of Paul (c.5–c.65), later to become the great travelling apostle. He came to faith following a powerful personal encounter with the risen Lord on the road to Damascus. He then spent time in Arabia and received the apostolic gospel through a direct personal revelation from the risen Lord.[2]

Any narration of the spread of early Christianity must begin with Luke's account of Paul's four extensive missionary journeys which laid the foundations of Christianity in the Roman Empire. Acts 13 recounts Paul's first missionary journey. Beginning in 46, he was sent out with Barnabas

---

[1] Eusebius, *History of the Church* II.1.
[2] Galatians 1:11–12 and 17–19.

by the leaders of the church in Antioch. Passing through Cyprus, they eventually reached Pisidian Antioch in Asia Minor,[3] where on one sabbath day "almost the whole city gathered to hear the word of the Lord".[4] They then travelled on through South Galatia, visiting Lystra and Iconium before returning to Antioch in Syria.[5] Paul was accompanied during this period by several different companions including Silas, Timothy and Epaphroditus. Together they developed a mission strategy of first going to the synagogues where they often found a welcome. Once they had established a community of believers, they appointed elders to lead and deacons to serve them. Paul's second missionary journey, which lasted from 49-52, took him through Lystra, Philippi, Phrygia, Thessalonica, Athens, Corinth and Macedonia.[6] Among many encouragements were Paul's very successful preaching in Berea, the coming to faith of Lydia in whose home a church was established, the conversion of the Philippian jailer and his family, and the debates with the philosophers in Athens.

The third journey began in 53 and was largely focused on Corinth where Paul was assisted by Silas, Timothy, and Aquila and Priscilla, a married couple who had come from Rome.[7] He spent an entire year in the city teaching and preaching.[8] He then devoted his time to Syria, Ephesus[9] and Macedonia,[10] ending up in Jerusalem in 57.[11] It was there while he was in the temple that some Jews from Asia created a major uproar against him for teaching "everyone everywhere against our people and our law and this place".[12] This resulted in Paul's arrest, trial and final journey to Rome which began in 59.

---

[3] Acts 13:14.
[4] Acts 13:44.
[5] See Acts 13 and 14.
[6] Acts 16.
[7] See Acts 18:23—21:14.
[8] Acts 18:1-28.
[9] Acts 19:1-41.
[10] Acts 20:1-12.
[11] Acts 21:1-26.
[12] Acts 21:27-8.

He arrived in the Imperial City "in chains"[13] in about the year 62 and was allowed to live there under guard[14] in his own rented house. People came in large numbers to visit him "from morning till evening" and he declared and explained the kingdom of God, trying to convince them about Jesus from the Law of Moses and the Prophets.[15] Both Paul and Peter, who had probably planted the first church in Rome, died in the city during the reign of the Emperor Nero (37–68) in about the year 64. The fourth-century church historian Eusebius of Caesarea recorded "that in his reign Paul was beheaded in Rome itself, and that Peter likewise was crucified".[16] Paul was not only a forthright preacher, he also frequently debated with philosophers, reasoned in synagogues, and testified to his faith in Christ before provincial governors and Roman authorities. In addition, his many letters were copied multiple times and read in hundreds of churches. They demonstrated that he was indeed a dynamic leader, gifted teacher and an able pastor. Without his life and ministry, it is doubtful whether the Christian faith would ever have had such a powerful early and lasting impact.

Other apostles and early leaders took the gospel in different directions. Andrew travelled to Scythia (modern Iran).[17] Matthew went to Ethiopia,[18] Bartholomew, also known as Nathaniel, preached in Armenia where he was martyred. Thomas carried the faith to India. Mark was said to be the first person to reach Egypt with the Christian message. There, according to Eusebius, "he preached the gospel he had himself written down and was the first to establish churches in Alexandria".[19] Philo (*c.*20 BC–AD 50), a Jewish scholar and exegete, who lived in the city, was so impressed by the rigorous faith of the Christian converts that "he wrote an account of their activities, gatherings, meals and everything about

---

[13] Acts 28:27–20.
[14] Acts 28:16.
[15] Acts 28:23–4 and 31.
[16] Eusebius, *History of the Church* II.25.1.
[17] Eusebius, *History of the Church* III.1.1.
[18] Socrates, *Ecclesiastical History* I.19.
[19] Eusebius, *History of the Church* II.14.4.

their way of living".²⁰ His teaching, which made use of allegory, came to have a significant influence on Egyptian Christianity and particularly on those in Alexandria, where Pantaenus (died *c.*190) served as Head of the Catechetical School.²¹ Alexandria, which was a flourishing port and a place of intellectual learning and culture, became a major Christian centre of theological excellence inspired by the teaching of Clement (*c.*150–*c.*215) and Origen (*c.*185–*c.*254). Their influence extended to many parts of the Eastern Mediterranean.

Rome was the centre of the Empire, the hub to which all roads were said to lead. Unsurprisingly the message of the cross and resurrection of Jesus soon spread far and wide through the diplomats, soldiers, traders and visitors who came on business to the city. By these means, the Church soon extended across the province of Italia. Christian symbols and remains dating from before the eruption of Vesuvius in 79 have been excavated in Pompeii. By the early second century, Christianity had penetrated Southern Gaul (France) possibly through Paul's disciple, Crescens.²² By 180, the coastal strip of Roman North Africa, which culturally and economically looked north to Europe, had come under Christian influence. Early North African centres of Christianity included Numidia and Carthage.

By the close of the second century, Christianity had probably arrived in Britain.²³ An English church was clearly well established by 314, in which year it sent three bishops to the Ecumenical Council of Arles.²⁴ By any standards, this was a very remarkable growth. It only really becomes comprehensible as the reasons for it are unpacked.

---

[20] Eusebius, *History of the Church* II.14.16.

[21] Eusebius, *History of the Church* V.10f.

[22] 2 Timothy 4:10.

[23] Bede, *Ecclesiastical History of the English People* I.4 gives 156 as a date when Christianity was in evidence in Britain. Some question this date, although it is known that Bede checked his sources carefully.

[24] *Council of Arles*, Canon 9 in J. Stevenson (ed.), *A New Eusebius* (London: SPCK, 1986), pp. 321–5.

The reasons for the expansion

Roman peace and Roman communications

The peace which resulted from Rome's total control of the Empire did a great deal to facilitate the spread of the gospel. The Emperor Augustus took a considerable interest in roads and made a board of senators responsible for their upkeep.[25] By 79, the Romans had even constructed 6,000 miles of well-engineered roads in Britain.[26] Roman roads were solid and straight, such that a person who had anything more than a donkey could cover 60 or 70 miles a day. Aurelius Aristides, a public orator of Smyrna, wrote in 150: "Wars have so far vanished ... A man can travel from one country to another as though it were his native land. To be a Roman citizen, nay even one of your subjects, is sufficient guarantee of personal safety."[27] More importantly, roads facilitated the swift and easy movement of troops who were able to preserve the *Pax Romana*. By the middle of the second century, Christians were discerning the hand of God in this peace. About the year 180, Irenaeus, Bishop of Lyons in Gaul, wrote: "The world has peace thanks to the Romans. Even Christians can walk without fear on the roads and travel withersoever they please."[28]

Greek language and culture

When the Romans conquered the Mediterranean area, they subsumed the last vestiges of the Greek Empire. One of the bonuses of this was that Greek remained the universal language or *lingua franca*. The result was that men and women of rank in particular, and indeed almost everyone in the Roman Empire, at least spoke some Greek. We see this well illustrated by the memorial tablets to some of "the good and the great" in the Roman city of Butrint in modern Albania. We also find it in Tacitus' comment that Licinius Mucianus, the governor of Syria, was

---

[25] Michael Green, *Evangelism in the Early Church* (Grand Rapids, MI: William B. Eerdmans, 1970), p. 15.

[26] David Starkey, *Crown and Country: A History of England through the Monarchy* (London: Harper Press, 2010), p. 9.

[27] William H. C. Frend, *The Early Church* (London: SCM Press, 1991), p. 6.

[28] Irenaeus, *Against Heresies* IV.30.3.

"quite a graceful speaker, even in Greek"![29] Although the Jews in Palestine spoke Aramaic as their first language, most of them also spoke Greek. The apostle Paul had studied in Tarsus, a city with a Greek university.[30] His letters and those of the other apostles were written in Greek. All these documents which were gradually brought together to form the New Testament[31] were in Greek. The advantage of having Greek as a universal language meant that communication was straightforward and easy. As late as 325 the Emperor Constantine addressed the Council of Nicaea in Greek.

Judaism
The Jewish faith was an important means of assisting the spread of the Christian message. Indeed, some viewed it as the greatest preparation. Origen certainly thought of it in these terms when he wrote: "The beginning of the Gospel is nothing but the whole Old Testament."[32] From Origen's statement we learn that the early Christians were clear that the Old Testament Scriptures pointed to the coming of Jesus. Indeed, at the very beginning of his ministry, Jesus had entered the synagogue at Nazareth and read Isaiah 61:1–2. He had then closed the book and said: "Today this scripture is fulfilled in your hearing."[33] On another occasion, Jesus told a crowd of unbelieving Jews that "Moses . . . wrote about me".[34]

Judaism also prepared the world for Christ's coming because in almost every Mediterranean city and town there was a community of Jewish worshippers with their synagogue and school. It has been estimated that in the second century there were twice as many more Jews outside Palestine than there were inside. The Greek geographer Strabo (*b*.63) wrote in 7; "Jews have gone into every city, and it is hard to find a place on earth which has not admitted them and come under their control."[35]

---

[29] Tacitus, *The Histories* II.80.
[30] Acts 21:37–9.
[31] Socrates, *Ecclesiastical History* I.8.
[32] Origen, *Commentary on John* 1:14.
[33] Luke 4:21.
[34] John 5:46.
[35] Strabo in Josephus, *Antiquities of the Jews* XIV.7.2.

Synagogues were recognized places where visitors could find the regular worship of "the one true God". Gentiles who had embraced the Jewish faith were also welcomed. In view of this, Brox aptly stated that Judaism became "a bridge for the Christian mission".[36]

Synagogue preaching

Michael Green wrote in his *Evangelism in the Early Church*: "The synagogue provided the seedbed for evangelism among the Jews", and again " . . . undoubtedly it was one of the most important factors in the early spread of the faith."[37] Paul's sermon in the synagogue at Antioch of Pisidia is a typical example of his mission strategy.[38] It had three main points which were aptly suited to the occasion. It began with a brief history of God's people leading to the coming of the Messiah. This was followed by the exposition of the good news of Jesus and ended with an exhortation to the hearers to embrace the forgiveness of sins available through the death and resurrection of Jesus.[39] The Acts of the Apostles records six sermons which were preached by one of the apostles. In Acts 2, we have Peter's preaching on the Day of Pentecost. In the following chapter we have his sermon at the gate called Beautiful following the healing of a crippled man.[40] Acts 4 gives the substance of Peter's address to the Jerusalem Council,[41] and Acts 10 recounts his message at a meeting in the house of Cornelius.[42] Acts 13 details Paul's long speech at Antioch,[43] and Acts 26 his defence of his faith before King Agrippa.[44] Significantly, in all of these, there is a specific mention and focus on the cross of Christ. Even in the brief mention of Philip's preaching to the Ethiopian official

---

[36] Norbert Brox, *A History of the Early Church* (London: SCM Press, 1994), p. 24.
[37] Green, *Evangelism in the Early Church*, p. 194.
[38] Acts 13:14ff.
[39] Acts 13:38–41.
[40] Acts 3:11–26.
[41] Acts 4:8–12.
[42] Acts 10:34–43.
[43] Acts 13:13–41.
[44] Acts 26:1–27.

on his way back to Ethiopia, Luke records that he told him the good news resulting from the sacrificial death of Jesus.[45] In his First Letter to the Corinthians, Paul reminded the church that he and his fellow labourers "preach Christ crucified: a stumbling block to Jews and foolishness to Gentiles, but to those whom God has called, both Jews and Greeks, Christ the power of God and the wisdom of God".[46]

The early Christians explained the cross as God self-sacrificing himself to save the human race from sin. As Paul put it in his Second Letter to the Corinthians, "God was in Christ reconciling the world to himself."[47] Again, as he explained to the Colossians, "God was pleased to have all his fullness dwell in [Christ] . . . making peace through his blood, shed on the cross."[48] In Jesus, God sacrificially substituted himself for the human race, dying the death that human sins deserve in order that those who would receive it could find forgiveness.[49]

Open-air preaching

Open-air preaching had long been a feature in Judaism, Palestine and elsewhere. So, it is no surprise that the apostles in no way restricted their preaching to the synagogues. The Acts of the Apostles recount many examples of their speaking and teaching in the open air. Peter's Jerusalem sermon on the Day of Pentecost immediately comes to mind.[50] Philip preached with great effect to the crowds in Samaria who had been astonished and attracted by his miracles.[51] Other instances of effective open-air preaching included Paul's stay in Athens where he met and debated with some of the Epicurean and Stoic philosophers at the Areopagus. His message had a mixed reception, but a few men believed.[52] At Lystra, he and Barnabas spent a "considerable time speaking for the

---

[45] Acts 8:32–5.
[46] 1 Corinthians 1:23–4.
[47] 2 Corinthians 5:19.
[48] Colossians 1:19–20.
[49] 2 Corinthians 5:21.
[50] Acts 2:14–41.
[51] Acts 8:4–8,13.
[52] Acts 17:18–28,34.

Lord who confirmed the message of his grace by enabling them to do miraculous signs and wonders".[53]

Prophetic preaching
Prophetic preaching and speaking were a recognized feature in the New Testament churches[54] and appear to have assisted in their evangelism. This was distinct from a prepared homily; it was a gift of the Spirit,[55] which was for the most part spontaneous rather than prepared beforehand. Prophecy varied in content and was exercised by both men and women alike. It could range from Agabus' prediction about a coming widespread famine,[56] to a plea to hearers to decide for Christ and be baptized.[57] Paul taught the Christian households in Corinth that the essential ingredient of prophetic preaching was that it must bring strength, encouragement and comfort to those who heard it.[58] The *Didache* and other early Christian writings of the beginning of the second century make it clear that the early Christian churches valued contributions from their prophets.[59] Prophecy remained strongly in evidence in the early Church until the late second century. The Montanist prophetic movement was no isolated outburst of enthusiasm, Eusebius recording that Melito (*d. c.*190), Bishop of Sardis, was also a prophet and that "he lived in all things in the Holy Spirit".[60] Ignatius, too, spoke under direct inspiration as a Christian prophet. In his Letter to the Romans, he reminded them that "Jesus Christ will make it clear to you that I am speaking the truth; he is a faithful mouthpiece, by which the Father's truth finds utterance ... for I am not writing now as a mere man, but I am voicing the mind of God".[61]

---

[53] Acts 14:3.
[54] 1 Corinthians 14:9,29–33; Romans 12:6; 1 Thessalonians 5:19–21.
[55] Romans 12:6.
[56] Acts 11:28; 21:10.
[57] Acts 2:38.
[58] 1 Corinthians 14:3.
[59] *Didache* 2.11.
[60] Eusebius, *History of the Church* V.24.8.
[61] Ignatius, *The Letter to the Romans* 8.

Teaching evangelism

There was no clear-cut distinction between teaching and evangelism in the early Christian churches. Both Paul in the first century and Origen in the third evangelized through teaching. In fact, Origen (c.185–253) taught Christianity in an evangelistic manner at the Catechetical School in Alexandria. Both Jews and gentiles came in order to hear him proclaim the word of God. Justin Martyr (c.100–c.165) opened a similar school in Rome in the early part of the second century where he taught both philosophy and Christianity. Among his pupils was Tatian (120–180) who became a Christian at some point between 150–165 and went on to become a prominent apologist and the author of the *Diatessaron*, a history of the life of Christ compiled from the Gospels. This mixture of teaching and evangelism seems to have been taken up by a number of other second-century converts from the ranks of the intellectuals. Among them Quadratus, Aristides, Athenagoras, Pantaenus and Clement.

Testimony and personal evangelism

Testimony was a frequent aspect of early Christian evangelism. Acts reports at least three occasions on which Paul gave his testimony. They included the defence of his commitment to Christ before Felix, Festus and King Agrippa.[62] The New Testament as a whole provides us with a number of instances of effective evangelism coming through testimony. John the Baptist brought Andrew to Christ, and Andrew brought Peter to Christ.[63] Philip, one of the seven deacons, led an important Ethiopian official to Christ on the road to Gaza. Eusebius reminds us that Dionysius the Areopagite who "was converted to the Faith by Paul, was the first appointed bishop of Athens".[64] Lydia, a dealer in purple cloth in the city of Thyatira, became "a believer in the Lord" as a result of talking with Paul and his companions.[65] The Philippian jailer and all his household were led to faith in Christ by the witness and testimony of Paul and

---

[62] Acts 24:10–27; 25:1–12; 26:1–32.
[63] John 1:35–42.
[64] Eusebius, *History of the Church* IV.23.
[65] Acts 16:14–15.

Silas.[66] Onesimus became a Christian as a result of conversation he had when visiting Paul during his imprisonment in Rome.[67] The philosopher and teacher Pantaenus (120–200) was influential in bringing Clement of Alexandria to faith. Augustine's (354–430) journey to faith began as he discussed Christianity with his friend Alypius. But it was the voice of a child coming from over a garden wall, "Pick it up and read", that proved to be the decisive moment. The words caused him to locate a Bible and as he read Paul's Letter to the Romans, he felt himself flooded with the presence of God and knew himself to be converted. He wrote of it as follows:

> I seized, opened, and in silence read that section, on which my eyes first fell: not in rioting and drunkenness, not in chambering and wantonness, not in strife and envying; but put on the Lord Jesus Christ, and make no provision for the flesh, in concupiscence. No further would I read; nor needed I; for instantly at the end of this sentence, by a light as it were of serenity infused into my hearing. All the darkness vanished away.[68]

Use of the home

Another vital feature of early Christian evangelism was the use of the home. In fact, it is clear that early Christianity was a home-based religion. Jesus delighted in the home and visiting people in their houses. He celebrated the Passover at which he instituted the Lord's Supper in a house.[69] When he rose from the dead he appeared to the disciples in a house.[70] The power of the Holy Spirit came on the disciples in a house on the Day of Pentecost.[71] There are many references in the New Testament to churches being established in people's homes. Luke reported that day after day the first Christians in Jerusalem were eating and praising God

---

[66] Acts 16:29–33.
[67] Philemon 10 and 16.
[68] Augustine, *Confessions* VIII.29.
[69] Matthew 26:18; Mark 14:14–15; Luke 22:7–38.
[70] John 20:19.
[71] Acts 2:2.

together in their homes.[72] During Paul and Silas' visit to Philippi, Lydia, a dealer in purple cloth, came to faith in Jesus and she and all the people of her house were baptized.[73] Following this, a church was formed in her home.[74] Interestingly, when the Philippian jailer came to faith in Christ he and all his household were baptized.[75] Events like this must have happened hundreds of times over across the Roman Empire. Even in Paul's lifetime, there is record of home-based churches in Corinth,[76] Laodicea[77] and Colossae.[78] Paul's Letter to the Romans ends with a list of greetings from more than 20 Christian leaders in the city, some of whom would have pastored churches which met in their own homes.[79] Among those Paul greeted were two women, Tryphena and Tryphosa, and Priscilla and Aquila, a married couple.[80] Eusebius recorded that by the mid-third century the church in Rome consisted of more than 40 home-based congregations.[81]

Other religions had their temples and the Jews had their synagogues, but during the first three centuries the great majority of Christians continued to meet for worship in their homes. This of course was largely on account of their being persecuted for their faith. The home was central to Jewish culture and provided a secure and relaxed environment in which to share and talk. Archaeological evidence suggests that early Christians may have decorated their homes in ways that might have attracted comment and led to opportunities for witness. Examples of this can be seen in the Roman villas at Hinton St Mary, Lullingstone and Corinium (Cirencester) in Britain. Recent excavations of Paquius Proculus' house in Pompeii have unearthed a Christian palindrome and

---

[72] Acts 2:46–7; 12:12.
[73] Acts 16:12–15.
[74] Acts 16:40.
[75] Acts 16:33.
[76] Acts 18:7; 1 Corinthians 16:19.
[77] Colossians 4:15.
[78] Philemon 1 and 2.
[79] See Romans 16.
[80] Romans 16:3–12.
[81] Eusebius, *History of the Church* VI.43.8.

rich mosaics including images of the fish, an early symbol of the Christian faith.[82]

Visiting and charitable care for the poor and needy

Jesus had taught the disciples that visiting was a priority and had organized them into pairs,[83] telling them to go and share the message of the kingdom from house to house. In his parable of the Sheep and the Goats, Jesus taught that visiting, especially the hungry and those in prison, was a vital aspect of his kingdom.[84] The early churches followed in his steps with some members selling goods and possessions and even in some cases fields, in order to provide for the needs of the poor.[85] Paul wrote to the Galatians of his "eager" concern for the poor.[86] Hermas, a second-century church leader in the vicinity of Rome, urged the readers of his book *The Shepherd* to "practise goodness; and from the rewards of your labours, which God gives you, give to all the needy in simplicity, not hesitating as to whom you are to give or not to give. Give to all, for God wishes His gifts to be shared among all."[87] Tertullian of Carthage described in his *Apology* how Christians contributed money to the church to feed the hungry, bury the dead and support those in any kind of need. At the time when Cornelius was Bishop of Rome, the churches in the city provided for the needs of 1,500 widows and distressed persons.[88] Dionysius, Bishop of Corinth (*d*.171), wrote a *Letter to the Romans* in which he commended their concern for the poor:

> From the start it has been your custom to treat all Christians with unfailing kindness, and to send contributions to many churches in every city, sometimes alleviating the distress of those in need, sometimes providing for your brothers in the

---

[82] Green, *Evangelism in the Early Church*, p. 218.
[83] Mark 6:7.
[84] Matthew 25:31–46.
[85] Acts 2:45 and 4:32–7.
[86] Galatians 2:10.
[87] Hermas, *The Shepherd* II.2.
[88] Eusebius, *History of the Church* VI.43.

mines by contributions you have sent from the start. Thus, you have observed the ancestral Roman custom, which your revered Bishop Soter has not only maintained but enlarged, by generously providing abundant supplies distributed among God's people, and by encouraging with inspired words fellow-Christians who come to the city, as an affectionate father encourages his children.[89]

It comes as no surprise that in later times we find the pagan Emperor Julian (361–3) writing, "It is disgraceful that ... the impious Galileans [Christians] support not only their own poor but ours as well. All men see that our people [pagans] lack aid from us."[90]

Literary evangelism and apologetics
The early Christians developed the new literary form of biography into something that would carry their message across the world, the Gospels. They were not history or biography but rather a confession of faith, a testimony from many witnesses collected together, so that in the words of John 20:31, "you may believe that Jesus is the Christ, the Son of God, and that by believing you may have life in his name". Mark's Gospel was the earliest of the three, with Matthew and Luke both making full use of it. Papias, the second-century Christian leader, informs us that Mark's Gospel was simply a record of Peter's preaching material. It presents a very down-to-earth picture of Jesus, the Son of Man, who came to seek and to save the lost. Matthew was a Jew and wrote for Jews, emphasizing the ways in which Jesus fulfilled the Old Testament prophecies and endorsed the Jewish Law. Luke wrote primarily for Gentiles and presented Jesus as the Saviour and sacrifice for all the world. John's Gospel came much later and was written in Ephesus about the year 100, addressing a time when the Church was no longer predominantly Jewish. At a very early point, these four Gospels became fully accepted as genuinely apostolic

---

[89] Eusebius, *History of the Church* IV. 22.
[90] Julian, *Letters* 290–291 in Birger A. Pearson, *The Emergence of the Christian Religion: Essays on Early Christianity* (Harrisburg, PA: Trinity Press International, 1997), p. 211.

and were widely read in all the churches. They were a major means of teaching and spreading the faith.

Apologetic writings
The word apologetic derives from the Latin *apologia* meaning "a defence". As the persecutions widened, a number of Christians began to write apologies as a means of commending their faith and their fellow men and women from unjust treatment and persecution. In particular, they made strong pleas for the same justice enjoyed by the non-Christian citizens of the Empire. The apologists helped to win many over to Christianity including some in high places.

These defences of the faith which are considered in more detail in Chapter 4, were largely a second-century development, prominent examples being Justin's *Dialogue with Trypho the Jew,* written about 135, and his pupil Tatian's passionate defence of the Christian faith entitled *Oratian to the Greeks*. The apologists stressed Jesus' fulfilment of Old Testament prophecies, the superiority of Christian morality, the good citizenship of Christians and their loyalty to the Empire.

Women were treated with equality and respect
Many first-century Jewish men began their day with a prayer in which they thanked God that they hadn't been born a gentile or a woman. In addition, in Roman law and Roman society women were also treated in a subservient manner. Jesus had stood out strongly for the equality of women. He had spoken with women in public, something no self-respecting rabbi would ever have considered.[91] Jesus included women in his travelling ministry of teaching, preaching and healing. He also opposed the Jewish law which made it much easier for men to divorce than women. Jesus' teaching was followed by the assertions of Paul and the apostles that "there is neither Jew nor Gentile, neither slave nor free, nor is there male and female, for you are all one in Christ Jesus".[92] The apostles welcomed women as leaders of house churches and as

---

[91] See John 4:1–42.
[92] Galatians 3:28.

co-workers.[93] This equal treatment had wide appeal to women in Roman and Jewish societies, both of which were highly patriarchal.

During the first three centuries, many thousands of Christians died bravely for their faith in Jesus in every part of the Roman Empire from Carthage to Verulamium where Alban became the first English Christian martyr. With the passing of time their witness began to win over the pagans in ever growing numbers. Along with many others, Henry Chadwick observed that the early persecutions, rather than halting the growth of the Church, gave it more publicity.[94] Tertullian, a second-century Christian leader, aptly declared, "The blood of the martyrs is the seed of the church."

Conclusion

No one factor can account for this prolific and rapid expansion of the Christian faith. Rather it was the unique combination of the factors which have been considered in this chapter. Judaism had provided a solid base and starting point in many of the early Christian communities. The Roman peace and road system, along with the Greek language, enabled easy travel and exchange of ideas and teaching.

Perhaps above all else the lifestyle and caring compassion of the early Christians gave people a glimpse of the Jesus who they proclaimed. Christians knew from Paul's First Letter to Timothy that slave trading was wrong,[95] but they went further and treated slaves as fellow human beings as indeed Paul himself did in the case of Onesimus the runaway slave.[96] They treated women with equal respect and gave them leadership roles. They provided for the poor and needy and cared for their families and children.

---

[93] See Romans 16:2,6,12,15; Philippians 4:2.
[94] Henry Chadwick, *The Early Church* (Harmondsworth: Penguin Books, 1993), p. 29.
[95] 1 Timothy 6:1–10.
[96] Philemon 8–21.

It seems appropriate to conclude with a quotation from an unknown early-second-century *Letter to Diognetus*. It demonstrates why the early Christians were so effective in sharing their faith:

> For the Christians are distinguished from other men neither by country, nor language, nor the customs which they observe. For they neither inhabit cities of their own, nor employ a peculiar form of speech, nor lead a life which is marked out by any singularity .... They marry, as do all [others]; they beget children; but they do not destroy their offspring. They have a common table, but not a common bed. They are in the flesh, but they do not live after the flesh. They pass their days on earth, but they are citizens of heaven ... They love all men and are persecuted by all. They are unknown and condemned; they are put to death and restored to life. They are poor yet make many rich; they lack all things, and yet abound in all; they are dishonoured, and yet in their very dishonour are glorified. They are evil spoken of, and yet are justified; they are reviled, and bless; they are insulted, and repay the insult with honour; they do good yet are punished as evildoers. When punished, they rejoice as if quickened into life; they are assailed by the Jews as foreigners and are persecuted by the Greeks; yet those who hate them are unable to assign any reason for their hatred.[97]

---

[97] *Letter to Diognetus* 5.

3

The blood of the martyrs: Triumphant Christians in times of persecution

Jesus warned his disciples that they would face persecution in the same way that he had. This first happened at the hands of the Jews. It was their authorities who had engineered Jesus' capture, trial and death. Later, following his resurrection and ascension, their council the Sanhedrin[1] instigated a surveillance movement led by men such as Saul of Tarsus. They tracked down prominent Christians, some of whom such as James, the Lord's brother, and Stephen[2] suffered violent deaths at their hands.

Persecution by the Romans

When the Romans overcame the Greek Empire, they also adopted many of their deities, giving some of them Roman names. All religions in the Empire were required to be formally recognized, and once this had been done, they were granted status as a *religio licita*. This allowed them to have a statue or symbol of their faith erected in the Pantheon. This is a huge circular building dating back to 29 BC, its name meaning "all the gods".

The major difficulty the early Christians faced was that all citizens were required to acknowledge all the official gods of the Empire. At many times during the first three centuries, this involved appearing before the local magistrate and publicly declaring, "Caesar is Lord" and paying

---

[1] Acts 6:15.
[2] Acts 7:59.

homage to the Roman deities. For the followers of Jesus, this was a step too far to which they could not agree. As far as they were concerned, Jesus was the *only* Lord. Indeed, they believed he was the "Lord of Lords" before whom one day every knee would bow.[3] They had no wish for his statue to be placed in the Pantheon as just another "also-ran" among all the Roman gods. Because of their refusal to compromise the Christians suffered almost continuous persecution until the early years of the fourth century. The intensity and nature of the punishments they endured varied from province to province and emperor to emperor. A number of differing accusations were brought against them, some trumped up, and others based on rumours or misunderstandings.

Reasons for the Roman persecutions

Refusal to worship the Roman gods

Strangely, the most basic and constant accusation brought against the Christians was the charge of "atheism". This was because of their refusal to honour or worship the Roman gods. This claim was made following their resistance to the Emperor Domitian (81–96), who demanded in addition that all his subjects should worship him as both "Lord and God". Domitian's scourge even fell on his cousin Flavius Clemens and his wife Domitila who both, it seems, had embraced the Christian faith. Dio Cassius (*b*.165), a Roman historian, wrote, "Domitian slew many others . . . Against them was brought the charge of atheism . . . some were put to death, while at the least deprived of their property."[4] This was an ideological conflict which increased significantly during the later second and third centuries. The Christian claim to the exclusive sovereignty of Christ stood in opposition to those of Caesar.

---

[3] Philippians 2:10–11.
[4] J. Stephenson (ed.), *Documents of the Christian Church*, 2nd edn (Oxford: Oxford University Press, 1967), p. 8.

Accused of cannibalism

The heart of early Christian worship was the Lord's Supper at which bread and wine were shared in the context of an ordinary meal; the broken bread and the outpoured wine symbolizing "the body and blood of Christ". This immediately suggested to those who had no understanding of Christianity that the believers were engaging in a crude form of cannibalism. Eusebius quoted from a letter written by "the servants of Christ at Vienne and Lyon in Gaul" during the reign of the Emperor Marcus Aurelius (121–80). In it, they recounted that "arrests went on, and day after day those who were worthy filled up the number of martyrs". At the soldiers' instigation, they were falsely accused of holding "Thyestean banquets". In Greek mythology, Thyestes, King of Olympia, seduced the wife of his brother Artreus. In retaliation, Artreus then murdered Thyestes' sons and served them to him at a feast.[5]

Hated for their upright behaviour

Early Christians often suffered persecution because they were a "separate people". Their clean living and exemplary behaviour frequently shamed the Roman authorities and the people living in their local neighbourhood causing them to take offence. Citizens in Rome were expected to show loyalty to their city by participating in the rites of the state religion which had numerous feast days and pagan processions. Christians found they simply could not participate and as a result their absence was noted and they were punished as members of an illicit religion.[6] Early in the second century, a Christian leader wrote in a *Letter to Diognetus*, a Roman official, that "the world hates Christians without provocation, because they are opposed to its pleasures . . . it is Christians who hold the world together".[7]

Christians understandably avoided taking part in public banquets or feasts in honour of various Roman gods. They also kept away from what Irenaeus, a second-century church leader in Lyons, referred to as "that

---

[5] Eusebius, *History of the Church* V.1.15.
[6] A. Douglas Lee, *Pagans and Christians in Late Antiquity: A Sourcebook* (New York: Routledge, 2016), Chapter 7 "Christ or Caesar".
[7] *Letter to Diognetus* 6.

bloody spectacle hateful both to God and men, in which gladiators either fight with wild beasts, or singly encountered one another".[8] Christians who shared Irenaeus' firm and godly stance were doubtless strengthened by recalling Jesus' assertion that "the world hates you because you are not of the world".[9]

Made scapegoats

Christians were often made scapegoats following disasters, mistakes or tragic circumstances. Such was the case in 64 when, according to Tacitus (b.6), the Roman historian, "the most terrible and destructive fire which Rome had ever experienced broke out".[10] The conflagration began in the Circus Maximus and quickly spread over the Palatine and Caelian hills and then outstripped every counter measure. When the flames were finally extinguished, "only four of Rome's fourteen districts remained intact".[11] Tacitus recorded that many people believed Nero himself had either instigated or promoted the fire, for they believed he was ambitious to found a new city to be called after himself. Nero tried to make amends by authorizing the construction of temporary emergency accommodation and had food aid brought in from Ostia, but neither this nor the appeasement of the gods did anything to eliminate the suspicions that he was to blame for the fire. Nero therefore fabricated reports that the "depraved Christians", as they were popularly called, were responsible. He first ordered all "self-confessed Christians" to be acknowledged.[12] Then using their information, large numbers of others were arrested, not for incendiarism but for "their anti-social tendencies". Tacitus recorded:

> Their deaths were made farcical. Dressed in wild animals' skins, they were torn to pieces by dogs, or crucified, or made into torches to be ignited after dark as substitutes for daylight. Nero provided his gardens for the spectacle, and exhibited displays in

---

[8] Irenaeus, *Apology* I.1.11–12.
[9] Cf. John 15:19.
[10] Tacitus, *The Annals of Imperial Rome* II.15.
[11] Tacitus, *Annals* II.15.
[12] Tacitus, *Annals* II.15.

the Circus, at which he mingled with the crowd—or stood in a chariot, dressed as a charioteer. Despite their guilt as Christians, and the ruthless punishment it deserved, the victims were pitied. For it was felt that they were being sacrificed to one man's brutality rather than to the national interest.[13]

Eusebius reported similar instances of Christians being blamed for natural disasters or failure in policies or government. Among them, he mentions that following an earthquake in Cappadocia during the rule of the Emperor Maximinus (235-8) the pagan masses blamed the Christians and attacked them.[14] Tertullian (c.155-220) commented in his *Apology*, "If the Tiber reaches the walls, if the Nile does not rise to the fields . . . if there is famine, if there is plague, the cry is at once, 'The Christians to the lions.'"[15]

Perceived as a threat to stability
In the first and early second centuries, many Christians were persecuted because they were regarded as a secret society and did not acknowledge or worship the Roman gods. By the beginning of the third century, however, the number of Christians had increased considerably and they came to be regarded as a threat to the stability of the Empire. This was most obvious during the reign of Decius (c.201-51) who was Emperor from 249-51. During his short time in office, he sanctioned the first empire-wide persecution of Christians. It began in 250 with the issuing of an edict which required everyone in the Empire, except Jews, who were exempted, to make a sacrifice to the Roman gods in front of the local magistrate who would then provide them with a certificate of proof known as a *Libellus*. Those who refused were to be examined with torture, followed by imprisonment and death.

---

[13] Tacitus, *Annals* II.15,44.
[14] Eusebius, *History of the Church* VI.28.
[15] Tertullian, *Apology* 40.2.

Persecuting emperors and their motives

Various attempts have been made to analyse the intensity of the Roman persecution into distinct time spans, but it is not easily done. It seems preferable therefore in a short chapter such as this to highlight significant persecuting emperors.

The first century

The extent of persecution often varied from province to province and place to place with much resting on the attitudes and inclinations of each individual emperor. Eusebius recorded that Tiberius (42 BC–37 AD), who ruled the Empire during the whole of Jesus' earthly ministry, made it clear to the Senate that he favoured Christian doctrine and "he threatened to execute anyone who accused the Christians".[16] In contrast, Nero was a serial killer who murdered both his second wife Poppaea and his mother and sometime lover Agrippina the Younger. He practised lewdness with young boys and every kind of sensual indulgence, Tacitus recording that he used to go out to Milvian Bridge where "he could enjoy himself more riotously outside the city".[17] Nero's brutal inhumane persecution of the Christians, mentioned already in this chapter, is best understood as the pinnacle of his obscene savagery. It was in this conflict that the apostles Peter and Paul were martyred, Clement of Rome writing:

> Let us set before our eyes the good apostles; Peter, who by reason of unrighteous jealousy endured not one or two but many labours, and having thus borne witness went to his place in glory. Paul . . . having taught righteousness to the whole world, even reaching the bounds of the West, and having borne witness before rulers, he thus left the world and went to the holy place, becoming the greatest pattern of endurance.[18]

---

[16] Eusebius, *History of the Church* II.2.
[17] Tacitus, *Annals* 13.
[18] Clement, *Letter to the Corinthians* 5. The letter is usually dated c.AD 95.

The second century

Trajan (45–117), who took office in 98, was a successful soldier-emperor. During his rule, he had a lengthy correspondence with Pliny, the governor of Bithynia, who had written to him expressing his alarm at the number of Christians being put to death for their faith. Pliny explained that the sum total of their guilt or error had amounted only to this, "that on an appointed day they had been accustomed to meet before daybreak and to recite a hymn to Christ as a god, and to bind themselves by an oath, not for the commission of any crime but to abstain from theft, robbery, adultery and breach of faith". He also went on to mention that it was "their custom to meet together and share ordinary and harmless food";[19] this probably being a reference to the meal taken with the Lord's Supper.

Pliny informed Trajan of his method of dealing with the Christians in his province. First he asked them if they were Christians. If they admitted to it, he repeated the question two further times threatening capital punishment. "If they still persist", he stated, "I sentence them to death. For I do not doubt that whatever kind of crime it may be to which they have confessed their pertinacity and inflexible obstinacy should certainly be punished."[20] In his reply, Trajan commended Pliny for having taken the right line in examining those who had been denounced to him as Christians but he advised that "no hard and fast rule can be laid down, or universal application". Trajan's ruling was:

> They are not to be sought out; if they are informed against, and the charge proved, they are to be punished, with this reservation—that if any denies that he is a Christian, and actually proves it, that is by worshipping our gods, he shall be pardoned as a result of his recantation, however suspect he may have been with respect to the past.[21]

Among those martyred during Trajan's rule was Ignatius (*c*.35–*c*.107), the leader of the church at Antioch, who was sent from Syria to face death

---

[19] Pliny, *Letter to Trajan* 10.7.
[20] Pliny, *Letter to Trajan* 10.3.
[21] Trajan, *Letter to Pliny* 10.96.

in Rome. During his long journey under the strictest of military guards, he wrote letters to the churches of Asia encouraging them to hold fast to the apostles' teaching.

Hadrian, who was initiated into the Eleusinian Mysteries at Athens in 133, followed Trajan as Emperor and attempted to ensure that Christians were fairly treated. As far as he was concerned, being a Christian was not enough for action to be taken and "slanderous attacks" against them were not to be initiated.[22] He sent an order to Minucius Fundanus, proconsul of Asia, "forbidding him to try anyone unless properly charged and prosecuted in a reasonable manner".[23] Furthermore, Hadrian stated that if anyone started proceedings against Christians in the hope of financial reward, then for goodness sake arrest him for his shabby trick, and see he gets his deserts.[24]

Hadrian's successor, Marcus Aurelius, was Emperor from 161–180, and made initial attempts to reason with the Christians. When this failed, he turned persecutor and authorized widespread persecutions in Rome, North Africa and other places.[25] There were a number of notable martyrdoms during his time, including Justin (c.100–65), the apologist, in Rome and a series of Gallic martyrdoms at Lyons and Vienne. Eusebius recorded that Christians were "hunted out" and "falsely accused of things we ought never to speak or think about". Among those martyred were Sanctus, a deacon from Vienne, who was burned with red hot copper plates, Maturus and Blandina. All three were taken to the amphitheatre to face wild beasts.[26]

Septimus Severus, Emperor from 193–211, was another brutal persecutor of the Church with numerous martyrdoms occurring during his rule in Alexandria and other parts of Egypt. Writing during his reign Clement of Alexandria recorded, "we have exhibited before our eyes every day abundant scores of martyrs that are burnt, impaled

---

[22] Eusebius, *History of the Church* IV.8.5.
[23] Eusebius, *History of the Church* IV.8.5.
[24] Eusebius, *History of the Church* IV.8.9.
[25] Eusebius, *History of the Church* V.1.24.
[26] Eusebius, *History of the Church* V.1.39 and V.1.51.

and beheaded".[27] Among them was Origen's father, Leonides, who was beheaded leaving his wife, Origen and six younger brothers. His father's property was seized for the imperial treasury so that the family lacked even the necessities of life.[28] Among the many who suffered were three very brave women, Potamiaena (*d. c.*205) and her mother Marcella, both of whom were burned, and Aquila, who had boiling pitch poured over different parts of her body from her toes to the crown of her head.[29]

Third century

The Emperor Decius (*c.*201–51) instigated the first Empire-wide persecution of Christians from 250–1. Before his edict provincial governors had a certain amount of discretion in their jurisdictions and could choose how to deal with local incidents of mob violence and persecution. This provision was now removed. Many notable martyrdoms now occurred, among them Alexander, Bishop of Jerusalem (*d.*251), who died in prison and Origen who endured agony in iron chains and torture in the stocks.[30] Eusebius wrote of the vast numbers who fled from the persecutors. "They wandered," he wrote, "over deserts and mountains till hunger, thirst and cold, sickness, bandits, or wild beasts destroyed them."[31] Among their number Eusebius singled out Chaeremon, "the very aged Bishop of Nilopolis who fled with his wife into the mountains of Arabia".[32] W. H. C. Frend estimated that between 3,000 and 3,500 Christians were killed in the Decian persecution.[33]

Valerian, who followed Decius two years later, ruled the Empire from 253 to 260. He spent much of his time away from Rome fighting the Persians who had conquered Antioch where he was eventually taken captive. Initially, he "was kind and sympathetic in his attitude to

---

[27] Clement, *Stromata* 2.20.
[28] Eusebius, *History of the Church* VI.2.
[29] Eusebius, *History of the Church* VI.5.
[30] Eusebius, *History of the Church* VI.39.5.
[31] Eusebius, *History of the Church* VI.42.5.
[32] Eusebius, *History of the Church* VI.42.5.
[33] William H. C. Frend, *Martyrdom and Persecution in the Early Church* (Cambridge: James Clarke & Co Ltd, 2008), pp. 393–4.

Christians and a number of his palace staff were people of faith. But the situation changed dramatically following a meeting with Macrian, a leading magic practitioner, who urged him to kill, or prosecute pure saintly men as rivals."[34] In consequence, in 257, Valerian ordered all Christian clergy to perform sacrifices to the Roman gods and forbade Christians from gathering for worship in cemeteries. Worse came in the following year when he ordered that bishops and other high-ranking church officials to be put to death.[35]

A second Empire-wide persecution took place under Diocletian (c.242–305). He was born to a family of low status but rose through the ranks of the military early in his career to become a cavalry commander for the Emperor Carus. He became Emperor in 284 and ruled until his abdication in 305. Diocletian was a brutal and unrelenting persecutor who purged the army of Christians and made sure that only opponents of the faith were appointed to high office. In the nineteenth year of his reign, as "the festival of the Saviour's Passion" was approaching, he issued an imperial-wide decree "ordering churches to be razed to the ground and the Scriptures to be destroyed by fire". Further decrees followed requiring that "the presidents of the churches were to be committed to prison and then coerced into offering sacrifice".[36] "Many", Eusebius reported, were "subjected to a series of different tortures, one flogged unmercifully with the whip, another racked and scraped beyond endurance, so that their lives came to a most miserable end."[37] All over Syria, the heads of churches were fettered and imprisoned. In every town, the gaols were crowded with bishops, presbyters and deacons, readers and exorcists.[38] Eusebius recorded:

> Words cannot describe the outrageous agonies endured by the martyrs in the Thebais. They were torn to bits from head to foot with potsherds like claws till death released them. Women were

---

[34] Eusebius, *History of the Church* VII.10.9.
[35] Eusebius, *History of the Church* VII.10.11.
[36] Eusebius, *History of the Church* VII.2.2.
[37] Eusebius, *History of the Church* VII.2.3.
[38] Eusebius, *History of the Church* VIII.6.4.

tied by one foot and hoisted high in the air, head downwards, their bodies completely naked without a morsel of clothing, presenting thus a most brutal, and inhuman of all spectacles to anyone watching ... Sometimes ten or more, sometimes over twenty were put to death, at other times thirty, and yet others not far short of sixty; and there were occasions when in a single day a hundred men as well as women and little children were killed, condemned to a succession of ever-changing punishment.[39]

Eusebius wrote, "I was in these places and saw many of the executions for myself. Some suffered death by beheading, others punishment by fire. So many were killed in one day that the axe was blunted and worn out by the slaughter."[40] It is hard not to conclude that the brutality of the battlefield had prompted Decius and Diocletian to embark on empire-wide campaigns against the Christians. Both men would have been intolerant of non-compliance from their subjects and driven to enforce complete submission.

Diocletian finally ran out of energy and appointed three others to share in the government of the Empire, one of whom was Constantius "Chlorus". Eusebius noted that "he saved God's servants among his subjects from injury and ill-usage, and he neither pulled down church buildings, nor caused any mischief".[41] On his death, the legions immediately proclaimed his son Constantine as his successor.[42] In 312, already acclaimed as Augustus Caesar, he arrived on the outskirts of Rome with a large army which overcame the forces of the usurper Maxentius in a decisive victory at Milvian Bridge. This was followed a year later in 313 by the Edict of Milan which brought toleration for all religions and saw Christianity become the privileged religion of the Empire.

---

[39] Eusebius, *History of the Church* VIII.9.4.
[40] Eusebius, *History of the Church* VIII.9.4.
[41] Eusebius, *History of the Church* VIII.14.1.
[42] Eusebius, *History of the Church* VIII.14.1.

The results of the persecution

The most obvious result of the persecution was a multitude of Christian martyrs whose number will never be fully known. Estimates of those who died during the first three centuries differ considerably. They range from 6 million to upwards of 15 million by the year 300. Eusebius simply stated that "the number was immense". He described the horrific ordeals of 146 men and women who were martyred naming 97 of them.[43] Those who died came to be known as "The Noble Army of Martyrs". Their courage and deep Christian faith lived on in the lives of the generations who followed them. Some of their number are still remembered in the Christian Calendar. Among them was Ignatius (c.35–c.107), the Bishop of Antioch, who was commanded by the Emperor Trajan himself to walk to Rome where he was martyred. As he journeyed with two other prisoners and escorted by soldiers, he wrote astonishing and memorable words of encouragements to the churches of Asia Minor. Among them, "Now I begin to be a disciple".[44] "When I am close to the sword I am close to God."[45] And "I am His wheat, ground fine by Lions' teeth to be made the purest bread for Christ."[46]

Another inspirational martyr was Polycarp, Bishop of Smyrna, (c.69-155) who in his youth had been taught by the apostle John. As the city games reached fever pitch, someone shouted "Away with the atheists." As a result, soldiers were despatched to collect the aged Polycarp, Bishop of Smyrna. When it was seen how old and frail he was, the governor said: "Just curse Christ and you can go back to your cottage." Polycarp replied: "Eighty and six years I have served him and he has done me no wrong. How then can I blaspheme my King whom I serve?"[47] He was first committed to the flames which proved insufficient and then finally stabbed by the executioner with a dagger. Others long remembered were Cyprian (d.258), the Bishop of Carthage, who was executed on

---

[43] Eusebius, *History of the Church* VIII.13.
[44] Ignatius, *Letter to the Romans* 5.
[45] Ignatius, *Letter to the Smyrnaeans* 4.
[46] Ignatius, *Letter to the Romans* 4.
[47] *The Martyrdom of Polycarp* 9 and 12–15.

the orders of Proconsul Galerius Maximus.[48] Many of the martyrs were brave women who stood firm in their faith despite the most brutal and inhumane treatment. Among their number was Blandina (c.162–77), a slave girl with no rights of citizenship. She was among the Christians that the Emperor Marcus Aurelius ordered to be put to death in the city of Lyon (Lugdunum). She was scourged, burned and thrown to wild beasts.[49] Fifty years later Perpetua and Felicity were among those who were martyred in Carthage. Vivia Perpetua (c.182–c.203) was a recently married noble woman, said to have been 22 years old at the time of her death. She died leaving her infant son to be cared for by her family.[50] Martyred with her was Felicity, a slave girl who had also recently given birth to a son.[51] Catherine (c.287–c.305) of Alexandria was alleged to have been of noble birth and to have become a Christian when she was 14. She is not mentioned in western literature until the eighth century, and this late tradition suggests that her witness brought hundreds to faith in Christ. Catherine was put to death in the early years of the fourth century on the order of the Emperor Maxentius. She was first attached to a chariot wheel and then executed.[52]

Persecution gradually increased the churches' popularity as people came to see that the Christians not only lived upright lives, but that they practised hospitality and demonstrated charitable care and compassion for the poor and those in need. Justin Martyr (100–65) declared that he had become a Christian for the reason that "the martyrs are like a vine under the pruning knife, the more they are bled under the pruning knife the more fruitful they become".[53]

---

[48] William H. C. Frend, *The Rise of Christianity* (London: Darton, Longman & Todd Ltd, 1984), p. 319.
[49] Eusebius, *History of the Church* V1.39.
[50] Tertullian, *The Passion of Perpetua and Felicity* 1 and 6.
[51] Tertullian, *The Passion of Perpetua and Felicity* 8.
[52] There are no known primary sources for Catherine's death. See Catherine Walsh, *The Cult of St Catherine of Alexandria in Medieval Europe* (Aldershot: Ashgate, 2007), p. 142. Walsh examines the way traditions about Catherine developed from the early fourth century.
[53] Justin, *Apology* I.7.

The emergence of Apologies

As the persecution of the Church intensified in the second and third centuries, Christian leaders and others began to write apologies; the word "apology" coming from the Latin *apologia*, meaning "defence". Apologies were addressed to the Roman authorities and in some instances directly to Roman emperors. In the early days of the Christian Church, Paul and other apostles frequently defended their faith before the Roman authorities. Towards the end of the second century, more detailed philosophical and written defences began to emerge. Prominent among these early apologists were Aristides (*d*.134), Athenagoras (133–90), Origen (185–254), Justin (*c*.100–65), Tertullian (*c*.160–*c*.220) and Theophilus (*d. c*.180). An analysis of their writings reveals that in the main they used several key arguments in their defence of Christians and the Christian faith. They refuted the charges made against them, they explained Christian beliefs and practices clearly, they demanded equal treatment with other citizens of the Empire, they exposed the weaknesses of the Roman and Greek gods, they emphasized the superiority of the Christian deity and the upright moral living of Christians.

Refuted the charges against them

As has been noted, Christians were wrongly accused of atheism on the ground that they did not worship the Roman or Greek gods. Justin wrote: "We do no wrong but are put to death as offenders because of our worship, though others everywhere worship trees, rivers, mice, cats and crocodiles and many irrational animals."[54] To those concerned about rumours of meals called "love feasts" and the practice of members greeting one another with a holy kiss, Athenagoras pointed out "people are not allowed to give the kiss of peace a second time".[55] To those who accused Christians of cannibalism because of talk that they were "eating the body and blood of Christ", Athenagoras responded by saying, "We

---

[54] Justin, *First Apology* 24, in Cyril Richardson (ed.), *Early Christian Fathers* (London: SCM Press, 1953), p. 234.

[55] Athenagoras, *A Plea Regarding the Christians* 32.

believe in the resurrection. You would not eat the body of another if you believed that body will rise in the resurrection."[56]

Demands for equal treatment

The apologists and Christians in general were quick to demand a fair hearing and a just trial. Tertullian in his *Apology*, written about the year 200, and addressed to "Rulers of the Roman Empire" began by complaining, "You do not deal with us in the ordinary way of judicial proceedings against offenders … you with your tortures force us to confession." He asked why it was that Christians couldn't defend themselves when even criminals were allowed to do so. He pointed out that Pliny, the Governor of Bithynia, found nothing wrong with the Christians in his province and that even the Emperor Trajan had made it clear that Christians were not to be hunted down without good reason.[57]

Exposed the weaknesses of the Roman and Greek gods

For Athenagoras, "Greek gods are of very recent origin" and it is "demons that draw men to idols".[58] The Egyptians, he reminded Marcus Aurelius and Commodus, "reckon among their gods cats and crocodiles, and serpents, and asps and dogs".[59] All the apologists stressed that the Greek and Roman gods engaged in vulgar and foul practices. Theophilus reminded his readers that Greek gods were "handmade".[60] Aristides wrote, "Great then is the error into which the Barbarians wandered in worshipping lifeless images which can do nothing to help them."[61] Aristides was adamant that "much evil has been arisen among men, who to this day are imitators of their gods and practise adultery and defile themselves with their mothers and sisters and by lying with males."[62]

---

[56] Athenagoras, *A Plea Regarding the Christians* 36.
[57] Tertullian, *Apology* 2.
[58] Athenagoras, *A Plea Regarding Christians* 32.
[59] Athenagoras, *A Plea Regarding Christians* 1.
[60] Theophilus, *Apology* 1.
[61] Theophilus, *Autolycus* I.1.
[62] Aristides, *Apology* 3.

The superiority of the Christian faith

Justin explained that the Trinity does not mean that Christians believe in three gods. Athenagoras also wrote of the "triad nature of God" and of his being the "artificer" (creator). "God", he asserted, "is eternal mind and had his eternal Word within himself from the beginning, being eternally wise."[63] Tertullian also endeavoured to articulate the Trinity explaining that "when a ray is shot from the sun, it is still part of the parent mass ... there is no division of substance. Thus Christ is Spirit of Spirit, and God of God, as light of light is kindled."[64] Origen of Alexandria wrote his apology about the year 245 in the form of a dialogue with Celsus, an educated Jew. In it he gives a very full picture of Jesus. Beginning with Jesus' character, he makes it clear that Jesus was not arrogant but truly humble; a fact made clear when he washed his disciples' feet.[65] Origen argued that Jesus revealed his divinity by his behaviour on the cross. He also focused on Jesus' "genuine death"[66] and resurrection which was testified by "many witnesses" who recognized his wounds were real.[67]

The fulfilment of Old Testament promises

Tertullian made the point that Christianity was not totally new since its roots were in the Old Testament.[68] Justin stressed the fulfilment of the predictions of Isaiah's Old Testament prophecies. "Hear", he continued, "how it was literally prophesied by Isaiah, that he would be born of a virgin. He said, 'Behold the virgin shall conceive and bear a son and they will call his name Immanuel, God with us'."[69] In the following paragraph he added, "Hear also in what part of the Earth he was to be born, as the prophet Micah foretold. He wrote, 'You Bethlehem ...'"[70] Since these and other predictions have come to pass Justin urged that "it must similarly be

---

[63] Athenagoras, *A Plea Regarding Christians* 10.
[64] Tertullian, *Apology* 2.1.
[65] Origen, *Against Celsus* 2.7.
[66] Origen, *Against Celsus* 2.36.
[67] Origen, *Against Celsus* 2.61.
[68] Tertullian, *Apology* 16.
[69] Justin, *First Apology* 51.
[70] Justin, *First Apology* 51.

believed that those things that have also been prophesied and are yet to happen will certainly take place". "Christ as has been foretold will come again in glory with his angelic host."[71]

The upright moral living of Christians
Apologists were quick to point out that all Christians were loyal citizens of the Roman Empire. Tertullian stressed that they prayed for the Emperor and were "chaste and virtuous" people who did not engage in wife swapping. "They offer prayer for the safety of our princes to the eternal, the true, the living God, whose favour, beyond all others, they must themselves desire."[72] Tertullian was forthright stating, "Among us nothing is ever said, or seen, or heard, which has anything in common with the madness of the circus, the immodesty of the arena, or the useless exercises of the wrestling ground."[73] Athenagoras underlined that Christians uphold marriage, live chaste lives and don't permit abortions to take place. They don't take part in or watch gladiatorial sports or criminals made to fight with wild animals. In short, they "exhibit good works; when struck they do not strike again; when robbed they do not go to law; they give to those who ask them, and love their neighbours as themselves".[74] Aristides wrote, "Much evil has arisen among men, who to this day are imitators of their gods and practise adultery and defile themselves with their mothers and sisters and by lying with men."[75] These detailed and sometimes lengthy apologies bore testimony to the fact that Christianity was taking strong root among sections of the upper classes of society. They also bear witness to the evidence that despite the increasing level of persecution the Christian Church was expanding. Indeed, as Tertullian observed, "the blood of the martyrs is the seed of the church".[76]

---

[71] Justin, *First Apology* 52.
[72] Tertullian, *Apology* 30.
[73] Tertullian, *Apology* 38.
[74] Athenagoras, *A Plea Regarding the Christians* 35.
[75] Aristides, *Apology* 10.
[76] Chadwick, *The Early Church*, p. 29.

4

Uniting a divided house: Persuading Novatians and Donatists to be more lenient with those who denied the Faith

The persecution of the early Christians brought a number of issues to the surface which the Church soon recognized demanded immediate attention. The most pressing question was how the churches were to treat those who had denied their faith in Jesus in order to save themselves during the persecutions. Should they be forgiven in the way that Jesus had extended forgiveness to Peter following his denial or should they be required to demonstrate their penitence by undergoing some form of discipline and probation? The followers of Novatian, who was based in Rome, and those of Donatus, who resided in North Africa, were rigorists who maintained that the Catholic Church was in serious error by allowing the lapsed back into fellowship on terms that were far too lenient.

This issue became particularly urgent in the wake of the Empire-wide persecutions in the reigns of the Emperors Decius (249–50) and Valerian (253–60). The chronicler Lactantius described Decius as "a bad man" and "a persecutor of righteousness".[1] Eusebius recorded that he commenced a persecution of the churches in the city of Rome during which its bishop Cornelius was martyred.[2] Decius was particularly threatened by the strength of the church in Rome and five bishops were martyred between 250 and 258. Eusebius also detailed Valerian's persecutions which, he

---

[1] Lactantius, *On the Death of the Persecutors* 3.
[2] Eusebius, *History of the Church* VI.39.

stated, "raged so fiercely that to give all the names of those who died would be quite impossible".[3]

Cornelius and Novatian

Cornelius (c.180–253) was elected Bishop of Rome in 251 with the consent of nearly all the bishops, clergy and people in preference to Novatian.[4] However, on taking office he was immediately confronted by many Christians in Rome who had denied their faith in the persecution but wanted to be received back into the church. Cornelius' way of dealing with the issue was to require a period of penitence with appropriate penance. When this was completed, they would be restored to fellowship and the Lord's Supper.[5]

However, Cornelius' views were soon challenged by his former rival Novatian who declared that those who had lapsed should not be received back into the church on what he felt and believed were far too easy terms. This disagreement sowed the seeds of what turned out to be a long-lived schism which lasted several hundred years and both sides of which quickly gained many supporters across the Roman Empire. Cornelius therefore promptly held a Synod that confirmed his election as bishop and then immediately excommunicated Novatian.

Cornelius' opponent Novatian (200–58) came from Phrygia. Eusebius, who was strongly on the side of the of the Catholic Church, described him as "a presbyter being lifted up with arrogance".[6] Cyprian, Bishop of Carthage, in contrast, it should be said, wrote of Novatian's power of language and in some of his letters spoke of "his good reputation in his congregation and of his learning and eloquence".[7] Novatian saw things very differently from Cornelius. He maintained that the lapsed,

---

[3] Eusebius, *History of the Church* VII.11.
[4] Cyprian, *Letter* 56.1–2.
[5] Cyprian, *Letter* 54.1.
[6] Eusebius, *History of the Church* VI.43.
[7] See for example, Cyprian, *Letter* 55.4.

by offering incense to the Roman gods in order to escape persecution,[8] were guilty of idolatry. More than that they had in fact committed the unpardonable sin and that the Church had no authority to forgive apostates.

Cornelius responded to Novatian's challenge by calling together at Rome a meeting of 60 bishops and a great number of presbyters and deacons. Together they took the view that Novatian and his followers should be considered as "strangers" and "cut off from the Catholic Church".[9] They also agreed that those who had denied their faith in Jesus during the persecution should be offered "the medicine of repentance". Cornelius wisely sent details of what had been agreed to churches in Asia Minor, Italy and Africa.[10]

Meanwhile Novatian withdrew from Cornelius and the official diocese of Rome and formed a separate community who soon elected and consecrated him as their bishop. They referred to themselves as the *katharoi*, meaning "the pure ones", but became widely referred to as the Novatians, after their founder. Novatian proved to be a gifted organizer who quickly established a separatist movement which extended from the cities of Rome and Carthage as far west as Spain and as far east as Asia Minor with Constantinople becoming one of its major centres. Bishop Cyprian of Carthage wrote that Novatian even assumed the primacy in Rome and sent out his new apostles to many cities to set up a new foundation for his establishment.[11] Cyprian rebuked him because even where there were "bishops of pure faith and tried virtue" in all provinces, he dared to create "false bishops" over their heads.[12] Novatian and the leaders he appointed, it should be said, were strictly orthodox in their theology. He himself had written on several theological subjects and his book on the Trinity was widely judged to be orthodox.[13]

---

[8] Cyprian, *Letter 51.2*.
[9] Eusebius, *History of the Church* VI.43.
[10] Eusebius, *History of the Church* VI.43.
[11] Cyprian, *Letter 59*.
[12] Cyprian, *Letter 55.24*.
[13] Frederick F. Bruce, *The Spreading Flame* (Carlisle: The Paternoster Press, 1992), p. 213.

The issues of dispute between Novatian and the Catholic Church

The treatment of the lapsed

Cornelius and the Catholic Church strongly disagreed with the Novatians on this issue of the lapsed. In light of the fact that Jesus had reinstated Peter after his denial of Jesus they were strongly of the view that compassionate forgiveness to those who demonstrated genuine repentance was the way forward. They therefore prescribed a period of penitence with penance and instruction after which they could be welcomed back into fellowship and the Lord's Supper.

In contrast, Novatian argued that those who had denied their Lord in the persecution had committed a mortal, unpardonable sin which only God could forgive. They needed to make a completely new start with basic teaching and eventually re-baptism. Many Novatians further extended mortal sins to include murder and adultery.

The validity of the clergy

Then there was the question of the validity of the clergy. The Novatians maintained that many of the Catholic bishops and priests were tainted either because they had denied their faith or gone into hiding to escape the persecution. Some were *traditors* (i.e. someone who had betrayed the Church by handing over the sacred Scriptures to the authorities) and yet others had compromised the integrity of the Church by allowing the lapsed to be restored to communion with the Church on too easy terms. Such clergy were therefore not able to minster valid sacraments which conveyed the true grace of God. The Novatians were adamant that ordinations conducted by bishops who had themselves denied Jesus in these ways could not be regarded as valid.

The validity of the sacraments

Then there was the validity of the sacraments of baptism and the Lord's Supper. The Novatians took the view that sacraments conducted by Catholic clergy who had denied Jesus in times of persecutions could not be regarded as valid. It was not possible for God's grace to flow from apostate hands. In response, Cornelius, supported by Cyprian and the

Catholic clergy, put forward the view that no matter how pure Novatian Communion services and baptisms were, they were out of communion with the Catholic Church and its bishops. Cornelius, who was strongly supported by Cyprian, held that only within the Catholic Church was salvation possible and that only there were the true sacraments to be found. "There could", he added, "only be one true bishop in every city."[14] With the passing of time, the Catholic Church took the view that sacraments ministered by bishops and presbyters who had denied or compromised their faith were still valid because God's grace was not dependent on the worthiness of the one ministering. Put another way, the sacraments were God's, not the Church's.

Cornelius died in the persecution on 25 June 253 and Novatian suffered martyrdom the following year in the same conflict. Their disagreements were the basis of a dispute which impacted the Christianity of the Empire for several centuries.

A long-standing schism

The official Catholic Church did not find it easy to respond to the challenges posed by the Novatians. Indeed, we learn from the Church historian Sozomen (400–50) that they soon had churches and followers in almost every province of the Roman Empire. And even at the end of the fifth century there were still some Novatian churches in existence. The main reason for this survival was their strong orthodox biblical theology, their articulate preaching, their many godly, caring leaders and their ability to present themselves as serious uncompromising Christians. It is significant that the Council of Nicaea recognized the substantial orthodoxy of the Novatians, Canon 8 stating, "those who call themselves 'Cathari' who come over to the Catholic and Apostolic Church and are ordained shall continue among the clergy". Cathari bishops who crossed back over were to be given the rank of presbyter unless the Catholic bishop "sees fit to share the honour of the title with him".[15] In 326, the

---

[14] Cyprian, *Letter to Jubianus* 73.2.
[15] *Council of Nicaea*, Canon 8, "On the Novatians", in Joseph Cullen Ayer, *A Source Book for Ancient Church History: From the Apostolic Age to the Close of the Conciliar Period* (New York: Charles Scribner's Sons, 1913), p. 295.

Emperor Constantine distinguished the Novatians from other heretics, and ruled that "they may retain their long-held buildings without any molestation".[16]

The Emperor Valens (328–78), who ruled from 364–78, was initially hostile to the Novatians. Later, however, he back-tracked on account of Marcian, one of their presbyters who had taught his daughters Anastasia and Carosa.[17] Some time later Arcadius (*c.*377–408), who was Emperor from 383–408, expressed his admiration for Agelius' leadership of the Novatians[18] and his clear articulation of the distinctives of the Trinity.[19] The Church historian Socrates recorded: "The decision caused the Novatians to flourish again, and hold their meetings within the city: for the Emperor delighted with the agreement of their profession with that which he embraced, promulgated a law securing to them the peaceful possession of their own church buildings, and assigned to their churches equal privileges and with this he gave more special sanction."[20]

The Novatians were strengthened and increased in number by the strong leadership of Bishop Agelius whose episcopate lasted for 40 years from the reign of Constantine to the sixth year of the Emperor Theodosius. There was some disagreement in the Novatian ranks over the dating of Easter and a Synod of their bishops was convened at Angarum to consider the matter. They ruled in what became known as "the Indifferent Canon" that each church was at liberty to celebrate the festival either after the Equinox or according to the Jewish Christian practice.[21] The historian Socrates wrote in great praise of Sisinnius who had been consecrated the Novatian Bishop of Constantinople by the aging Agelius. He was "celebrated for erudition", and on account of it "all the bishops and the members of the senate loved, esteemed and admired

---

[16] *Codex Theodosianus* 16.5.2 (AD 326), in Ayer, *A Source Book for Ancient Church History*, p. 296.
[17] Socrates, *Ecclesiastical History* IV.9.
[18] Arcadius was co-Emperor with his brother Honorius from 389 until his father's death in 395.
[19] Socrates, *Ecclesiastical History* V.10.
[20] Socrates, *Ecclesiastical History* V.10.
[21] Socrates, *Ecclesiastical History* V.21.

him".²² After the death of Sisinnius, Chrysanthus was consecrated in his place, Sozomen recording that "he established and enlarged the churches of the Novatians in Constantinople".²³ Sozomen gives further details of prospering Novatian churches in Constantinople and differing opinions regarding the Eucharist held by the Novatians of Phrygia.²⁴

Denouement

Novatianism was the first great schism in the Church based solely on a question of discipline. It could perhaps be seen as a conservative protest against the growing liberalism of the Catholic Church. Gradually, over the course of more than 200 years, it appears to have slowly merged with the mainstream Catholic Church. The last recorded mention of the Novatians is contained in the 95th Canon of the *Second Trullan Council*, known as the Quintisext, held in 692.²⁵

The Donatists

In 303, the Roman Emperor Diocletian (284–305) was responsible for the fiercest and most brutal persecution of Christians that had yet been seen. Diocletian ordered that all church buildings were to be destroyed and the Scriptures were to be handed over and burnt. At the same time, those who held official positions in the government or had other public honours were stripped of their office if they continued to profess the Christian faith.²⁶ All citizens were required to honour the Roman gods and declare "Caesar is Lord" before the local magistrate. Eusebius, who personally witnessed some of the persecutions, recorded that many believers had to face brutal floggings at the hands of the military which were then followed by "the ordeal of facing man-eating beasts when they were attacked by panthers, bears of different kinds, wild boars, and bulls

---

[22] Socrates, *Ecclesiastical History* VI.22.
[23] Sozomen, *Ecclesiastical History* VI.9.
[24] Sozomen, *Ecclesiastical History* VI.4. See also VII.12.
[25] Ayer, *A Source Book for Ancient Church History*, p. 295.
[26] Eusebius, *History* VIII.2.2.

goaded with red-hot irons".[27] Some of the punishments meted out under Diocletian's tyranny were barbaric in the extreme. Eusebius reported the following episode:

> Words cannot describe the outrageous agonies endured by the martyrs in the Thebais. They were torn to bits from head to foot with potsherds like claws till death released them. Women were tied by one foot and hoisted high in the air, head downwards, their bodies completely naked without a morsel of clothing, presenting thus the most shameful, brutal, and inhuman of all spectacles to anyone watching.[28]

Eusebius ended this same paragraph by remarking that "there were occasions when on a single day a hundred men as well as women and little children were killed, condemned to a succession of ever-changing punishments".[29] Christians reacted in different ways in response to these terrors. Many church leaders "bore up heroically under horrible torments, an object lesson in endurance of fearful ordeals", while countless others, "their souls already numbed with cowardice, promptly succumbed to the first onslaught".[30]

The fundamental issue that brought the Donatists to the fore was in essence the same as that which had earlier provoked the emergence of the Novatians; how to handle those Christians who had denied their faith in Jesus rather than die amid such terror and bloodshed. The Donatist movement was deeply rooted and predominant in the North African provinces of the Empire, while the Novatians flourished in the northern provinces. Donatism was also intertwined with political issues and a strong resistance to high taxation. Donatists also strongly rejected the Emperors interfering with the affairs of the Catholic Church. This was never more memorably expressed than by Donatus himself who

---

[27] Eusebius, *History of the Church* VIII.7.
[28] Eusebius, *History of the Church* VIII.9.
[29] Eusebius, *History of the Church* VIII.9.
[30] Eusebius, *History of the Church* VIII.2.

emblazoned the cause with the words, "What has the emperor to do with the Church?"

The touch paper of this dispute which ignited the Donatists was the compromising behaviour of Mensurius, the Catholic Bishop of Carthage. He had agreed to suspend public worship in the hopes that he could lie low until the persecution died away. At the very same time, a number of the city's brave Christians had boldly professed their faith from prison. Understandably they denounced Mensurius as a cowardly, compromising traditor.

When Mensurius died towards the end of 311, there was an unseemly struggle to appoint his successor. Eventually his archdeacon, Caecilian,[31] was chosen. Contrary to the established tradition, however, he was quickly consecrated by only three bishops, one of whom was Felix of Aptunga in Byzacena who was also believed to be a traditor. There was also a feeling that Caecilian was himself a traditor. Although he had the support of most of the Roman citizens, he was regarded with suspicion by many of the local church leaders. They thought him cowardly, cruel and intolerant and particularly so of the confessors and martyrs. As far as many in the city were concerned, this was a good enough reason to reject Caecilian's appointment. Strife began in earnest when the opposition party sent an invitation to Secundus of Tigisis, the Primate of Numidia, to intervene. He duly arrived together with 70 Numidian bishops and a council was held which declared the consecration of Caecilian as invalid on the grounds that correct procedures had not been followed and that Felix was a traditor. The Council appointed Marjorinus in his place. His candidature had been strongly supported by Lucilla, a wealthy and devout lady whom he served as her private chaplain. Caecilian, it emerged, had offended her by publicly rebuking her for kissing a relic during a communion service. Marjorinus remained in office from 311-15. On his death, Donatus (*d. c.*355), Bishop of Casae Nigrae, was immediately elected Bishop of Carthage in his place. It is after him that the Donatists were named.

---

[31] The date of Caecilian's death is unknown, but he was present at the Council of Nicaea in AD 325.

Caecilian and his followers widened the whole issue still further when they appealed to the Emperor Constantine in Rome, claiming that the schism was likely to cause a public disorder. Probably in the spring of 317, the Emperor Constantine dispatched the most severe law to North Africa decreeing that the Donatist churches should be confiscated and their leaders sent into exile. But Donatus was made of sterner stuff and refused to surrender the churches he held in Carthage, and the Christians there were at once a divided community. Away from the city, all the old Donatist bishops were left untouched and continued to minister to their clergy and people. Finally, in May 321, Constantine realized it was going to be no easy matter to restore unity to the churches in North Africa and he therefore granted the Donatists toleration. In a subsequent letter to the Catholics, he urged moderation and patience.

Meanwhile, Donatism spread rapidly with many new churches being constructed. Their basilica at Theveste was reckoned as one of the finest monuments in Roman Africa, its massive stone blocks still standing unweathered.[32] Donatist worship was vigorous and lively and made use of the same Latin text of the Bible current in Cyprian's time. The reading of Scripture and Bible-based sermons played a central part in the proceedings. Agape meals, particularly those in conjunction with the anniversary of a martyr's death, were highly valued. It has been pointed out that many of the inhabitants of North Africa lived in fear of evil spirits and believed that there was a constant and dire need to propitiate the gods on this score. The strong Donatist emphasis on the Holy Spirit and their faith in the power of the third person of the Trinity over malevolent forces was therefore a particularly attracting feature of their message.[33] Their view of baptism was that the Holy Spirit was actually present in the water and had a powerful cleansing and protecting impact on those who received the sacrament.[34] Such was the appeal of Donatism that it even gained a foothold among the African community in Rome and Donatus

---

[32] William H. C. Frend, *The Donatist Church: A Movement of Protest in Roman North Africa* (Oxford: Oxford University Press, 1942), p. 162.

[33] Frend, *The Donatist Church*, p. 113.

[34] Frend, *The Donatist Church*, p. 119.

dispatched Victor of Garba, to establish himself as the true bishop of Rome.

Donatist concerns

Penance and the lapsed

This big issue which the two sides hotly debated was whether or not the sacrament of penance could effect a reconciliation that was sufficient to allow traditors and those who had denied Jesus in other ways back into full communion. The Catholic Church took the view that the sacrament of penance was exactly designed and effective for this purpose. The Donatists on the other hand maintained that such a crime of denying Jesus disqualified a person from any leadership role in the Church.

The Donatists for their part were clear that lapsed clergy could not celebrate valid sacraments because their denial of Jesus had lastingly tainted them. Put another way, their denial of Jesus meant that no grace or blessing could flow through them when they ministered the sacraments. In short, they were permanently corrupted individuals and no spiritual grace could be conveyed through their ministries. In response, the Catholic Church argued that what made the sacrament valid was not dependence on the spiritual state of the church leader but on God alone. This meant that even if a priest was in mortal sin the sacrament would still convey God's presence and blessing simply for the reason that the right form of words had been recited. As far as the Catholic Church was concerned, a person who received the bread and wine from the hands of an unrepentant priest could still receive the presence of Christ.

The sacraments

The Donatist position was that the sacraments operated on account of the moral fitness of the minister. This view was rebutted by bishop Optatus (*d. c.*390) who penned *Optatus of Milevis against the Donatists*. Optatus' main point was that the sacraments derived their validity from God and not from the minister. True baptism was therefore conferred by the name of the Trinity and not in the name of the minister. The Donatists strongly disagreed and took the view that those who had been baptized in the Catholic Church should be re-baptized after penance, a practice which Bishop Cyprian of Carthage had used in previous times when restoring the lapsed into the Church. The Donatists also advocated the re-ordination of leaders who joined their ranks from the Catholic churches. Augustine was later to express his disagreement and to contend that valid baptisms could be conferred outside the Catholic Church as well as in it. His point was that the sacraments are God's sacraments even when administered in schism.[35] Donatus was strongly of the view that there was no true baptism outside his communion and yet he was still able, on occasions, to be bendable. Thus when he discovered that a number of congregations in Mauretania were willing to join him if they could do so without undergoing what they considered to be a second baptism, Donatus allowed himself to be persuaded by them.[36]

The result of this major disagreement was that the Church in many towns and cities of North Africa became divided. This matter also brought the very recently converted Roman Emperor, Constantine, into the controversy and in 314, he called together the Council of Arles. The decision of the assembled Christian leaders, which included representatives from Britain, went against the Donatists who needless to say did not accept the judgement. In fact, they despised those compromising bishops who collaborated with Rome and they strongly opposed the notion of a state church over which the recently converted Emperor was exerting a growing influence. In consequence, the Donatists rapidly became a second church, setting up their own hierarchy in 316. In fact, their threat was to grow so rapidly that a later Emperor, Valerian I, passed further laws against them. By 350, they outnumbered the Catholic Christians in Africa, and each city had its own opposing Donatist bishop. It wasn't until the time of Bishop Augustine of Hippo's campaigns against them that the official Church began to gain the upper hand. Augustine's view was that it was the office of the priest that was important rather than his character. He argued on the basis of legal documents that the Emperor Constantine had chosen the Catholic Church of the Empire rather than

---

[35] Augustine, *Writings in Connection with the Donatist Controversy* (Edinburgh: T&T Clark, 1872), p. 3.
[36] Frend, *The Donatist Church*, p. 168.

the Donatists as the official Church of the Empire. The result of all this was that the Donatists faced considerable persecution.

The two sides had completely opposite views regarding the nature of the Church. The Catholics held the Church to be an inclusive and mixed body consisting of both saints and sinners. They saw this pictured in Jesus' parables of the wheat and the tares[37] and of the dragnet,[38] and possibly symbolized in Noah's taking both clean and unclean animals into the ark. The Donatists on the other hand saw those very same passages as referring to the world and therefore held that the sorting and separation happens here and now to produce a pure body of Christ. At heart, therefore, the Donatists were a holiness movement and declared themselves to be the true church on the ground of holiness.

The spread of Donatism

Resonance with North African culture

Unlikely though it seemed, it was the Donatist church rather than the official Catholic Church under the Emperor, which grew rapidly across the North African provinces of the Roman Empire. As Frend observed, "Within a generation, Donatism was the religion of nearly all Africa and neither force nor argument could root it out"[39] and again, "Southern Numidia remained for three centuries the heart of Donatism."[40] This rapid spread was borne out by a 1930s excavation which studied 72 Romano-Berber villages and brought to light over 200 Donatist churches and chapels with a uniform local culture and distinctive art forms[41] based on veneration of the martyrs.[42] There were a number of reasons for this burgeoning movement. Perhaps most obvious was the fact that many of the North African peoples were readily convinced by the Donatist view

---

[37] Matthew 13:24–30,36–43.
[38] Matthew 13:47–50.
[39] Frend, *The Donatist Church*, p. 23.
[40] Frend, *The Donatist Church*, p. 24.
[41] Frend, *The Donatist Church*, p. 66.
[42] Frend, *The Donatist Church*, p. 53.

that traditors who had renounced Christ could not have the Spirit of God in them. Conversely, they easily saw the Donatists as the true church who were wholly committed to following Jesus and standing without fear in times of persecution.

The Donatist gospel also found a ready hearing on the part of the tribal peoples who lived south-west of Carthage between the sea and the Aures mountains. In pre-Christian times, they had been fanatical and rigorous worshippers of the pagan god Saturn. The uncompromising stance of the Donatists and their willingness to face martyrdom had an immediate appeal to their serious-minded natures. Symbols such as the palm, dove, lion and crown were common in both Saturn and Donatist worship which they subsequently embraced. The acceptance of Christian teaching from Donatist evangelists did not appear to them as a radical rejection of the African tribal religion but rather as a transformation of it.[43]

Support from the Circumcellions

Groups of people known as Circumcellions began to attach themselves to the Donatists about the year 340. They were bands of social revolutionaries who hailed from Upper Numidia and Mauretania. Combining religious enthusiasm with violence, they protested against the poverty which they believed resulted from the harsh taxes of the Roman establishment who they perceived as working hand-in-glove with the newly emerging state church.

Circumcellions delighted in Donatist inscriptions that have been recently uncovered in village churches, hailing Jesus as the champion of justice and the refuge from toil and hardship.[44] They also shared the Donatist resentment and rejection of imperial authority. As far as they were concerned, the Donatists were a pure church and the Catholics who were in league with the persecuting authorities were "Babylon".

---

[43] Frend, *The Donatist Church*, p. 104.
[44] Frend, *The Donatist Church*, p. 111.

The impact of Donatus of Carthage

Donatus' literary works have not survived and little is known about his personal life and friendships. What is clear from the writings of Augustine, however, is that he was a great orator and leader of men. Wherever he went, he stirred enthusiasm, and his charisma was remembered even 50 years after his death.[45] As Frend aptly put it, "He seems to have personified popular loathing for the worldly ecclesiastics who thought that they would do well in this life and the next." Frend also described him as "a prophet and religious leader who could converse directly with the Lord and maintain stringent control over his following".[46] According to Augustine, he was known as the man "who purged the church of Carthage from error".[47] Augustine noted that towards the end of Constantine's reign Donatus' authority was acknowledged by nearly 300 bishops.[48] Indeed, when the Emperor died in May 337, Donatus was at the height of his power with strong and solid support in Carthage and Numidia and his authority extended to every corner of Roman Africa. Donatism remained the predominant religion in North Africa for another 50 years. Frend noted that many literate Africans regarded the Donatist Church "as the true Catholic Church in Africa and the successor of the Church of Cyprian's time".[49]

Donatism in the years after Donatus

The end of Donatus' influence and the decline of his movement began about the year 346 when he decided to appeal to the Emperor Constans (*c*.323–50) for recognition as the sole Bishop of Carthage. Constans sent a commission to investigate the matter. Unfortunately for Donatus, the African Catholic bishops had primed the members of the Emperor's

---

[45] Frend, *The Donatist Church*, p. 153.
[46] Frend, *The Donatist Church*, p. 165.
[47] Augustine, *Contra Cresconium* III.56.62, cited in Frend, *The Donatist Church*, p. 154.
[48] Augustine, *Letter* 93.43, cited in Frend, *The Donatist Church*, p. 167.
[49] Frend, *The Donatist Church*, p. 170.

Commission even before they set off to meet him, and it was clear on their arrival that they were not going to support him or his followers. Several violent clashes ensued and Donatus was exiled and never again set foot in Africa. His death, which probably took place in 355 away from his homeland, did, however, enable his followers to claim him as a martyr as well as a reforming religious leader. Donatus was clearly a dynamic and strong leader. Indeed Augustine went so far as to call him a "precious jewel" in the Church.[50] He was gifted with spiritual and administrative talents and shared a high view of the office of a bishop.

Following Donatus' death, the leadership passed to Bishop Pontius and Macrobius, the Donatist Bishop in Rome, who had previously been a presbyter in the Catholic Church. Macrobius sent encouraging letters to the North African churches. After the death of the Emperor Julian on 26 June 363, the Donatists were led for nearly 30 years by Parmenian (*d. c.*392), the Donatist Bishop of Carthage. He was a man of integrity, a powerful speaker and a strong opponent of the Catholics. Parmenian made worship a priority and wrote "new psalms" that proved very popular and were still sung in Augustine's day and indeed in much later times.[51]

Parmenian had considerable teaching gifts, and under his instruction Donatist theology was developed and strengthened. Parmenian set out his ideas in a five-volume set entitled *Adversus Ecclesiam Traditorum*, a work that has survived only in snippets quoted by Bishop Optatus of Milevis in Numidia. Parmenian was adamant that African Catholics had proved themselves to be false Christians because they had betrayed their Lord during the persecution. Return to the true Church could only be gained by penance and followed with a new initiation with baptism at the hands of a pure minister. Parmenian therefore reinforced the views of Donatus that the Christian Church must be separated from the state.

---

[50] Augustine, Sermon 37.3, cited in Frend, *The Donatist Church*, p. 181.
[51] Augustine, *Letter* 55,18.34, cited in Frend, *The Donatist Church*, p. 194.

Radical Donatism under Optatus and Gildo, 386–98

The closing years of the fourth century were dominated by Optatus who was elected Donatist Bishop of Thamagadi which was the most important see in southern Numidia. He was a powerful orator and under his influence, aided by the Circumcellions, he set about creating a more just social order. During his leadership from 388 to 398, Donatism came nearest to achieving complete mastery in Africa.[52] In this period, there is evidence that many literate Africans continued to prefer Donatism to Catholicism and even Augustine himself was unable to dissuade some of his own clergy from leaving the Catholic fold.

The Donatist supremacy came to an end when Optatus gambled on trying to force the imperial authorities to recognize their right to be the official Church of northern Africa. The method he chose was to hold the corn fleet back in North African ports until his request was granted. In consequence, the Emperor Honorius (384–423) sent in troops and Optatus was put to death along with his friend and ally Gildo. Their deaths marked the end of the Donatist bid for supremacy in Africa. They had nevertheless been hugely successful. They had won the battle for popular support. They had set up their own diocesan structures and raised up many able leaders and strategists of considerable ability and spirituality. In the end, they never finally succeeded in finding an alternative to the state church. Although Donatism was to live on for many years to come, the future of the African church gradually came into the hands of pro-Catholic administrators and church leaders. In their Primate, Aurelius, Bishop of Carthage, and Augustine, Bishop of Hippo, the Catholics finally found men who could debate the issues with them in a more convincing way.

---

[52] Frend, *The Donatist Church*, p. 210.

Augustine and the decline of Donatism

It was their teaching, writings and the public debates of Augustine that gradually turned the tide in favour of the Catholics. Of great significance were the conferences that Augustine organized between the Catholic and Donatist bishops at Carthage in 411. Together with Aurelius, Augustine gathered 286 Catholic bishops. They were joined by 284 Donatist bishops who were led by Primianus, the Donatist Bishop of Carthage, and Petilian, Bishop of Constantine. Their discussions lasted for three days. During the debate, Augustine appealed to a text in Luke's Gospel, "Compel them to come in", as justification to come over to his side. After three days in the presence of Marcellinus, the imperial commissioner, a vote was taken and he decided in favour of the Catholics. Following this the Emperor Honorius pronounced an edict against the Donatists requiring Donatist properties to be handed over to the Catholics.

Whilst Donatism declined in influence after the conference, it was by no means dead and buried. In the 17 remaining years of Roman rule in Africa, the Donatists did not return to the Catholic fold in large numbers as Augustine had hoped. Donatist bishops remained in control in centres such as Caesarea and Thamugadi.[53] Significantly, as late as 594, we find Pope Gregory writing to the new Bishop of Carthage urging him to hold a council against the Donatists. Little decisive action can have taken place, however, since Donatism continued in many areas until the Arab conquests of the seventh and eighth centuries.

Denouement

Donatism and Catholicism were clearly two fundamentally opposite ways of understanding what the Church is. While it is plain that the Catholic approach was both practical and inclusive, it failed, like most state religion, to deliver on a number of key issues: most obviously, the social evils and injustices that were being meted out to the slaves and poverty-stricken workers on the big estates run by the Roman authorities. For all its inclusiveness, a Catholic Church which sided with the oppressors could never appeal to the Berber poor of northern Africa. In short, the

---

[53] Frend, *The Donatist Church*, p. 299.

issue was whether these injustices were to be tolerated for the sake of Christian unity or were they to be challenged in the name of Jesus? For the Donatists, there would only ever be one answer!

In conclusion, it is hard not to escape the fact that we are seeing a repetition of these two movements in the contemporary Church of England where sections within the dioceses are setting up alternative forms of episcopal and pastoral oversight. There are certainly lessons to be learned from the history of both the Novatians and the Donatists and their relationships with the Catholic Church. On the positive side, the establishment mellowed over time and in many places in North Africa there were cordial good relationships between Catholics and Donatists. One thing is clear and that is that Christianity went on spreading and growing both through the Catholics and through the Novatians and the Donatists.

5

Deliverance from evil within: Overcoming Gnosticism within the Church

Gnosticism is the name given to a broad-based speculative movement which began to have significant impact on the Christian churches in the early second century. There has been some debate as to whether its Christian forms were an erroneous development of apostolic teaching, as some early Church fathers believed, or whether it emerged from earlier pagan religions and esoteric mystery cults.[1] However, one thing is clear: by the beginning of the third century Gnosticism had ceased to have any major influence on the life and worship of the early Church.

The meaning of Gnosticism

The name derives from the Greek word *gnosis*, meaning "knowledge", but it was not achieved by learning or study; rather it was revealed. It was experiential knowledge or enlightenment by which redemption could be received. Some Christian versions of Gnosticism asserted that this body of secret knowledge was necessary in addition to repentance, faith and baptism. Gnosticism also sought to offer answers to the questions about God, man and the universe. In particular, and most importantly,

---

[1] See Benjamin Walker, *Gnosticism: Its History and Influence* (Wellingborough: The Aquarian Press, 1989), pp. 1, 17–18; Arland J. Hultgren and Steven A. Haggmark, *The Earliest Christian Heretics* (Minneapolis, MN: Fortress Press, 1996), pp. 5–7.

it sought to explain how God could be considered good when there was evil and suffering in the world.

Some Gnostics organized themselves into coteries, but Gnosticism was not a church or religious institution. There were many Gnostic teachers, but there was no centralized organization. Although Gnostic teachers came from a variety of backgrounds, there were a number of major ideas and beliefs which most of them held in common.

Common threads in Gnosticism

The nature of God

The Gnostic deity is "the supreme ineffable God of the Universe"; ineffable, meaning that he is both beyond words and comprehension. He was held to be formless, without a body and could not be named or thought of in earthly terms. Many Gnostics spoke of God as "infinite" and "eternal light and love". The true God, they maintained, was far above and beyond the material world with which he had no connection. In some of the Christian Gnostic schemes, the Supreme God is identified with the God and Father of Jesus who is holy and perfect love. In contrast, "Jehovah", the God of the Old Testament, was believed to be the creator of this world and in his own words was jealous, wrathful and avenging.

The world

Gnostics maintained there were two distinct and entirely separated worlds. One was the perfect and complete world of the Supreme God identified in Christian Gnosticism with God the Father of Jesus Christ. The other was this present imperfect, material world separated from it by vast distances in time and space. The Gnostics believed that between these two worlds there were many intermediate heavens, every one of which were governed by angels. Each of these ethereal beings declined in goodness the further away they were from the world of perfection. It was one of these fallen beings, sometimes described as Satanel or the

Demiurge,[2] and even in some instances, Yahweh, who created the present material world. This accounted for the evil, suffering and pain within it.

In some Gnostic schemes, there was a strong belief that there is an ongoing cosmic battle or struggle between good and evil or light and darkness. This concept may have derived from Zoroastrianism, Zoroaster (*c*.700 BC) teaching the existence of a constant universal struggle between Ormazd, the ruler of light, and Ahriman, the ruler of darkness.

Aeons

A common thread running through most Gnostic systems was a belief in aeons. These were held to be projections which beamed out from the Godhead in much the same way that rays beam out from the sun. Some of them were associated with abstract qualities such as mercy, truth and power. Other such ideals became personalized and were spoken of as messengers or even angelic beings. In Jewish and Christian Gnosticism, aeons were regarded as angels who provided assistance in helping to bring salvation by releasing the soul from the body. This might be why at a very early point the apostle Paul warned in his Letter to the Colossians against worshipping angels.[3] In Gnostic thought, some of these heavenly beings were given responsibility for managing various levels of the heavens and the "many mansions" within them. There is perhaps a glimpse in the Gospel of John against this.[4]

Men and women

Gnostics followed the Greek philosopher Plato (*c*.427–348 BC) maintaining that all human beings possessed an immortal soul which was trapped inside a physical body. They were of the view that despite the fleshly and corrupt nature of human beings the Supreme God managed to put a divine spark or soul into every individual. The author of the Gnostic *Gospel of Thomas* made this very point: "How marvellous it is", he wrote, "that such a treasure as the soul can find a habitation in such

---

[2] A word meaning "craftsman".
[3] Colossians 2:18.
[4] John 14:2.

poverty, and can even exist in the body."[5] With the passing of time, the soul was believed either to become increasingly trapped in the body or to gradually break free. The result depended on either succumbing to evil and darkness or resisting them.

Some Gnostics held the view that there were three categories of human beings. The *Sarkikoi* were people driven by the desires of the flesh in consequence of which they had little hope of salvation. The *Psuchikoi* were dominated by a rational and intellectual nature and were capable of responding to the light of the Supreme God. The *Pneumatikoi* were people of the spirit who more naturally responded to the promptings of the divine light of their soul.

Because women were involved in giving birth to human flesh, which substance all Gnostics believed to be evil, they tended to be accorded a low status. Marcion (85–160), a second-century Christian leader some of whose views were similar to those held by the Gnotics, wrote in very harsh and sickening terms of people "created in loathsome matter, conceived in the filth of sexuality, born amid the unclean, excruciating and grotesque convulsions of labour, into a body which is 'a sack of excrement', until death turns it into carrion, a nameless corpse, a worm-filled corpse".[6]

Mediators

Mediators came to play an important role within Gnostic schemes of salvation. Their function was to prompt each individual to respond to divine light. In this way, they helped to prepare the way for mediators to release the divine spark or soul trapped within the individual and enable it to find its way back to God. When this was achieved, enlightenment and salvation were experienced. Two prominent mediators in Christian Gnostic schemes were John the Baptist and Simon Magus.[7] The central mediator in the majority of Christian Gnostic schemes was Jesus, but he was not the Jesus of the New Testament Gospels. Because Gnostics took the view that the human body was flesh and blood it was, like all matter,

---

[5] *Gospel of Thomas* (The Gnostic Library, 1994), 29.
[6] J. F. Bethune-Baker, *An Introduction to the Early History of Christian Doctrine* (London: Methuen & Co., 1903), p. 82; Walker, *Gnosticism*, p. 61.
[7] Acts 8:9–11.

corrupt and sinful. They therefore taught that Jesus only appeared to have a material body. He was, in their view, a spirit being who could appear and disappear at will. This led theologians to speak of the Gnostic Jesus as "docetic", the word deriving from the Greek word *dokein* meaning "to appear" or "seem".

Gnostic schemes of salvation

John the Baptist

There were a number of Gnostic groups who made use of various Christian themes, theology and practices. Early among them was the John-the-Baptist Sect who may have practised baptismal rites as part of their ritual and as a means of experiencing enlightenment. Several New Testament scholars have argued that the Gospel of John presupposes there was a John-the-Baptist Sect who believed him to be the eschatological Messiah. John the Baptist certainly had his own disciples.[8] The *Apocryphon of John*, or secret book of John, purports to reveal a number of mysteries which Jesus had taught him. The book, which is strongly tinged with Gnostic ideas, was cited by Irenaeus and a version of it was found in Nag Hammadi, where a library of Gnostic texts was discovered by shepherd boys in the Egyptian desert in 1947.[9] In the prologue of the Gospel of John, there is an emphatic statement of John the Baptist that "he himself was not the light; he came only as a witness to the light, the true light that gives light to everyone".[10] Clearly, John the Baptist had disowned any notion of his being a Messiah[11] or even an intermediary. It seems clear that he encouraged at least two of his disciples to become followers of Jesus.[12] The Gnostics, as we have noted, believed that God had nothing at all to do with the creation of this material world, but John begins his Gospel with the words, "Through him [Jesus the Word] all things

---

[8] John 1:35.
[9] Walker, *Gnosticism*, pp. 12 and 87.
[10] John 1:8–9.
[11] John 1:19–28.
[12] John 1:35–7.

were made; without him nothing was made."[13] Clearly after his death,[14] there were many who counted themselves as followers of John the Baptist and worshipped him. This is particularly apparent in the writings of the Mandaeans.[15]

Manda is the Aramaic word for "knowledge", which Mandaeans personified as *Manda de Hayye* meaning "Knowledge of Life". Manda was believed to have been on Earth and to have conquered the powers of darkness. He was seen as one of the mediators who could guide souls into redemption. The Mandaean Psalm Book dates from the third to fourth centuries. *The Ginza* or *Treasure* and most of their other extant writings date from the seventh century. Mandaeans did not believe John to be their founder but nevertheless regarded him as their greatest teacher and the messenger of light who was full of *manda* (*gnosis*). There are still a small number of scattered Mandaean communities in the Middle East and elsewhere. They maintain that Jesus was a false Messiah who perverted the teaching entrusted to him by John.

Basilides (85–145)
Basilides hailed from Alexandria where he was employed as a lecturer from 120–40. His system began with "the Ineffable Father", at the top of a hierarchical tree, who presided over 365 heavens, each one cared for and supervised by angels. Fallen humanity was at the bottom of the pile, estranged and cut off from God. Basilides' scheme of redemption focused on the Father's first begotten, *Nous*, the Greek word meaning "mind". *Nous* appeared in a kind of personalized form and reached down to release the spiritual element trapped in each body. Basilides believed Jesus was not a human being because all material including human flesh was evil. His Jesus was therefore "the first begotten mind" who came from the Supreme God. Thus Jesus only seemed to have been a man and to have had a physical body. Needless to say Basilides' form of Gnosticism did not accept either the reality of the incarnation or salvation through

---

[13] John 1:3.
[14] Josephus, *Antiquities* 18.5.2; Matthew 14:10–12.
[15] See also Carlos Gilbert, *The Teachings of the Mandaean John the Baptist* (Fairfield, NSW: Living Water Books, 2017).

the cross. His Jesus did not himself suffer and at the time of the crucifixion changed places with Simon of Cyrene who carried his cross.[16] Jesus then walked amid the crowd while Simon carried the cross to Golgotha and suffered and died in his place. For the Gnostics salvation was of the soul only. There could be no resurrection of the body and life beyond the grave.

Valentinus (110–175)
Valentinus was a priest in the mainstream Catholic Church who was very nearly elected Bishop of Rome. He came to the fore shortly after Basilides and taught for a while in the Imperial City. At the top of his system was "God the Father", whom he designated *Bythos* meaning "life". On either side of Him were *Sige*, meaning "silence", and *Ennoia,* meaning "thought". Below them, in a way similar to Basilides' system, there were a series of aeons or intermediaries, one of whom was the ungovernable *Sophia*, meaning "wisdom", who succumbed to an all-consuming desire to discover the true nature of God. In the process of her fall from his presence she gave birth to the demiurge who, according to Valentinus, was the God of the Old Testament who created the world and everything in it. Redemption was brought about by an immaterial Jesus who reached down and released the trapped spirit from within each body.

Cerinthus (c.100)
Cerinthus taught in both Asia Minor and Alexandria. The central core of his Gnostic system was that the world was not made by "the Principal God" but by a separate and far removed and distant Virtue. Jesus was an ordinary human being born of Joseph and Mary but "superior to all others in justice, prudence and wisdom".[17] Later, at his baptism, "Christ descended upon him in the form of a dove from the 'Principality' who is above all things. He revealed the Unknown Father and the deeds of Virtue."[18] Christ remained in Jesus for the rest of his earthly ministry of preaching, healing and caring for the needy. Then, at a time very shortly

---

[16] Mark 15:21.

[17] Irenaeus, *Against Heresies* I.26.1–2.

[18] Irenaeus, *Against Heresies* I.26.1.

before his crucifixion, the Christ Spirit flew back to the Principal God so that only the human Jesus suffered and rose again but Christ remained spiritual and suffered no fleshly pain.

Marcion (*d*.165)
Marcion was a native of Sinope in Pontus on the Black Sea coast. He was born about the year 85 and, according to Epiphanius, he was the son of a Christian bishop who excommunicated him on grounds of immorality. With the passing of time, he grew up to be a wealthy ship owner and travelled widely in the Mediterranean area. His journeys brought him into contact with both pagan and Christian thinkers who began to impact his thinking. About the year 140, he settled in Rome and joined the Catholic Church. All of Marcion's writings have been lost, but it has been possible to reconstruct the basics of his system from the writings of some of his opponents, most notably Tertullian. Marcion rejected the idea that the Supreme God and Yahweh the God of the Jews were one and the same. He maintained that the Supreme God is the Father of Jesus Christ who is unseen and whose nature is boundless love and peace. He has no connection with the creation, which was brought into being by the demiurge, sometimes called "the architect", who was revealed in the Old Testament as Yahweh. It was this that accounted for the evil and suffering in the present world.

Marcion drew a sharp distinction between Yahweh as the God of the Jews who he described as despotic, angry, vindictive and vengeful. He took a literal view of the Old Testament rather than an allegorical one as men such as Philo had done in the past. This led to his being troubled by texts such as in Isaiah where God confesses, "I create evil" and another in 2 Samuel where it is said, "The Lord sent evil".[19] In his book entitled *Antithesis*, Marcion drew up a list of all the ways in which the Old Testament ran counter to the teaching of Jesus and Paul. Hippolytus informs us that Marcion held that "Christ is the Son of the good Being and was sent by him for the salvation of souls". He also asserted that

---

[19] Cf Isaiah 45:7 and 2 Samuel 16:14.

Christ "appeared as a man though not being a man, and as incarnate though not being incarnate".[20]

As a result of this, Marcion left the Church and set up independent communities of his own. They made no use of the Old Testament in their worship, and they read only those New Testament books which they considered to be worthy of a loving God. According to Irenaeus, "he mutilated the Gospel of Luke, removing all the narratives of the Lord's birth" and those discourses of the Lord where "he described the maker of this universe to be his father".[21] In a similar way, "he mutilated the Epistles of the Apostle Paul" removing "whatever is manifestly spoken concerning the God who made the world".[22] Marcion maintained that the rest of the apostolic gospel and letters had been corrupted by Judaizers.

The challenge and the Church's defeat of Gnosticism

The apostles
At an early point, the Church was quickly provoked into action against the Gnostics. As the first century drew to a close, the Gospel and Letters of John were written against early expressions of Gnosticism to defend the Orthodox Christian understanding of God, the world, Jesus and salvation. John forcefully highlighted crucial Gnostic terms and demonstrated that Jesus had in fact superseded them. Jesus was not just a light, as the Gnostics perceived their aeons and intermediaries to be. He was "the true light" which no amount of darkness could ever overcome. He was "the Light of the world" and those who put their trust in Him would never walk in darkness but have everlasting life. Far from the world being made by a demiurge, the God who came into the world in the person of Jesus made all things and "without him nothing was made that has been made".[23] In his Gospel, John deliberately stressed the humanity of Jesus in opposition to Docetism (from the Greek *dokein* to appear, to

---

[20] Hippolytus, *Refutation of All Heresies* 10.15.
[21] Irenaeus, *Against Heresies* I.27.2–3.
[22] Irenaeus, *Against Heresies* I.27.2–3.
[23] See John 1:1–18.

seem), the view that Jesus only appeared to have a human body but was in fact divine. He recorded Jesus being tired and needing rest, thirsty and drinking water at the well in Samaria, hungry and eating fish with the disciples, mourning and weeping at Lazarus' grave and blood and water flowing from his side at the crucifixion.

Irenaeus, Tertullian and Hippolytus

The main orthodox theologians who opposed the second- and early-third-century Gnostics were Irenaeus (*c*.130–*c*.202), Tertullian (155–220) and Hippolytus (*c*.170–*c*.234). They focused on the key areas where Gnostic teachers had departed from the apostolic Christian faith. All three would have agreed with Justin Martyr (*c*.100–*c*.165) who saw the Gnostics as being among the many "false Christs", "pretend apostles" and "sheep in ravening wolves clothing", who, Jesus warned, would arise in the last days. "They are all", he declared, "outside of our communion, for we know them for what they are, impious atheists and wicked sinners who profess Jesus with their lips, but do not worship Him in their hearts."[24]

The ground on which early Christian theologians attacked the Gnostics was their departure from the faith enshrined in the four widely acknowledged and later canonized Gospels and the genuine apostolic letters. In *Against Heresies*, written sometime between 174–89, Irenaeus rebuked Marcion because "he persuaded his disciples that he himself was more trustworthy than the apostles, who handed down the Gospel".[25]

A wrong view of creation

Gnosticism held that both the world and the matter from which it was created was evil. This caused its followers to adopt unhealthy attitudes towards the world and its pleasures. It led to some of them being unable to enjoy even the simplest pleasures of their daily living such as eating and drinking and to reject other perfectly decent relationships and activities. In contrast to Gnosticism, the early Christians rooted their faith in the Genesis creation story in which God saw that everything that he had made was good. More than that they rejoiced in the Jesus

---

[24] Justin, *Dialogue with Trypho* 35.
[25] Irenaeus, *Against Heresies* I.27.2–3.

of the apostolic Gospels who delighted in the created world in all its aspects and ate and drank and enjoyed the company of publicans and sinners. From an early point, the apostolic Church was conscious of the need to rebut the teaching of the Gnostics. Many Gnostics asserted there was an ongoing cosmic struggle between light and darkness. John, in the prologue of his Gospel, declared that Jesus was "the true light that gives light" and "without him nothing was made that has been made".[26] Justin was similarly unequivocal that Jesus the Divine Logos was the one who revealed God and was the instrument by which God created and instructed the world.

The Godhead

All the early Christian theologians disagreed with Gnostic separation of the "Supreme God", who they depicted as "the God and Father of Jesus Christ", from the second and "Inferior Creator God" who they identified as Yahweh, the God of law and the Old Testament. They totally rebutted the Gnostic contention that Jesus who revealed Yahweh was without flesh and blood. Tertullian regarded "the separation of Law and Gospel" as "this heresy".[27]

They rejected the Christian doctrine of salvation

Most significant of all, the Gnostics totally rejected the apostolic doctrine of salvation. They all held that salvation was of the soul only and amounted to its release from captivity in the body and its uniting with the Supreme God. Gnostics mistakenly believed that everything in the material world was tainted with evil. Therefore, they could not even begin to contemplate the idea that the Supreme God became a human being. All flesh, in their eyes, was evil and it was therefore impossible for Jesus to have been "the spotless lamb of God". For the same reason, the Gnostics rejected the very idea of mankind being saved through the shedding of human blood on a cross. Jesus of the Gnostics was therefore docetic. He only appeared to have a human body and, as far as they were concerned, he was a phantom and not a reality. In opposition to

---

[26] John 1:3 and 9.
[27] Tertullian, *Against Marcion* I.19.4–5.

such thinking, the apostle Paul had much earlier asserted that Jesus "was manifest in the flesh".[28]

Tertullian took Marcion to task on this very point in his book entitled *Against Marcion* (written c.208). Among other things, he pointed out that if, as Marcion asserted, Jesus' having flesh was a lie then,

> it follows that all things that were done by means of Christ's flesh were done by a lie, his meetings with people, his touching of them, his partaking of food, his miracles besides. For if by touching someone, or being touched by someone, he gave freedom from sickness the act performed by the body cannot be credited as truly performed apart from the verity of the body itself.[29]

Tertullian continued his disenchantment with Marcion by going on to state that few people would want to believe in a Jesus who has not truly suffered and indeed has not suffered for all.[30]

Irenaeus strongly rejected the Gnostic view that "salvation belongs to the soul alone for the body is by nature subject to corruption".[31] He likewise dismissed their contention that they would be "entirely and undoubtedly saved, not by means of conduct, but because they are spiritual by nature".[32] He totally rejected Valentinus' assertion that just as gold lost none of its beauty and character when submersed in mud so his followers could not lose their spiritual substance regardless of their behaviour.[33]

They had wrong attitudes to the body and behaviour

Gnostics held that since matter is evil, the body must be evil. This meant that there were seemingly two alternatives; either it must be conquered with ascetic practices or its desires satisfied with freedom and pleasure.

---

[28] 1 Timothy 3:16 (KJV).
[29] Tertullian, *Against Marcion* III.8.2–7.
[30] Tertullian, *Against Marcion* III.8.2–7.
[31] Irenaeus, *Against Heresies* I.24.1.
[32] Irenaeus, *Against Heresies* I.6.2.
[33] Irenaeus, *Against Heresies* I.6.2.

Gnosticism therefore led its followers into one of two wrong attitudes to the flesh and the body: antinomianism or lawlessness on the one hand and austerity and asceticism on the other.

First, there were many in the days of the apostles who had fallen under the influence of incipient Gnosticism. This led the apostle Paul to denounce those at Colossae for demanding abstinence from meats. "Do not let anyone", he wrote to them, "judge you by what you eat or drink" and engage in "harsh treatment of the body".[34] Hippolytus condemned the followers of Marcion, writing, "You forbid marriage, the procreation of children, [and] the abstaining from meats which God has created for participation for the faithful, and those who know the truth." Both Irenaeus and Hippolytus challenged their Gnostic opponents who advocated sparse diets with the plainest of food and drink. Macarius the Younger is said to have eaten palm leaves and John of Egypt survived on seeds and water.[35] There was a decidedly monastic emphasis among a number of Gnostic groups. For many, vigils, fasts and self-flagellation became the order of the day. Other ascetics abstained from sexual relationships and some tried castration and excision of sexual organs as a means of suppressing sexual desires.

Second, there were Gnostics who argued that as the flesh was evil all that mattered was the Spirit. So, why not be free and "eat, drink and be merry"? It was against this backdrop of Gnostic thinking that the apostle Jude wrote his warning letter counselling his readers against "certain godless men who have secretly stepped in among you".[36] These men, he continued, "pervert the grace of our God into a license for immorality and deny Jesus Christ".[37] In the same way, they "pollute their own bodies" and are blemishes at their Love feasts "eating with you without the slightest qualm".[38] They are "wild waves of the sea foaming up their

---

[34] Colossians 2:16,20–3.

[35] Walker, *Gnosticism*, p. 109.

[36] See William Barclay, *The Letter to Jude* (Edinburgh: St Andrew Press, 1965), pp. 190–4.

[37] Jude 4.

[38] Jude 8,12.

shame".[39] Paul may also have been addressing some such people in the church at Corinth who had slipped into Gnostic beliefs and lifestyle. Those he addressed were bragging that "everything is permissible for me", were eating gluttonously and consorting with prostitutes in the city's brothels.[40] A little later in the second century, Irenaeus condemned the followers of Carpocrates (78–138), the Alexandrian Gnostic, who

> practice magic arts and incantations, love potions and love feasts, familiar spirits and dream inducers and other evil things, saying that they have power to prevail over the archons and creators of this world, and not only that, but over all that crossed it.[41]

Clement of Alexandria also condemned the followers of Carpocrates "who think wives should be common property" and gather together for agape feasts at which "they overturn their lamps and so extinguish the light that the shame of their adulterous 'righteousness' is hidden and they have intercourse where they will and with whom they will".[42] The Church historian Eusebius condemned Cerinthus, the early-second-century Gnostic, who "taught that the kingdom of God would come on Earth, and that carnal humanity will dwell in Jerusalem, once more enslaved to lusts and pleasures". These would include "a thousand years given over to unlimited indulgence in lechery at banquets, drinking bouts and wedding feasts".[43]

Irenaeus wrote of the Gnostics, "The most perfect among them addict themselves to all kinds of forbidden deeds of which the Scriptures assure us that they who do such things shall not inherit the kingdom of God." A little later in the same document he added, "Then again, at every heathen festival celebrated in honour of the idols, these men are the first to assemble; and to such a pitch do they go, that some of them do not even keep away from the bloody spectacle hateful to both God and men,

---

[39] Jude 13.
[40] 1 Corinthians 6:12–16.
[41] Eusebius, *History of the Church* IV.7.
[42] Clement, *Stromata* III.2.5.
[43] Eusebius, *History of the Church* III.28.1.

in which gladiators either fight with wild beasts, or singly encounter one another."[44]

The early Christian theologians included secrecy as an aspect of unacceptable Gnostic behaviour. Irenaeus maintained that the hidden practices of many Gnostic societies were contrary to orthodox Christian principles which emphasized openness. "Gnostics", he stated, "do not disclose membership of the sect" and "declare that it is not fitting to speak openly of their mysteries, but right to keep them secret by preserving silence".[45]

The speculative nature of Gnosticism

Orthodox Christian theologians were highly critical of the speculative nature of Gnostic systems of redemption. Irenaeus attacked Basilides for his assertion that there were 365 heavens which is why, he jibed, "there were three-hundred and sixty-five days in a year"![46] Irenaeus also understandably opposed the Gnostic Jesus who Basilides described as "Mind" and "the first-born of the unborn Father".[47] Furthermore, he pointed out that Basilides' Jesus "did not suffer death, but a certain Simon of Cyrene was compelled to bear the cross in his stead. Simon was then transfigured by him, that he might be thought to be Jesus, and was crucified, through ignorance and error, while Jesus himself received the form of Simon, and, standing by laughed at them."[48] Irenaeus denounced those Gnostics who continued to assert that "anyone who confesses Jesus crucified is still a slave, and under the power of those who formed our bodies".[49] Tertullian also took issue over this Gnostic contention that Jesus did not die, arguing that if he did not die then neither can there be any assurance of the resurrection. He then quoted from chapter 15 of Paul's First Letter to the Corinthians, where the apostle wrote, "For I delivered to you, first of all that Christ died for our sins, and that he

---

[44] Irenaeus, *Against Heresies* I.6.3.
[45] Irenaeus, *Against Heresies* I.8.5.
[46] Irenaeus, *Against Heresies* I.19.1–4.
[47] Irenaeus, *Against Heresies* I.19.1–4.
[48] Irenaeus, *Against Heresies* I.19.1–4.
[49] Irenaeus, *Against Heresies* I.24.1–4.

was buried, and that he rose again the third day."⁵⁰ Eusebius of Caesarea wrote that "Basilides under the pretence of deeper mysteries, extended his fantasies into the infinite, inventing monstrous fictions to support his impious heresies".⁵¹

Denouement

Most orthodox theologians of the second and third centuries would have agreed with Justin Martyr's conclusion that, "As we look about us, we see events actually taking place which He [Jesus] predicted would happen." Indeed, Justin continued:

> Jesus foretold: 'Many shall come in My name, clothed outwardly in sheep's clothing, but inwardly they are ravening wolves. And there shall be schisms and heresies. And beware of false prophets who come to you in the clothing of sheep, but inwardly are ravening wolves. And there shall arise many false Apostles, and they shall deceive many of the faithful.'⁵²

The study of these forms of Gnosticism with which the early Christians grappled is still profoundly relevant in the twenty-first century. Many "New Religions" (so called) which are growing hugely across the globe work on the basis that there is a "divine spark", "immortal divinity" or "spiritual energy" within every individual person which can only be released by their meditation, mantras, fasting or ceremonial rituals. Among them are Sahaja Yoga, Krishna Consciousness and Elan Vital.⁵³

After a long struggle the early Christians gradually overcame the threat posed by the Gnostics. Clement of Alexandria even put forward the idea of "a [Christian] Gnostic".⁵⁴ In conclusion, it is clear the early Christian leaders and theologians gained much from their struggles to overcome

---

50   Tertullian, *Against Marcion* III.8.2–7.
51   Eusebius, *History of the Church* IV.7.
52   Justin, *Dialogue with Trypho* 35.
53   See Nigel Scotland, *A Pocket Guide to Sects and New Religions* (Oxford: Lion Hudson, 2005), pp. 11,18 and 28.
54   For a full discussion of this see Chadwick, *The Early Church*, pp. 96–7.

Gnosticism. They learned from Marcion the necessity of defining the Canon of Scripture. Gnosticism caused Irenaeus to emphasize the fact that there were only four genuinely apostolic Gospels.[55] It also gave Christian leaders the impulse to engage in serious study of the apostolic writings and to re-affirm the essential core doctrines of their faith. The heart of this was their insistence on one good creator God fully revealed in the humanity of Jesus Christ, salvation through the cross and the basic goodness of the material world. Irenaeus counteracted the Gnostics by giving a summary of the teaching of the Catholic Church. Perhaps above all, Gnosticism, with its huge output of literature, challenged the Church to be sure which documents were undoubtedly from the apostles. It also led churches to keep lists of orthodox bishops and church leaders reaching right back to the apostolic age. This in turn caused church leaders to begin keeping lists of all books which were genuinely known to have come from the pens of the apostles. It is this issue which is the subject of the following chapter.

---

[55] Irenaeus, *Against Heresies* 3.11.

6

On solid ground: A faith founded on apostolic teaching and the formation of the New Testament

As we have seen in the previous chapter, Gnostics believed that the material world is essentially evil, and this led to their rejection of much of the Old Testament and those sections of the New which affirmed the goodness of the material world. This challenged the early churches to make clear the authority they placed on the Old Testament Scriptures and the teaching of the apostles. From the very beginning, the early Christians met together to sing, pray and read the Jewish Scriptures and the writings of the apostles. By the year 100, almost all the books which came to make up the New Testament were widely accepted and by almost all congregations. However, it took nearly another 300 years before what finally became known as the Canon of New Testament Scripture was formally agreed and ratified by the Catholic Church.

The word canon means "rod" or "rule" and came to be used to signify a measuring standard by which orthodoxy could be tried and tested. So when in later times Christians spoke of the Canon of Scripture or the Canon of the New Testament they were referring to those writings which were genuinely believed to be orthodox and endorsed by all the churches. In other words, they were sure that they were teaching the true Christ-centred faith "once for all entrusted to the saints".[1]

---

[1] Jude 3 (NRSV).

Why was the New Testament put together?

The challenge of the sects

Not only were the churches provoked by the Gnostics into defining the orthodox Gospels and letters, other challenges were also emerging. In the late second century, Montanus, a church leader who placed a strong emphasis on the gifts of the Holy Spirit, and his followers, claimed to be having revelations and prophecies about the end times.[2] Some of these were being written down and treated as equally authoritative as the apostolic writings. This was particularly the case when it came to their predictions that the town of Pepusa in Phrygia was destined to become the New Jerusalem and place of Jesus' return in 177. This further prompted church leaders to ensure that their members were grounded in the teachings of the apostolic Gospels and Jesus' assertion that no-one would know the time of his return.

Among those who were imparting unorthodox teaching was Marcion (c.85–160) who, along with his followers, presented a major challenge to the apostolic Christian faith. Marcion was a wealthy ship owner and merchant based in Rome. He taught that there were two gods—Yahweh the cruel and vindictive God of the Old Testament, and Abba, the kind loving God of the New Testament. Marcion therefore eliminated the entire Old Testament and scrubbed out three Gospels altogether, retaining only a pruned version of Luke and ten letters of Paul. He set out his teaching in writing in a work entitled *Antitheses* for which he was eventually excommunicated by the church of Rome about the year 144. Marcion was of great significance because his action forced the Christian Church to come clean and make plain what was the true faith proclaimed by the apostles.

Written traditions were part of the Jewish culture

The Jews were a people who wrote things down and remembered them with great accuracy. It is known that some Jews in the first century knew the whole Pentateuch by heart. Not only did they memorize their traditions and laws, they had scribes who wrote out in detail how they were to be

---

[2] Eusebius, *History of the Church* V.14.

interpreted and kept. The New Testament scholar Oscar Cullmann aptly wrote: "Jesus and the Early Church lived in an atmosphere permeated with tradition."[3] It was therefore only natural that the apostles and those close to Jesus would have written down his teachings and parables. Many of these small documents would have then been collected up by the Gospel writers and by the apostles as they wrote their letters. This process would have continued until all the text and orthodoxy of all the books of the New Testament were finally fixed, acknowledged and accepted by the whole of the Catholic Church.

The apostles were passing from living memory
By about the year 150, there were very few people still living who had personally known any of the apostles. Papias (c.60–c.130), who was Bishop of Hierapolis in Asia Minor, was said to have been taught by the apostle John, but he died in 130. His companion Polycarp (c.69–155), who was Bishop of Smyrna, was recorded by Irenaeus to have "had intercourse with John and with the rest of those who had seen the Lord".[4] But he had been martyred in 156.

By this time, the early Christians came to the realization that they were reaching a point where they were becoming too distant from the apostolic age to guard the purity of their original doctrines and traditions. When they died who would be left who could truly say for certain, "This is what the apostles of Jesus taught" or that "This letter or document was written by one of Jesus' disciples or close followers"? A number of scholars have therefore argued that the year 150 was probably about the time when all the churches began to specify which documents were genuinely apostolic. They were still near enough to the apostolic age to be able, with the help of the Holy Spirit, to assert and select genuine written traditions.

These, therefore, were the main reasons why the early Christians formed the New Testament. However, it leads on to the further question, "On what basis did they select the books of the New Testament?"

---

[3] Oscar Cullmann, *The Early Church* (London: SCM Press, 1956), p. 63.
[4] Irenaeus, Entry in *The Oxford Dictionary of The Christian Church*, 2nd edn, eds F. L. Cross and E. A. Livingstone (Oxford: Oxford University Press, 1998), p. 1306.

The basis on which the books of the New Testament were selected
Roman Catholics have always maintained that it was the Church, given authority and commissioned by Jesus, who, under the guidance of the Holy Spirit, made the final decision regarding which books were to form part of New Testament. This view asserts that the Scriptures were written by members of the early Christian Church which is the body of Christ, and it was he who guided them. On this understanding, it is the Church who decides what is Scripture and what is not. It's a position which generates some problems, the most obvious being that it infers that if the Church has the power to decide what is Scripture and what is not, it is the Church who shall decide what is the true meaning of the text.

At the time of the sixteenth-century Protestant Reformation, this caused the Roman Church to re-visit the question of the Canon. This in turn raised further concerns about the authority of the Bible. The early Church had produced other books, some of which may have predated those in the New Testament. Even in later centuries, some of these were mistakenly regarded as of equal importance and authority as the books written by the apostles. In fact, the Counter Reformation Council of Trent (1545–63) went on to decree that "Catholic tradition is of equal importance with the New Testament".[5] It was small wonder that visitors to Canterbury Cathedral at the time were surprised to find a copy of the apocryphal *Gospel of Nicodemus* on the lectern.

Protestants have been happy to accept that the Church, guided by the Holy Spirit, decided the Canon. That said, they also wanted to assert that the Church recognized that the New Testament books carry authority within themselves. Put very simply, this view says that when we read the Gospel of Mark, it is "a unique book", particularly if we were to set it alongside the Gnostic *Gospel of Peter* or the *Gospel of Thomas*. This Protestant view asserts that the New Testament books carry their own inherent authority. Christ is encountered through their pages in a way not found in other literature. Oscar Cullmann expressed it with clarity, writing: "Among the numerous Christian writings the books which were

---

[5] Bernard M. G. Reardon, *Religious Thought in the Reformation* (London: Longman, 1981), p. 306, citing Council of Trent, Session 8 April 1546.

to form the New Testament Canon imposed themselves on the church by their intrinsic authority as they still do, because Christ speaks in them."[6]

Initially, this understanding can appear subjective, but Protestant scholars have taken the view that the New Testament books have this authority because they all derive from the apostles themselves or from apostolic sources. Added to this is the fact that the apostles were unique and personally chosen by Christ himself. By "apostle", the early Church meant one of the original twelve disciples who had been with Jesus from the beginning and had witnessed his resurrection.[7] Paul was added to their number since he had seen the risen Lord on the road to Damascus and had received the same gospel independently by divine revelation.[8] The apostle John recorded in his Gospel Jesus' promise to his disciples that they would be enabled by his Holy Spirit to remember all that he had taught them: "The Advocate, the Holy Spirit, whom the Father will send in my name", Jesus declared to his disciples, "will teach you all things, and will remind you of everything I have said to you."[9]

In the weeks and months following the Day of Pentecost, Jesus' teachings would have been passed on by word of mouth. Inevitably oral tradition was soon supplemented by written sources. And so we find Paul in his First Letter to the Corinthians stressing that what he was teaching about the resurrection was an apostolic tradition that he was now handing on just as he had received it: "For what I received I passed on to you."[10] In his Letter to the Colossians, Paul reminded the church to depend on legitimate apostolic traditions that come from Christ and not on "deceptive philosophy which depends on human tradition".[11] The Letter to the Ephesians sums up the matter, informing readers that the Church is "built on the foundation of the apostles and prophets with Christ Jesus himself as the chief corner stone".[12]

---

[6] Cullmann, *The Early Church*, p. 91.
[7] Acts 1:21–2.
[8] Galatians 1:12.
[9] John 14:26.
[10] 1 Corinthians 15:3.
[11] Colossians 2:6–8.
[12] Ephesians 2:20.

Papias (*c*.60–*c*.130), a second-century church leader, underlined this same fact stating that Mark's Gospel was based on apostolic traditions which he had personally received from Peter:

> Mark who was Peter's interpreter, wrote down accurately, though not in order all that he recollected of what Christ had said or done. For he was not a hearer of the Lord or a follower of His. He followed Peter, as I have said, at a later date, and Peter adapted his instruction to practical needs, without any attempt to give the Lord's teaching systematically. So that Mark was not wrong in writing down some things in this way from memory, for his one concern was neither to omit or falsify anything that he had heard.[13]

Mark's Gospel has 661 verses of which Matthew reproduced 606 and Luke 320. Generally speaking, Matthew and Luke follow Mark's order of events. Matthew was an apostle of Jesus, but although Luke was not, it is clear that he derived much information from apostolic sources and in particular from the apostle Paul with whom he travelled for at least two years.[14] The apostle John's Gospel was published towards the close of the first century and is different in style and emphasis from the other three, stressing the universality of Jesus' message. It is therefore clear that well before the end of the first century all four Gospels were widely accepted as apostolic literature and read in all the churches.

From this, it can be seen that even in the earliest New Testament period of Christian history, all the churches applied this same test. Was this Gospel, letter or document they had received of apostolic origin? This same fundamental principle can be traced throughout the centuries until the Canon of Scripture was finally fixed at the Third Council of Carthage in 397.

---

[13] Papias, The Sayings of the Lord, cited in Eusebius, *History of the Church* III.39.11.

[14] See Luke 1:1–4 and Acts 1:1–2.

The sub-apostolic period

The "sub-apostolic period" extended roughly from 100 to about 130. The sub-apostolic writings are those which came in succession to or immediately after the time of the apostles. One of the earliest such documents was Clement of Rome's *Letter to the Corinthians*, which is dated about 98. It is conceivably possible that he may have been Paul's co-worker whom he mentions in his Letter to the Philippians.[15] Clement refers to Peter and Paul and writes of them as "the greatest and most righteous pillars of the church".[16] In paragraph 42 of the same letter, Clement made it abundantly clear that he regarded them as "the final, authoritative apostles of the Lord". He wrote: "The apostles received the gospel for us from the Lord Jesus Christ; Jesus Christ was sent forth from God, and the apostles are from Christ. Both therefore came of the will of God in their appointed order."[17] In these lines from his letter, Clement was making it clear that both he and the Church of Corinth to whom he was writing fully acknowledged the authority of the apostles to teach and minister in the name of the Lord.

Another early sub-apostolic document generally dated around 120 is *The Didache* which has as its full title *The Teaching of the Lord to the Gentiles through the Twelve Apostles*. This of itself indicates that the churches at this time believed that its teaching had come to them through the apostles. It should be noted in passing that *The Didache* sometimes uses the word "apostle" in a broader way to mean "missionary", but this doesn't invalidate the general point regarding the authority of the twelve apostles.

The Letter of Barnabas is generally agreed to have been written before 132. Its author did not claim to be an apostle in the sense that the New Testament writers did,[18] but he went on to state that "the Lord chose his own apostles who were to proclaim his gospel". By this he meant the twelve.

---

[15] Philippians 4:3.
[16] Clement, *Letter to the Corinthians* 5.
[17] Clement, *Letter to the Corinthians* 42.
[18] *Letter of Barnabas* 5.

Hermas was a merchant and possibly a church leader in Rome. About 130, he wrote an allegorical book entitled *The Shepherd*, which became a popular read in the first half of the second century.[19] The book has three sections: Visions (church), Mandates (behaviour), and Similitudes (values). In it, he speaks of the supreme authority of the apostles. In Vision 3, he describes them as "the first stones of the building that is being erected".[20] In Similitude 9, Hermas wrote that "the Son of God was preached by the apostles".[21] Again in Similitude 9, Hermas refers to the apostles as "pre-eminently those who preached unto the whole world, and who taught the word of the Lord with soberness and purity, and ... walked always in righteousness and truth, even as they received the Holy Spirit".[22]

The Letters of Ignatius were written by Ignatius (c.35–c.107), the second Bishop of Antioch, as he journeyed on his way to martyrdom in Rome. In his *Letter to the Ephesians*, he wrote of Paul as, "he who was sanctified, who obtained a good report, who is worthy of all felicitation, in whose steps I would fain be found treading, when I shall attain unto God; who in every letter makes mention of you in Christ Jesus".[23] Writing in his *Letter to the Magnesians*, Ignatius referred to "the council of the apostles" so as to emphasize their supreme authority. "Do your diligence therefore", he pleaded, "that you be conformed in the ordinances of the Lord and the apostles."[24] Again in his *Letter to the Romans*, Ignatius urged his readers to pray earnestly for him but at the same time being careful not to issue an order as if he were an apostle. He wrote, "Intercede ... for me ... that I may be made a sacrifice to God. However, I am not issuing orders, as though I were a Peter or a Paul. They were apostles, and I am a condemned criminal."[25]

---

[19] *The Muratorian Canon* (c.180) suggests that the author was the brother of Pope Pius I (d.155).
[20] Hermas, *The Shepherd*, Vision 3, para 5.
[21] Hermas, *The Shepherd*, Similitude 9, para 17.
[22] Hermas, *The Shepherd*, Similitude 9, para 25.
[23] Ignatius, *Letter to the Ephesians* 12.
[24] Ignatius, *Letter to the Magnesians* 13.
[25] Ignatius, *Letter to the Romans* 4.

Another sub-apostolic document of particular note was Polycarp's *Letter to the Philippians*. Polycarp (*c*.69–155), who was Bishop of Smyrna, wrote to the Philippian church at some point probably shortly before his martyrdom: "Let us therefore serve Him [Jesus] with fear and all reverence, as he himself gave commandment and as the apostles who preached the gospel to us and the prophets who proclaimed beforehand the coming of the Lord."[26]

Not only did the sub-apostolic writers acknowledge the supreme authority of the twelve apostles and Paul, the same was also true of both the Early Christian Fathers of the second and third centuries and the Post-Nicaean Fathers of the fourth and fifth centuries.

The Early Christian Fathers

About the year 150, Justin Martyr (*c*.100–165) wrote in his *First Apology*: "On a day called Sunday there is an assembly of all those residing in the cities and in the country, and then the memoirs of the apostles or writings of the prophets are read as long as time allows."[27] Perhaps of even greater significance is the testimony of Irenaeus (*c*.130–200), who was Bishop of Lyon in the province of Gaul. In his extensive volume *Against Heresies*, he asserted the unique and authoritative character of both the apostles and the apostolic writings. In Book 1, he referred to the writings of "the evangelists and apostles" and of "the law and the prophets" and then designated them as "Scripture". In another lengthy passage, in which he was defending the biblical faith against his heretical Gnostic opponents, he asserted the uniqueness of the four New Testament Gospels:

> We have learned from no others the plan of salvation, than those from whom the gospels came down to us . . . . For, after our Lord rose from the dead, [the apostles] were invested with power from on high when the Holy Spirit came down [upon them], were filled from all his gifts, and had perfect knowledge

---

[26] Polycarp, *Letter to the Philippians* 6.
[27] Justin, *First Apology* 67.

> .... Matthew also issued a gospel among the Hebrews in their own dialect, while Peter and Paul were preaching in Rome, and laying the foundations of the Church. After their departure, Mark, the disciple and interpreter of Peter, did also hand down to us in writing what had been preached by Peter.... Afterwards, John, the disciple of the Lord, who also leaned on his breast, did himself publish a gospel during his residence in Asia Minor.[28]

These words from Irenaeus make it clear that in the later second century he and other church leaders were still emphasizing the supreme importance of apostolic authority. Here he made a point of telling his readers that both the first and the fourth Gospels were apostolic, having come from the pens of Matthew and John, while Mark's Gospel was clearly based on the apostolic preaching of Peter.

In another somewhat quaint passage in *Against Heresies*, Irenaeus once more impressed on his readers the uniqueness of what the Church later recognized as the four canonical Gospels:

> It is not possible that the gospels be either more or fewer than they are. For since there are four regions of the world in which we live, and four principal winds, and the church is scattered over the whole earth ... it is fitting that she should have four pillars breathing forth immortality on every side.[29]

Irenaeus' testimony is very important because he travelled around a good deal and would have been fully aware of what was happening in the different churches across Asia Minor where he had lived before becoming the overseer of the churches in Gaul. He had also visited Rome and knew the situation and practice of the city's churches. Irenaeus emphasized that the apostles' teaching is the only foundation of the church. He stressed that it was they who through the Holy Spirit were given perfect ability to proclaim the gospel in its final form.

---

[28] Irenaeus, *Against Heresies* 3.1.
[29] Irenaeus, *Against Heresies* III.2.8.

A little later in time, Tertullian (c.160–225), who was a theologian and Christian leader in Carthage, remarked that the church in his locality recognized the four Gospels of Matthew, Luke, Mark and John. One of his major writing projects was entitled *Against Marcion*. Written in Latin about the year 208, it was a defence of the Church's teaching against the Gnostic views of Marcion and his followers.

At one point in the book, Tertullian gives some insights into the ways in which the churches came to decide which books could be recognized as Scripture and so eventually were included in the New Testament. He wrote: "It is evidently true that what is earlier is more true, that from the beginning is from the apostles. It is evidently true that what was handed down from the apostles is what has been a sacred deposit in the churches." A little further on he added, "the gospels also, which we possess ... I mean the Gospel of John and the Gospel of Matthew, but that which Mark published may be affirmed to be Peter's, whose interpreter Mark was. For even Luke men universally ascribe to Paul."[30] Here Tertullian highlights the fact that both Mark and Luke are to be regarded as authoritative because both were based on apostolic sources, namely the lives and teachings of Peter and Paul.

A little later, about the year 230, Origen of Alexandria listed all the books that later came to be accepted as Canonical Scripture. He did, however, mention that Hebrews, Peter's Second Letter, John's Second and Third Letters, The Letter of James and Jude are disputed by some.[31] It is plain to see that by Origen's time there was widespread agreement about most of the New Testament books.

Eusebius, writing about the year 327 in his *History of the Church*, followed in the steps of Tertullian and Origen and stressed the unique authority of the apostles. He wrote, "Those inspired and wonderful men, Christ's apostles, had completely purified their lives and cultivated every spiritual virtue, but their language was every day."[32] In Book 3 he stated, "It will be well, at this point to clarify the New Testament writings already

---

[30] Tertullian, *Against Marcion* IV.5.
[31] Bruce, *The Spreading Flame*, p. 235. He also cites Origen, *Commentary on John* 2:6 and *Homily on Jeremiah* 15:4.
[32] Eusebius, *History of the Church* V.24.

referred to." He then listed "the holy quartet of gospels, followed by the Acts of the Apostles". He then added all of Paul's letters and 1 Peter and 1 John. "These", he affirmed, "are classed as recognized books. Those that are disputed, yet familiar with most are the letters James, Jude, 2 Peter and 2 and 3 John." He also mentioned that "some are uncertain about Revelation".[33]

Spurious apocryphal books

In Chapter 5 of his *History*, Eusebius listed some of the many books which the churches had come to regard as spurious. He mentions *The Acts of Paul, The Shepherd, The Revelation of Peter*, "the alleged *Letter of Barnabas*", and *The Teachings of the Apostles*.[34] To his list, others which he does not mention could be added, for example, the *Gospels of Matthias, Philip, Thomas* and *Bartholomew*, the *Acts of John, The Revelation of Peter*, and *The Apocalypse of Thomas*. Although none of these writings came from the pens of the apostles whose name they carried, they nevertheless demonstrate the high regard in which the recognized churches continued to hold the genuine apostles and their writings. For example, in *The Preaching of Peter* we read: "I have chosen you twelve apostles, judging you to be worthy of me and esteeming you to be faithful apostles, sending you out into the world to preach the gospel to all nations."[35] Interestingly, some of the apocryphal documents endorse facts found in the genuine apostolic writings. *The Gospel to the Hebrews,* for example, gives an accurate piece matching 1 Corinthians 15:7 where the risen Jesus appeared to his brother James.[36] The *Gospel of Peter* also endorses a number of the facts concerning Jesus' death, burial and resurrection.[37]

---

[33] Eusebius, *History of the Church* III.25.

[34] Eusebius, *History of the Church* III.25.

[35] *The Preaching of Peter*, in Montague Rhodes James (tr.), *The Apocryphal New Testament* (Oxford: Clarendon Press, 1966), p. 17.

[36] *The Gospel According to the Hebrews, Fragment*, in James, *The Apocryphal New Testament*, p. 3.

[37] *The Gospel of Peter* 4.11–27 and 10.47–54 in James, *The Apocryphal New Testament*, pp. 91–3.

Canonical lists

As has been seen, from an early point in time churches kept lists of the Gospels, letters and other literature which they believed to be genuinely apostolic. One of the earliest known lists is the *Muratorian Canon*, which was discovered in the Vatican library by the eighteenth-century Italian historian Lodovico Muratori. It is generally held to date from the late second century, since Hermas, Montanus and others are cited as contemporaries of the author. It lists Mark, Luke and John, Acts and 13 letters of Paul, although not in their present order, 1 and 2 John, Jude and Revelation. The Canon was written in bad Latin and was possibly a translation from the Greek. It is believed that the beginning of the list was lost which may account for the lack of any mention of Matthew. From lists such as this a strong case can be made that all the books which later came to form the New Testament were recognized as Scripture before the year 200.

Syria played a significant role in the early growth and development of Christianity. It was therefore not surprising that there were early Syriac translations of the New Testament. The second-century *Peshitta* (meaning "Common") *Syriac New Testament* dates from about the year 170 and contains all the books of the present New Testament, except 2 Peter, 2 and 3 John and Revelation. Origen, in his *Seventh Homily on the Book of Joshua,* mentions Matthew, Mark, Luke, John, Acts, 14 letters of Paul, 1 and 2 Peter, James and Revelation. Cyril (313–86), Bishop of Jerusalem, in his *Catechetical Lectures,* listed all the books "openly read in church which are acknowledged among us all".[38] Athanasius of Alexandria (*c*.296–373) gave the first exact witness to the present New Testament in his *Festal Letter for Easter 367*.[39] He declared that these books "are fountains of salvation, that they who thirst may be satisfied with the living words they contain. In these alone is proclaimed the doctrine of godliness. Let no man add to these or take ought from these."[40] Athanasius also noted in the same festal letter that the apocryphal writings "are an

---

[38] Cyril, *Catechetical Lecture* 4.
[39] Athanasius, *Letter 39* (Easter 367).
[40] Athanasius, *Letter 39.7.*

invention of heretics, who write them when they choose, bestowing upon them their approbation, and assigning them a date, that so, using ancient writings, they may find occasion to lead astray the simple".[41]

Church councils

Following in the wake of Athanasius' definitive list of books, several church councils gave them official endorsement. In 382, at the Council of Rome, Damasus, Bishop of the city and diocese, issued a decree aptly titled "The Decree of Damasus" in which he listed the canonical books of both the Old and New Testaments. He then asked Jerome to make a new translation of the Bible which included the Old Testament with all the 46 books which were in the Septuagint and a New Testament which included the 27 canonical books. Jerome completed his Latin *Vulgate* in 404; "vulgate" meaning "the vernacular or common language of the people". The Old Testament Scriptures, it must be said, were never doubted by the early Christians. They saw them as the basis of Jesus' teaching, the source of his vision, the pattern of his calling and the foretelling of his coming, incarnation, life, death, resurrection and final return in judgement.

On 28 August 397, the Third Council of Carthage assembled and stated that "besides the Canonical Scriptures nothing is to be read in the Church under the title of 'divine Scriptures'". It then listed all the books of the Old and New Testament, the former including Tobit, Judith, Esther, the two books of Esdras, Ecclesiasticus, The Wisdom of Solomon and two books of Maccabees.[42]

---

[41] Athanasius, *Letter* 39.7.

[42] B. F. Westcott, *A General Survey of the History of the Canon of the New Testament* (Edinburgh: T& T Clark, 1881), pp. 440, 541–2.

Conclusion

It should now be clear that the early Christian churches were of one mind from a very early point in time as to what was genuinely canonical Scripture. All were agreed that the criterion was apostolicity. Throughout more than three centuries at the close of which the first Church councils finalized the Canon of the New Testament, this was always the decisive test of authenticity. There was also a strong sense that books which came from the pens of genuine apostles, or were based on their testimony, carried an inherent spiritual authority which other literature did not. The Church councils simply validated them rather than imposed them, their decisions being accepted with widespread and genuine unanimity. The Canon was closed by the beginning of the fifth century and the issue wasn't revisited until the time of the sixteenth-century Reformation. It was the early Christians' faith and trust in the apostolic books which enabled them to proclaim the good news of the gospel with great confidence and stand firm against the threat of persecution from without and false teaching from within.

7
Faith in a tri-personal God: Monarchianism and explanations of God as a Trinity

From its earliest days the church in Rome was known for its orthodox teaching, vibrant life and worship.[1] However, being located in the cosmopolitan capital city of the Empire, it was always going to meet with challenges from people who came seeking a hearing for their latest ideas and new doctrines. One such teaching which came into prominence towards the end of the second and early third centuries became known as "Monarchianism". A monarch is a sole leader or ruler, and Monarchianism was therefore about God's rule over his people and the affairs of the world. It raised the question: was there one sole ruler, namely God the Father, or were there three rulers, Father, Son and Holy Spirit? At its heart this was the issue of the Trinity in unity. It was a question that was bound to come to the surface sooner or later. For a long time, Christian believers had been content to picture the Father as God, the Son as God and the Spirit as God without trying to give a philosophical explanation of their relationship.

Although the Monarchian ideas were clearly erroneous, we should not be too hard on its teachers and preachers, some of whom had a missionary motive. They wanted to make it clear to their fellow citizens that although Jesus was equal with God, they weren't "ditheists" or believers in two gods. They were endeavouring to demonstrate that Christianity was above the level of the polytheism of the Roman Empire. Tertullian, who was one of the Church's leading opponents of Monarchism, wrote about

---

[1] Romans 1:8.

the year 213 in his book entitled *Against Praxeas*, that "Praxeas and his followers are constantly throwing against us that we are preachers of two gods and three gods, while they take to themselves pre-eminently the credit of being worshippers of one God".[2]

Types of Monarchianism

Several different types of Monarchianism began to emerge, each grappling with the same basic issue of how the Father and the Son could both be God and yet not two separate individuals. Put another way, how could Jesus be God and share God's monarchy or rule?

Dynamic Monarchianism
One solution that was put forward in an attempt to solve the problem was known as Dynamic Monarchianism, the word dynamic deriving from the Greek word *dunamis* meaning "power". "Christ", said the thinkers of this school, "was an impersonal power like a stream flowing from a fountain or a ray from the sun being sent out and then being drawn back into the sun." One prominent teacher of this view was Paul of Samosata who was Bishop of Antioch from about the year 260–72. Paul maintained that in the incarnation the Word descended on and dwelt in the man Jesus, who thus became the Son of God. Interestingly, Paul was the first person to use the term *homoousios*, meaning "the same substance" to express his conviction that Jesus the Son was the "same substance as the Father". It is strange that he was judged to be heretical for his use of this term which later came to be regarded as orthodox when used in a slightly different way by Athanasius. Bishop Paul appears to have used the term to try and deny that the Word or Logos was a hypostasis separate from the Father.

However, in the full light of day it emerged that Paul appeared to have held that the real incarnation of the divine Logos was physically impossible. The divine Logos, according to Paul, was an impersonal force which came on Jesus and gradually grew greater and greater until eventually he became the same substance (*ousia*) as the Father. Paul's

---

[2] Tertullian, *Against Praxeas* 3.

view clearly did not match the apostolic faith as expressed in the four Gospels that Jesus was totally divine from all eternity.

Adoptionist Monarchianism
Another very similar form of this heretical teaching was known as Adoptionist Monarchianism. Those who taught it maintained that at some point in his earthly life Jesus was either promoted to be, or adopted as, God's Son as a reward for his perfect and obedient life. It is interesting to reflect that this teaching found expression many centuries later in a line written by the seventeenth-century English poet John Milton in *Paradise Regained*, "This perfect man by merit called my Son".[3] The major problem which arose from this teaching is immediately clear: an adopted son can only be a son in a limited sense. There is no generic relationship, blood tie or anything which would indicate they were of the same substance. An adopted son can only be a son in some diminished or metaphorical sense. This form of Monarchianism implied that Jesus began his earthly existence as a mere man which meant he was not therefore God at the outset. Furthermore, it denied the eternal deity of Jesus. This didn't square with the opening lines of the Gospel of John that Jesus the Word "was God. He was with God in the beginning".[4] This same truth was endorsed by Paul's statement in his Letter to the Philippians that Jesus was "in very nature God".[5] It was also clear that Jesus was born "Immanuel ... God with us".[6]

Adoptionist Monarchianism was taught by a number of different teachers and fostered and promoted in small groups. Prominent among them were Theodotus and Artemon. Theodotus (second century) was a shoemaker[7] and leather trader who came from Byzantium,[8] where he had also developed an interest in philosophy. The core of his message was that Jesus was a man who was anointed with the Holy Spirit at his

---

[3] John Milton, *Paradise Regained*, Book 1.
[4] John 1:1–2.
[5] Philippians 2:6.
[6] Matthew 1:23.
[7] Eusebius, *History of the Church* V.28 describes him as a shoemaker.
[8] The name was later changed to Constantinople.

baptism and thus became Christ the Logos. Theodotus held him to be identical with the Father but a limitation of him. He came to Rome and began teaching during the time when Victor was Bishop (c.189–98).

Hippolytus (c.170–236), a bishop and orthodox theologian also based in Rome, gives a brief statement of Theodotus' views in his book *Refutation of All Heresies*:

> A certain Theodotus introduced a novel heresy... that Jesus was born of a Virgin, according to the counsel of the Father, and that after he had lived in a way common to all men, and had become pre-eminently religious, he afterward at his baptism in the Jordan received Christ, who came from above and descended upon him. Therefore miraculous powers did not operate within him prior to the manifestation of the spirit which descended and proclaimed him as the Christ.[9]

Theodotus was excommunicated by Bishop Victor about the year 195 for what Eusebius described as his "God denying apostacy, when he became the first to declare that Christ was merely human".[10]

Much later, possibly about the year 230, Artemon who was described as "an Aristotelian philosopher of mathematical learning but with little reverence", was also teaching in the Imperial City. Eusebius stated in a passing line that his heresy was "that the Saviour was merely human".[11] Artemon's doctrine was condemned by the anonymous author of *The Little Labyrinth*.[12] "The Artemonites", according to him, "say that all the early teachers and the apostles themselves received and taught what they now declare." But, he continued, "What they say might be credible if first of all the divine Scriptures did not contradict them."[13] The words of the author of *The Little Labyrinth* demonstrate that the orthodox Church

---

[9] Hippolytus, *Refutation of all Heresies* VII.23.
[10] Eusebius, *History of the Church* V.28.
[11] Eusebius, *History of the Church* V.28.
[12] See Eusebius, *History of the Church* V.28.5
[13] Eusebius, *History of the Church* V.28.

was securely anchored in what they knew and held to be the genuine apostolic faith and Scriptures.

Modalistic Monarchianism

Another form of Monarchian theology was modalism. Its teachers asserted "that one cannot believe in one only God in any other way than by saying that the Father, the Son and the Holy Spirit are the very same person".[14] Modalists therefore recognized that each of the three persons, Father, Son and Holy Spirit, were God but obscured their distinctions. This was taught by Praxeas (c.200), a priest who is said to have come from Asia and who arrived in Rome[15] around the beginning of the third century. Tertullian described him somewhat harshly as "a man of restless disposition" and "not having the love of God".[16] The core of his teaching is only known through the vigorous opposition of Tertullian in his treatise entitled *Against Praxeas*. In it, he accuses Praxeas of teaching that "the Father himself came down into the Virgin, was himself born of her, Himself suffered, indeed, was Himself Jesus Christ".[17] A little later he added Praxeas' assertion that "After a time, then, the Father was born, and the Father suffered—God himself, the Almighty, is preached as Jesus Christ".[18] Much later in his book, Tertullian further rebuked Praxeas and his followers for "understanding the Son to be the flesh, that is the man, that is Jesus; and the Father to be the Spirit, that is God, that is Christ".[19] Tertullian took the Modalists to task for blurring the distinction between the Father and the Son "which we [the orthodox Church] make by examples of the sun and the ray, and the fountain and the river".[20] Tertullian expressed his agreement with Praxeas that when the Son died the Father died but asserted "we do not say that He died after the divine nature, but only after the human ... They [the heretics] indeed fearing

---

[14] Tertullian, *Against Praxeas* 1.
[15] See Tertullian, *Against Praxeas* 1.
[16] Tertullian, *Against Praxeas* 1.
[17] Tertullian, *Against Praxeas* 1.
[18] Tertullian, *Against Praxeas* 2.
[19] Tertullian, *Against Praxeas* 27.
[20] Tertullian, *Against Praxeas* 27.

to incur blasphemy against the Father, hope to diminish it in this way, admitting that the Father and the Son are two; but if the Son, indeed, suffers, the Father is His fellow-sufferer."[21] Praxeas therefore appeared to have embraced ditheism. Tertullian urges that when Christ prayed to the Father we should not think in terms of the Son on earth and the Father in heaven because "God is in the depths and exists everywhere in might and power; and the Son being indivisible from the Father is everywhere with him".[22] As an example of this deep communion he cited Psalm 110:1. "The Lord said to my Lord, sit at my right hand" and Isaiah 53:1, "Who has believed our message?"[23]

Modalistic Monarchianism was also taught by Noetus, a presbyter of the church at Smyrna in Asia Minor, about the year 230. His opponent, Hippolytus, described him in rather strong terms as "a reckless babbler and trickster who derived his teaching from a certain Epigonus".[24] First and foremost, Noetus defended the monarchy or one rule of God by declaring that the Father and the Son were one and the very same. Hippolytus wrote in Chapter 10 of his *Refutation of all Heresies*: "For in this matter he thinks he establishes the Monarchy, alleging that the Father and the Son, so called, are not from one another, but are one and the same, Himself from Himself, and that He is styled by the names Father and Son, according to the changes of the times."[25]

In this same chapter, Hippolytus wrote that Noetus held that when the unbegotten Father "is born of a virgin; that He is not subject to suffering". Nevertheless, when his passion came upon him, Noetus was clear "that the Father dies". This meant that during his incarnation He would not have been able to experience or empathize with human pain and hurt. Hippolytus and other orthodox theologians took a different view that only the humanity of the Godhead died on the cross. At the end of this section, Hippolytus added: "The Noetians think that the Father is

---

[21] Tertullian, *Against Praxeas* 29.
[22] Tertullian, *Against Praxeas* 25.
[23] Tertullian, *Against Praxeas* 11.
[24] Hippolytus, *Refutation of All Heresies* 23.
[25] Hippolytus, *Refutation of All Heresies* 11.

called the Son according to events at different times."[26] This core aspect of Modalistic Monarchianism held that at some point in history God operated as the Father and on other occasions, when more appropriate, as the Son. In contrast, the early theologians recognized that God the Father, God the Son and God the Holy Spirit always acted in concert at any given time.

Hippolytus recorded that when the blessed presbyters heard Noetus' teaching, they summoned him before the church and examined him. Following his refusal to change his opinions they expelled him from the church. Hippolytus added: "He was carried away to such a pitch of pride that he established a school", which was based on the Mosaic Law, "I am the God of your fathers; you shall have no other gods beside me."[27]

Sabellian Monarchianism

Another form of Modalistic Monarchianism was that strongly propounded about the years 250–60 by Sabellius, an Egyptian presbyter. He and his followers maintained that there were three different phases of the one divine being who appeared first as the Father, then as the Son and then as the Holy Spirit. This view is sometimes referred to as the "Economic Trinity". He was not therefore the Father and the Son at the same time. Furthermore, Sabellius taught a "Subordinationist Modalism", in which the Father was greater than the Son and the Son slightly greater than the Holy Spirit.

Epiphanius (310–403), Bishop of Salamis in Cyprus, was a strong opponent of the Sabellians. He began his treatise *Against Heresies* by commenting that Sabellius' views were "similar to those of Noetus apart from some exceptions". He noted that most of his followers were to be found in Mesopotamia and at Rome. He then gave a summary of Sabellius' teaching:

---

[26] Hippolytus, *Refutation of All Heresies* 23.
[27] Hippolytus, *Fragment*, MSG, 10.84, which seems to be the conclusion of *Against the Heresy of Noetus*, in Ayer, *A Source Book for Ancient Church History*, pp. 177–8.

> Their doctrine is, that Father, Son and Holy Spirit are one and the same being, in the sense that three names are attached to one substance. A close analogy is the sun: it is one substance, but has three manifestations, light, heat and the orb itself. The heat ... is the Spirit; the light is the Sun; while the Father himself is represented by the actual substance.[28]

Sabellius, Epiphanius then explained, believed the Son was emitted like a ray from the sun into the world to accomplish humanity's salvation during the dispensation of the gospel. When that task was completed, "he was taken back into heaven just as a ray emitted by the sun is withdrawn again". The Holy Spirit was "then, and still is, being sent forth into the world and into the successive individuals who are worthy to receive it".[29] Epiphanius robustly opposed Sabellius because his constant stress on "only one God destroys as far as he can the divinity and subsistence of the Son and of the Holy Spirit".[30]

Patripassianism

A feature in some Monarchian schemes became known as Patripassianism, from the Latin *pater* (father) and *passio* meaning "to suffer", because by asserting God is one being it meant that the Father must have suffered on the cross. Indeed, some Monarchian teachers stated the fact in a very straightforward way. Noetus, for example, wrote that "Christ was the Father himself, and that the Father himself was born and suffered and died". Again Noetus was clear: "If therefore I acknowledge Christ to be God, he is the Father himself, if he indeed is God; and Christ suffered, being himself God; and consequently the Father suffered, for he was the Father himself." Hippolytus stated that Noetus was clear that when the passion took place the Father suffered and died.[31] Hippolytus attacked Patripassianism on the ground that "the Son offered himself to

---

[28] Epiphanius, *Panarion* 62.1.
[29] Epiphanius, *Panarion* 62.1.
[30] Epiphanius, *Panarion* 65.3.2
[31] Hippolytus, *Refutation of All Heresies* 23.

the Father"[32] and that "the Father raised up the Son in righteousness".[33] Such a resurrection empowered by the Father could not have taken place if Christ "is the Father Himself".[34]

In the first chapter of his treatise *Against Praxeas*, Tertullian clearly stated his opposition to Praxeas' teaching that "the Father himself came down into the Virgin, was Himself born of her, Himself suffered, indeed, was Himself Jesus Christ". Praxeas, "a man of restless disposition", was, he continued, "the first to import into Rome this sort of perversity".[35] Tertullian went on to condemn Praxeas not only for this but also for his dislike of charismatic beliefs. "He did", Tertullian wrote, "two pieces of the devil's work in Rome; he drove out the paraclete and he crucified the Father."[36] He began his second chapter making the same point: "After a time, then", he wrote, "the Father was born, and the Father suffered—God himself, the Almighty, is preached as Jesus Christ."[37] Tertullian was clear that "we teach in precisely the same terms but we do not say that He died after the divine nature, but only after the human".[38]

The challenge of Monarchianism

Some of the Monarchian teachers were trying to do what in many ways was laudable. They were seeking to defend the Christian faith against charges of polytheism. However, as far as the orthodox Church was concerned, Monarchianism had two basic weaknesses. First, it didn't do justice to the doctrine enshrined in the genuine apostolic Gospels and letters which stressed distinctive characteristics of the Father, Son and Holy Spirit. Second, Modalism didn't match the experience of ordinary Christian believers. They didn't encounter God in just one mode at a time

---

[32] Hippolytus, *Against the Heresy of Noetus* 2.
[33] Hippolytus, *Against the Heresy of Noetus* 4.
[34] Hippolytus, *Against the Heresy of Noetus* 4.
[35] Tertullian, *Against Praxeas* 1.
[36] Tertullian, *Against Praxeas* 1.
[37] Tertullian, *Against Praxeas* 2.
[38] Tertullian, *Against Praxeas* 27.

but often in all three modes simultaneously. They came to know God as Father, through the Son and in the indwelling presence of his Spirit. They prayed to God through the Son and in the Holy Spirit.

The main opposition to the Monarchians came from Hippolytus (c.170–c.236) and Tertullian (160–220). Hippolytus was a bishop based in Rome but seemingly without a See. He doesn't appear to have been particularly kind towards the official bishops of the city and described Zephyrinus, who was Bishop of Rome from 199–217, "as a simple man without education",[39] who "hurried headlong" into Monarchian views.[40] He was even less well disposed to Callistus who succeeded him from 218–22 and produced a heresy much like the Monarchians, asserting "there is one Father and God, and that He is the Creator of the Universe, and that He is regarded as the Son by name, yet that in Substance He is one".[41]

Hippolytus opposed Monarchianism in two main ways. First, he laid great stress on the need to treat and interpret Scripture as a whole and to avoid reading too much into isolated sentences or texts. Second, he made constant reference to the separateness of the Father and the Son from a wide range of Scriptural texts, early writers and hymns. This is clearly visible in his tract entitled *Against the Heresy of Noetus* (c.205). He began by pointing out that "the Scriptures teach that the Father raised up the Son". In Paragraph 4 he posed the question, "Of whom does the Father thus testify? It is the Son of whom the Father says, 'I have raised him up in righteousness.'" In Paragraph 6, Hippolytus focused on Jesus' clear statement that He was going to the Father. He wrote: "If Noetus says, that Jesus is the Father to what Father was he going when he says, 'I am going to my Father and your Father?'"[42] Hippolytus went on to point out that God existed in plurality from the beginning. In Paragraph 10, he wrote: "He while existing alone, yet existed in plurality." In the following paragraph, he clarified: "I do not mean that there are two Gods, but that it is only as light of light, or as water from the fountain, or as a ray from

---

[39] Hippolytus, *Refutation of All Heresies* 2.
[40] Hippolytus, *Refutation of All Heresies* 2.
[41] Hippolytus, *Refutation of All Heresies* 6.
[42] Hippolytus, *Against the Heresy of Noetus* 6.

the sun." At one or two points in his treatise, Hippolytus demonstrated that he was beginning to articulate a doctrine of the Trinity. In Paragraph 14, he wrote:

> If then, the word was with God, and was God, what follows? Would one not say that he speaks of two Gods? I shall not indeed speak of two Gods, but one; of two persons, however, and a third economy, viz., the grace of the Holy Ghost.

In this quotation, Hippolytus does not appear to regard the Holy Spirit as fully personal, equal of divine terms. He does, however, clearly articulate the distinctives of the Father and the Son while at the same time viewing them to be of one substance. He expressed this difference by speaking of them as "two persons", the word coming from the Latin *persona*, which strictly speaking meant "a role" in a stage play. In a somewhat surprising way, Hippolytus' use of word *persona* brought him a little closer to some of the Monarchians than he perhaps realized. Significantly, towards the close of *Against Heresies of Noetus*, Hippolytus gave a clear statement of the incarnation based on the "tradition of the apostles":

> Let us believe then, dear brothers, according to the tradition of the apostles. . . . God the Word came down from heaven, and entered into the holy Virgin Mary, in order that, taking flesh from her, and assuming also a human, by which I mean a rational soul, and becoming thus all that man is with the exception of sin, and conferring immortality on men who believe on His name.[43]

Tertullian, who was one of the first early theologians to write in Latin, left the orthodox Christian Church some time before 210 to join a charismatic sect known as the Montanists. About the year 213, he published a major attack against the Monarchians entitled *Against Praxeas*, an individual who, as has already been noted, was opposed to prophecy and the practice of spiritual gifts. In Chapter 3, Tertullian pointed out that the Scriptures clearly speak of Jesus as the Son, distinguishing him from

---

[43] Hippolytus, *Against the Heresy of Noetus* 17.

the Father. He then went on to stress that plurality doesn't necessarily amount to more than one rule. It is possible, he asserted, for a monarch to be a sole ruler and to administer his rule through a son or chosen agents or administrators.[44] Therefore, he concluded that "even if a monarchy is ministered by ten thousand times ten thousand angels [Daniel 7:10] ... it has not for that reason ceased to be the rule of one person".[45] In modern terms, we could think of King William IV and Queen Mary II sharing in one rule over the British Isles. Tertullian pointed out that the Son does not work separately or independently of the Father, rather he works under the Father's rule or Monarchy. In Chapter 4, he went on to point out that "the Son does nothing apart from the Father's will".[46]

In Chapter 7, Tertullian stressed the eternity of the Son who was present before time and had an equal part with the Father in the creation. He cited Proverbs 8 which speaks of the Father having formed the Son. He then drew attention to Paul's Letter to the Philippians 2:6, which emphasized that Jesus "had been a separate being with God from the beginning but being in nature God thought it not robbery to be equal with God". Tertullian gave a number of analogies in a bid to illustrate the way in which the Father and the Son were distinct and yet not separate. One of these was the tree and the root and another the river and the spring from which it flowed. Elsewhere he spoke of the threefold nature of a tree, its root and the fruit it bears as distinct parts of one complete whole.

Like Hippolytus, Tertullian made serious attempts to define the doctrine of the Trinity in unity. He titled Chapter 2 of *Against Praxeas* "The Catholic Doctrine of the Trinity" and stated what he took "to be the Catholic view of things":

> There is only one God ... this one God has also a son, His Word, who proceeded from Himself. Him we believe to have been sent by the Father into the Virgin, and to have been born of her ...

---

[44] Tertullian, *Against Praxeas* 3.
[45] Tertullian, *Against Praxeas* 3.
[46] Tertullian, *Against Praxeas* 4.

> who sent also from the Father according to His own promise, the Holy Spirit, the Paraclete.[47]

Tertullian didn't reach the crisp detailed theological clarity of the Athanasian Creed or the careful nuanced definitions of the Cappadocian Fathers, but he was important because he provided some of the terms which have since become the beginning point of many later Trinitarian theologies in the Western Church. Tertullian was the first person to speak of God as "Trinity"[48] and indeed stated that God could be counted. He also spoke of the Godhead being of "one substance", a term which he almost certainly adopted from his Monarchian opponents. In one paragraph where he wrote about the unity and trinity of the Godhead, he appears to come close to subordinationism. God is, he wrote:

> One by unity of substance, while mystery distributes the unity into a Trinity, placing in their order three persons—the Father, the Son, and the Holy Spirit; three, however, not in condition, but in degree; not in substance, but in form, not in power, but in aspect; yet one substance, and one condition.[49]

As is clear in this quotation, Tertullian was the first person to use the Latin word *persona* to refer to the distinctives of Father, Son and the Holy Spirit. In the early-third-century world in which Tertullian had been trained as a lawyer, the word *persona* meant someone who played "a role on stage" or in public life. This was not an altogether helpful term since the apostolic Church clearly understood God as a Trinity of being rather than of roles. A further difficulty has been that the word "person" in contemporary western society generally designates an individual human being. To think of God in terms of three people would be tritheism, and Tertullian well knew that was in total conflict with the apostolic faith in "one Lord". In order to assert the oneness of the three *personae*, Father, Son and Holy Spirit, Tertullian used the Latin term *substantia*. In

---

[47] Tertullian, *Against Praxeas* 2.
[48] See Tertullian, *Against Praxeas* 2.
[49] Tertullian, *Against Praxeas* 2.

many minds in today's world, this bespeaks materiality, but in Tertullian's day it meant "essence" or literally that which is underneath; *sub* being Latin for "under" and *stantia* Latin for "to stand". In other places, in order to indicate the triune nature of the Lord, Tertullian used the word "distinctions".[50]

Denouement

Monarchianism was clearly a major threat to the faith of the early Church in the first and second centuries. Nevertheless, its challenge played a significant part in helping Christians to speak with greater clarity about the nature of the God they trusted and the ways in which they experienced his presence in their lives. The labours of Hippolytus and Tertullian enabled Christian leaders to shake off accusations of polytheism and to be clear that God is one being with three distinctive aspects.

---

[50] Tertullian, *Against Praxeas* 11.

8

Guided by biblical scholars and theologians: Tertullian, Cyprian, Clement and Origen

Background

One of the reasons the early churches were able to stand firm in the apostolic faith and proclaim it with confidence was the teaching and writings of orthodox theologians. Reference has already been made to some of the early apologists and theologians who defended biblical doctrines from heterodox views, most notably Gnosticism and Monarchianism. There were, however, several late-second- and early-third-century biblical scholars whose teaching and public writings were of particular importance. Among them were Tertullian (*c*.165–*c*.240), Cyprian (*c*.200–58) of Carthage, Clement (*c*.150–*c*.215) and Origen (*c*.185–253), both of whom were based in Alexandria.

North Africa theologians

Tertullian
North African Christianity was the cradle of practical Christianity and Quintas Septimus Florens Tertullianus was perhaps its greatest exponent. He was born in Carthage about the year 165, but little is known about his early years. He came from a pagan family and was the son of a captain

of a Roman Legion. His family belonged to the educated classes[1] and no doubt aided Tertullian in his training as a lawyer.[2] As a young man, he indulged his sexual passions, attended gladiatorial games and witnessed the brutal persecution of Christians including the execution of young children. Having witnessed their courage, he began to investigate their faith which led to his conversion when he was about 40 years of age.[3] Sometime shortly after this, he became a presbyter in the church at Carthage. Tertullian was very focused on the practicalities of daily living, and this impacted both his intellectual and spiritual life. He was also impetuous and impatient in nature, which may help to explain why he later left the Catholic Church and joined the Montanist sect about the year 206. There is no evidence that he actually left the Church until much later.

Greek was the language of the intelligentsia and the main means of communication for commerce and travel.[4] However, by the later years of the second century, Latin was beginning to grow in popularity in many parts of the Roman Empire. Congregations began to speak the language and sermons were preached in it. Tertullian became the first important Christian to write in Latin; indeed he is sometimes spoken of as "the Father of Latin Western theology". As has already been noted, he played a major and significant role in the defending of Christians against unjust and foolish persecution[5] as well as the errors of Gnosticism and the Monarchians.[6] Regarding the former, he declared Christians were the best Roman citizens; in short, loyal, tax-paying, caring, living quiet lives and refusing to worship the Roman gods who were in their view not gods at all. In response to the latter, he articulated the clear doctrine of the Trinity.

---

[1] Hans Lietzmann, *The Founding of the Church Universal* (London: Lutterworth Press, 1953), p. 219.
[2] Richardson (ed.), *Early Christian Fathers*, p. 19.
[3] Tertullian, *Apology* 15.
[4] See Chapter 2.
[5] See Chapter 3.
[6] See Chapter 7.

Tertullian's writings

At the time of Tertullian's life, the Christian Church was facing many difficulties both from within and without, and he began to devote his energy and writing to many of them. In contrast to Irenaeus and some of the Alexandrian theologians, Tertullian was particularly strong in his denunciation of the ancient philosophers. He described them as "the patriarchs of the heretics". Believing that their writings led to factions and various heresies he once wrote: "What has Athens [the home of philosophers] to do with Jerusalem [the citadel of God's people]?"[7]

Doctrine

Tertullian wrote extensively on core Christian doctrine including the nature of God, creation and human nature. The incarnation, atonement, resurrection and apostolic lineage are all topics to which he frequently returned. In an important book entitled *On Prescription against Heretics*, he insisted that the basis of all orthodox doctrine is that which came to the Church through the apostles.[8] It was they "who then published to the nations the same doctrine of the same faith". They established churches in every city with the same apostolic doctrine. Tertullian felt it important that churches should be able to trace their link back to an apostle. He instanced the Church of the Smyrnaeans deriving from Polycarp who was appointed by the apostle John.[9] It is clear that for Tertullian, apostolicity and unity of doctrine were the irrefutable hallmarks of the one true Church. It is in his writings the Apostles' Creed occurs for the first time as "a rule of faith" binding congregations together.

God

God "is the supreme being, existing in eternity, unborn, uncreated, without beginning, without end".[10] Although God is Spirit, he is also

---

[7] Tertullian, *On the Soul (De Anima)* 3.1.
[8] Richardson (ed.), *Early Christian Fathers*, p. 18.
[9] Tertullian, *On Prescription against Heretics* (*De Praescriptione Haereticorum*) 20–1, 32 and 36.
[10] Tertullian, *Against Marcion* 3.

"substantial" and has a body and creates great substances.[11] "This", he asserts, "is a matter of general agreement."In the same passage he adds: "This body is seen in the Word who is called the Son of God, and given the name of God."[12] "All things which are were made through him."[13]

The Son

"The Father", Tertullian taught, "is the whole substance of deity while the Son is derivative and a portion of the whole." He points out that "Jesus himself confesses, 'The Father is Greater than I am' . . . so the father is other than the son, as being greater, as he who begets is other than the begotten, the sender than the sent, the creator than the agent of creation."[14] Strangely this assertion comes close to a subordinationist Christology, making Jesus appear to be less than the Father. Remarkably Tertullian also came close to anticipating the later Chalcedonian definition concerning Jesus' two natures: "a divine and a human . . . the divine being immortal, the human mortal". In the same paragraph, he explains that when the apostle says that "Christ the anointed died . . . that what died was that which was anointed, that is, his flesh . . . Therefore the Father did not suffer with the Son." Tertullian reiterated this point stating "the Father is distinct from the Son [in his humanity] not distinct from [the son] in his divinity".[15] A phantasm or "insubstantial being", as many Gnostics asserted, could not suffer.[16] "We should not", Tertullian stated, "imagine the Son here on Earth and the Father in heaven because the Son being indivisible from the Father is everywhere with him."[17]

Humanity

Tertullian attacked the Gnostic heretics who ascribed the creation of the material world, and hence human flesh, to an inferior deity. In direct

---

[11] Tertullian, *Against Praxeas* 7.
[12] All these quotations were taken from Tertullian, *Against Praxeas* 1.3.
[13] Tertullian, *Against Praxeas* 7.
[14] Tertullian, *Against Praxeas* 9.
[15] All these quotations taken from Tertullian, *Against Praxeas* 29.
[16] Tertullian, *Against Marcion* 3.8.
[17] Tertullian, *Against Praxeas* 23.

opposition, he asserted "the nobility of the flesh".[18] Humanity Tertullian held to be "mortal, corporeal, having shape simple in substance" and "having freedom of choice, affected by external events".[19] He asserted that every human being inherited a bias towards evil "for a wicked spirit will be found attached to every man lying in wait for him at the very gateway of birth".[20] This pull towards evil is not total. There is also in the soul "that original good, the divine genuine good, which is natural in the true sense". There is, he says, "some good in the worst men, and some evil in the best".[21]

The resurrection
With a constant eye on the dangers of Gnosticism, Tertullian asserted a literal fleshly incarnation of Christ as the second Adam. The Son of God then lived a perfect life on earth, was crucified, died, buried and rose again.[22] Following on from this basis, Tertullian anticipated Christ's exalted and triumphant return.[23] After this, there will be a first resurrection of the saints and martyrs "with a promised kingdom set up on Earth but before we attain heaven".[24] This will last for a thousand years in a city of God's making, Jerusalem, sent down from heaven. After the conclusion of this period of bliss there will be a second general resurrection and judgement will follow "with the most faithful mediator Jesus Christ restoring God to man and man to God".[25] Meanwhile, the persecutors of the Lord's name will find themselves groaning together in lowest darkness.[26]

---

[18] Tertullian, *On the Flesh of Christ (De Resurrectione Carnis)* 5–6.
[19] Tertullian, *On the Soul* 22.
[20] Tertullian, *On the Soul* 39–40.
[21] Tertullian, *On the Soul* 41.
[22] Tertullian, *On the bodily Resurrection of Christ* 17.
[23] Tertullian, *On the Spectacles (De Spectaculis)* 30.
[24] Tertullian, *Against Marcion* 3.25.
[25] Tertullian, *On the Resurrection of the Flesh* 63.
[26] Tertullian, *On the Spectacles (De Spectaculis)* 30.

Church life

Worship was very important to Tertullian who wrote on one occasion: "What betters man is worship."[27] His writings give us glimpses of the structure and nature of church life such as intercessory prayer, voluntary offerings, charitable works, the reading of Scripture and a strong system of discipline. In a moving passage in his *On the Spectacles (Games)* written between 197 and 202, Tertullian stormed against all the pagan pleasures such as the civic prize fights, the circus games and sports, and the theatre, which breed immorality and excess.[28] A Christian should not indulge in luxury, cosmetics, finery and costly adornments.[29]

Tertullian gives glimpses of worship in some of the North African churches. "We meet", he says, "to nourish our faith, we pray for Emperors, their ministers, those in authority and for the peace of the world" and "we refresh our memories with the sacred writings".[30] He mentions that our Presidents (presumably those who presided over home-based worship) are of "tested character".[31] Money is collected at times of worship and is used to pay for the burial of the poor and "to support boys and girls who are orphans and destitute". After prayer to God, they share food: "enough is eaten to satisfy hunger; as much drunk as befits the temperate".[32]

Tertullian, probably writing as a Montanist, records that the worship he shares in has "an absence of display, novel elaborations and any costly trappings".[33] Baptism, he notes, "is when a man is plunged and dipped in water to the accompaniment of a few words".[34] After coming up out of the waters, "the candidates are anointed with oil and hands are laid upon us invoking the Holy Spirit through the act of blessing.[35] The supreme priest [that is the bishop] has the right of conferring baptism and after

---

[27] Tertullian, *On Repentance (De Paenitentia)* 2.7.
[28] Tertullian, *On the Spectacles* 3.
[29] Tertullian, *On the Spectacles* 3.
[30] Tertullian, *Apology* 39.
[31] Tertullian, *Apology* 39.
[32] Tertullian, *Apology* 39.
[33] Tertullian, *On Baptism* 2.
[34] Tertullian, *On Baptism* 2.
[35] Tertullian, *On Baptism* 8.

him priests and deacons."[36] Writing possibly at a later stage in his life, Tertullian reminds us that "laymen are also priests" and can in time of need baptize. "It is", he concludes, "God's will that we should all be in a fit state to administer the sacraments at any time and in any place."[37] About 201, in *Of the Crown*, Tertullian records that the sacrament of the Eucharist is taken "in meetings before day-break and only from the hands of the presidents".[38] This early time of day was probably to avoid attracting the attention of the persecuting Roman authorities.

Tertullian sees fasting as a means of making satisfaction to God. The prohibition of food revives the salvation which had been extinguished by gluttony.[39] Other passages in Tertullian's writings, particularly his later works, reveal him to have been something of an ascetic rigorist. He denounced the Church's practice of voluntary fasting as indulgent, and in its place he advocated mandatory and long fasts.

Tertullian wrote of marriage being "an ancient discipline of Christians".[40] His mindset seems to have been much the same when it comes to issues of sex and marriage. Like many of the Fathers of the early Church he had a deep suspicion of sexuality,[41] seeming to have regarded marriage as a necessity for those who were naturally frail. He considered celibacy as preferable for both sexes.[42] Second marriages Tertullian regarded at adulterous. They also "greatly detract from faith and are a hindrance to sanctity".[43] Often held to be a misogynist, he devoted a whole work to the necessity of all women, of whatever age or status, covering their heads as a sign of submission.[44] In a work which was clearly written at a time when he was in the Catholic Church, Tertullian

---

[36] Tertullian, *On Baptism* 17.
[37] Tertullian, *On Exhortation to Chastity* 7.
[38] Tertullian, *Of the Crown* 3.
[39] Tertullian, *On Fasting* 3.
[40] Tertullian, *On Monogamy* 2.
[41] Elizabeth Carnelley, "Tertullian and Feminism", *Theology,* January 1989, pp. 31–5.
[42] Carnelley, "Tertullian and Feminism", p. 33.
[43] Tertullian, *To My Wife (Ad Uxorem)* 1.7.
[44] Tertullian, *On the Veiling of Virgins* 2–3.

also wrote, "A woman may not speak, nor baptize, nor claim the right to any masculine function, still less the priestly office." He did, however, concede that "the apostle shows that women have the right to prophesy, by making a woman wear a veil when prophesying".[45] Elsewhere perhaps we should note that Tertullian drew a parallel between Eve and the Virgin Mary. The wrong that Eve committed by believing the serpent was redressed, he suggested, by Mary's obedience to the words of the angel Gabriel. It is not clear whether Tertullian truly believed women to have been reinstated through Mary or not. Certainly, in his later years when he joined the Montanists, he appears to have held relaxed views, allowing women to hold leadership roles in the Church.

Writing *De Paenitentia* in about the year 192, Tertullian gives us a sense of the early Catholic Church's discipline. No sin, he asserts, is unforgivable by God who in response demands repentance. The solemn and binding sacrament of baptism was then "first penance" in which the one baptized pledged to live according to the precepts of Jesus' teaching. A "second penance" was necessary where sins of the gravest kind had been committed. These included "murder, idolatry, fraud, denial of Christ, blasphemy and fornication".[46] This penance required the wearing of sackcloth and ashes at the church doorway. Tertullian believed that the greater the misery the more beneficial the bishop's absolution would be.[47] Significantly Tertullian later strengthened his view on the matter of absolution when he joined the Montanists. Writing about the year 208 in *De Felicitia*, he rebuked the Church's lax penitential discipline as witnessed by Callistus, the Supreme Pontiff, who proclaimed easy remission after fornication and adultery. He wrote: "They are not sins but monstrosities."[48] For the sake of discipline, the Church must, if necessary, be strict in refusing absolution.[49]

---

[45] Tertullian, *On the Veiling of Virgins* 9.
[46] Tertullian, *On Penitence* 7.
[47] Tertullian, *On Penitence* 9–10.
[48] H. B. Swete, "Penitential Discipline in the First Three Centuries", *The Journal of Theological Studies* 4 (April 1908).
[49] Tertullian, *On Modesty* 16.

The Montanists

It is somewhat puzzling that Tertullian, who had spent so much of his time refuting heresies that were threatening the Catholic Church, should have joined the Montanists about the year 207. They were a group who were attempting to recover the prophetic emphasis and the practice of spiritual gifts of the apostolic period. The movement was noted for its rigorous ascetic demands and its conviction of an imminent end of the world. It seems likely that Tertullian was frustrated by the lack of passion and ecclesiastical trends of the second-century Catholic Church.[50] In his later Montanist writings, Tertullian was more critical of the established Church seen particularly in his denial of its right to forgive grave sins[51] and his assertion that there was no necessity for a clerical priesthood.[52]

Summary

For Tertullian, faith is always simple[53] and also practical. "What else does God want but that we live according to his discipline?"[54] Despite his Montanist convictions, it is clear that later Church Fathers read his works and were clearly influenced by him. His writings played a major part in the Church's struggles with the Gnostics and the Monarchians. His texts also became particularly useful during the fourth-century struggles with the Arians. Tertullian was the first significant theologian to write in Latin. Indeed he created a Latin ecclesiastical language which made it possible to convey Greek theological concepts. Tertullian died peacefully, a man with a passion for the Christian faith who greatly encouraged the believers in times of persecution. His influence has continued through the centuries.

---

[50] See K. Baus, *History of the Church from the Apostolic Community to Constantine* (London: Burns & Oates, 1980), p. 217.
[51] Baus, *History of the Church*, p. 325.
[52] Tertullian, *Exhortation to Chastity* 7.3 (written between 197 and 202).
[53] Tertullian, *Against Marcion* 5.20.
[54] Tertullian, *On Prayer* (*De Oratione*) 4.

Cyprian

Thacius Caecilius Cyprianus was born in the early years of the third century and grew up to be a rhetorician and member of the Carthaginian Bar. After searching for moral renewal, he was converted to Christianity about the year 246. He described his experience in the following lines:

> I was myself so entangled and constrained by very many errors of my former life that I could not believe it possible for me to escape from them ... But when the stain of my earlier life had been washed away by the help of the water of birth [baptism] ... and the second birth had restored me so as to make me a new man ... what before had seemed difficult was now easy.[55]

Remarkably, within two years he was elected Bishop of Carthage, having gained a deep knowledge of the faith through studying the Scriptures and reading the works of Tertullian. As noted earlier, his appointment caused resentment among some of the presbyters,[56] Felicissimus and Novatus being two of them. Only a few months after taking office the Decian persecution broke out and he was forced to flee but managed to administer his diocese from exile by letters. Cyprian returned to Carthage in 251 and soon became popular with the people of his diocese who called him "Papa".[57] He served as bishop for ten years until his martyrdom in 258. His years in office were a demanding time in which his leadership skills and practical faith were tested to the full. He is said to have read Tertullian daily but managed to transform his more radical ideas into practical organizational systems.

---

[55] Cyprian, *Letter to Donatus* 4
[56] See Chapter 4.
[57] Frederick W. Farrar, *Lives of the Fathers: Sketches of Church History in Biography* (London: Adam & Charles Black, 1907), p. 262.

Cyprian's significance

The issue of the lapsed

As noted earlier, Cyprian had been elected bishop at a time of intense persecution brought about by the Emperor Decius. When the brutality subsided and Cyprian had returned to the city, he was confronted with the issue of how to deal with those who had abandoned their faith in Christ. Many in his diocese were of the view that there should be no quick and easy return to the life and worship of the Church. Defectors should be required to start again with serious penitential discipline, new catechization and rebaptism. Cyprian took a much milder view that forgiveness should be extended to the lapsed after a period of penitence and rebaptism. Many strongly objected to Cyprian's leniency and joined the Novatians or Donatists who had formed separate churches. Meanwhile, Cyprian fell out with Stephen, the Bishop of Rome, over his policy of rebaptism.

This issue of the lapsed presented a further difficulty for Cyprian and some of the other bishops. In certain areas, some of the confessors who had stood firm in their faith and in consequence suffered persecution and imprisonment were either asked, or took it upon themselves, to pardon the lapsed. A group of them wrote to Cyprian as follows: "Know that we all have given peace to those concerning whom an account has been rendered to you as to what they have done since they committed their sin; and we wish to make this rescript known through you to other bishops. We desire you to have peace with the holy martyrs."[58] Cyprian, who had a high regard for these faithful confessors, commended them, writing, "Bravely you have resisted the world, you have been an example to your brethren that should follow you."[59] Nevertheless he was distressed that by taking it upon themselves to pardon the lapsed they were threatening the developing episcopal authority of bishops in the Church. Cyprian presided over the Council of Carthage in 251, when it was decided that the lapsed could be allowed to return after repentance and penance. He

---

[58] *Peace Letter* contained in Cyprian, *Letter 16*, in Ayer, *A Source Book for Ancient Church History*, p. 215.

[59] Cyprian, *On the Lapsed* 2.

urged people to turn to the Lord with all their hearts and express their repentance for their sin and grief.[60]

The unity of the Church

The issues surrounding the lapsed which brought about new groups such as the Novatians and the Donatists had a profound impact on the unity of the Catholic Church. It became a major concern for Cyprian who was worried about the Catholic Church splitting apart into factions and electing their own bishops and leaders. In particular, his own episcopal authority was being seriously questioned. This was particularly stressful for Cyprian who, in the words of Hans von Campenhausen, "had begun the line of 'curial' bishops who attempted to perform their ecclesiastical office in the magisterial style of the consuls and pro-consuls, with whom he did not shrink from being directly compared".[61] In 251, he published an important treatise entitled *The Unity of the Church* in support of Bishop Cornelius of Rome against his rival Novatian. In it, he argued that the only true church is the Catholic Church. It was not possible to leave it as Novatian had done. The schismatic who leaves the Catholic Church has cut himself off from salvation. In Chapter 4, Cyprian wrote:

> For the blessed Apostle Paul ... sets forth the sacrament of unity when he says, "There is one body, one Spirit, one hope of our calling, one Lord, one faith, one baptism, one God." This unity we ought firmly to hold and defend, especially we who preside in the Church as bishops, that we may prove the episcopate also to be itself one and undivided. Let no one corrupt the truth of our faith by faithless transgression.[62]

Most scholars are of the view that this text is unlikely to be exactly what Cyprian wrote but rather a version which has been emended along later Roman lines. Nevertheless, it is abundantly clear that he has a very

---

[60] Cyprian, *On the Lapsed* 29.
[61] Hans von Campenhausen, *The Fathers of the Latin Church* (London: Adam & Charles Black, 1964), p. 125. See also Cyprian, *Letter 37.2*.
[62] Cyprian, *On the Unity of the Church* 4.

hierarchical understanding of the nature of the Church with its authority rooted in a free union of bishops each having equal authority. Cyprian's view of an equal episcopal hierarchy stood in contrast to the monarchic idea of the primacy of Rome based on Peter being the rock on which Jesus would build his church. Cyprian did his best to take hold of the situation by calling together a council of 87 bishops at Carthage on 1 September, 256. He made it clear to the assembly that every bishop possessed the freedom and right to hold to his own opinion as he pleased. A delegation which was despatched to Rome was not even received by Stephen who declared Cyprian "to be a false Christ, a false prophet and a deceitful worker".[63] Their clash of views was brought to an end when persecution was resumed in 258 with the new Emperor Valerian ordering that all bishops, elders and deacons were to be executed. Stephen, Cyprian and Novatian all joined the ranks of martyrs.

In other passages in *On the Unity of the Church*, there are clear illustrations of the way in which those who leave the Catholic Church are cut off from salvation:

> If a branch is broken from a tree it cannot bud; if a stream is cut off from its source it dries up ... Nor can he who forsakes the church of Christ. He is a stranger, he is an enemy. Without the church as your mother, you cannot have God for your Father. If it was possible to escape outside the ark of Noah, then it may be possible to escape outside of the church ... There is only one baptism, but they [the schismatics] think that they can baptize. Although they forsake the fountain of life, they promise the grace of living and saving water. Men are not washed there, they are made foul; sins are not purged, they are piled up.[64]

In this passage, Cyprian clearly rejected the validity of heretical and sectarian baptism. It is clear that he was at odds with the church in Rome who affirmed the principle and validity of heretical baptisms. In fact,

---

[63] Von Campenhausen, *The Fathers of the Latin Church*, p. 56.
[64] Cyprian, *On the Unity of the Church* 5, 6.11, 13, 14.

they went even further and recognized Novatian ordination.[65] Despite being engaged in many conflicts, Cyprian was also commended for his preaching, wise council, generosity, abstinence and humility. He died an exemplary martyr's death surrounded by a huge crowd who wanted to die with him.[66]

Cyprian's view of bishops and priests

Cyprian was clearly seeking to build and strengthen a doctrine of episcopacy also viewing it as a bastion against the persecuting Roman authorities. "We are bound", he wrote, "to observe the precepts and admonition of our Lord; and he ordained the high office of bishop and the principle of his Church when in the gospel he spoke these words of Peter, 'You are Peter, and on this rock I will build my church.'"[67] So from this he asserted "the Church is established on the foundation of bishops, and every act of the Church is directed by those same presiding officers".[68] In another passage he makes bishops the *sine qua non* of the Church. "Hence", he wrote, "you should know that the bishop is in the church, and the Church in the bishop, and that if anyone is not with the bishop he is not in the Church."[69]

Considering the appointment of priests, Cyprian was adamant that "we ought to choose none but men of spotless and upright character as our leaders".[70] The selection procedure should always be in the presence of the people who can raise any doubts or merits of those being considered.[71]

Baptism is always in the name of the Trinity and should be granted, even to the worst offenders if they have repented and believed, and infants should not be shut out.[72] Cyprian makes mention that the baptized person must also be anointed, that by receiving the *chrism*, that is, the

---

[65] Von Campenhausen, *The Fathers of the Latin Church*, p. 53.
[66] See the reply of Nemesianus et al. to Cyprian, in *Letter 77*.1.
[67] Cyprian, *Letter 33*.1.
[68] Cyprian, *Letter 33*.1.
[69] Cyprian, *Letter 65*.7.
[70] Cyprian, *Letter 67*.2, 3–5.
[71] Cyprian, *Letter 67*.2, 3–5.
[72] Cyprian, *Letter 64*.5.

unction, they may be God's anointed and have themselves the grace of Christ.[73] Those who have been baptized in the Church are brought to the leaders of the Church and prayed for with the imposition of hands so that they may obtain the Holy Spirit and be perfected in the Lord.[74] Those who have been baptized and have obtained the Holy Spirit are "admitted to drink the cup of the Lord".[75]

Cyprian has much to say about the Eucharist. Among other things, he stresses that it was not in the morning but after supper that the Lord offered the "mingled"[76] cup. He warns that the bread and wine must not be taken without penance or lightly. That would be to do violence to the Lord's body and blood.[77] Cyprian was the first to expound the idea of the Eucharist being in some sense a "sacrifice" and "oblation". In the Eucharist, we remember his passion and sacrificial offering of himself. The priest, Cyprian is suggesting, "re-enacts the oblation of His passion".[78] The priest acts truly in Christ's stead, when he reproduces what Christ did and then offers a true and complete sacrifice to God the Father.[79] J. N. D. Kelly suggested that Cyprian conceived the eucharistic sacrifice as possessing objective efficacy.[80] "Ought we not, then", asks Cyprian, "to celebrate the Lord's cup after supper?"[81] It was necessary, he pointed out, that the Lord's Supper be held in the evening because the Passover which preceded it was held in the evening.

---

[73] Cyprian, *Letter* 70.3.
[74] Cyprian, *Letter* 73.9.
[75] Cyprian, *Letter* 52.8.
[76] Mingled because in Carthage the cup of wine was also mixed with water. The water represented the people and the wine the blood of Christ. The mingling illustrates the fact that believers are joined to Christ by an intermixed union. See Cyprian, *Letter* 63.16.
[77] Cyprian, *On the Lapsed* 15.1.
[78] Cyprian, *On the Lapsed* 15.1.
[79] Cyprian, *Letter* 53.14.
[80] J. N. D. Kelly, *Early Christian Doctrines* (London: Adam & Charles Black, 1980), p. 216.
[81] Cyprian, *Letter 63 to Caecilian* 13–17.

The school of Alexandria

Clement

Titus Flavius Clemens Alexandrinus was born about the year 150. Little is known of his early life, though he appears to have come from a pagan family in Athens. Like many other young men, he travelled widely and sat at the feet of a broad range of teachers, both pagan philosophers and Christian instructors.[82] The best of these proved to be Pantaenus (*d. c.*200) who founded and ran a Christian philosophical School in Alexandria. Clement enrolled as a pupil about 185 and settled in the city. He was evidently an able scholar, because when Pantaenus left Alexandria, he succeeded him as the head of the school. He remained in this post until the persecution of the Emperor Septimus Severus caused him to take refuge in Cappadocia in about the year 203 from which he never returned, dying about the year 215. The Bishop of Alexandria from 189 and for 43 years was Demetrius (*d.*232). He like Clement was a strong opponent against Gnosticism and was constantly teaching and lecturing in order to present an orthodox Christian faith that was intellectually viable.

Clement's writings

As was the case with many other early Christian writers, much of what Clement wrote has been either lost or destroyed. Apart from numerous fragments of a number of lost works, four others have survived. In all his books, it is clear that Clement was greatly indebted to earlier writers. He makes frequent quotations from the classical poets and from Plato and Philo as well as from the Old Testament and Christian writers.

The Exhortation to the Greeks (Protrepticus) was written by Clement around 195 with the specific aim of bringing the reader to faith in Christ. It is in the form of a challenge to listen to "The Song of the New Orpheus", the Logos proceeding from Zion. Following on from this there are a series of attacks on the folly of immorality and pagan myths. By contrast, full unclouded knowledge is only to be found in the prophets and above all in the Logos.

---

[82] Clement, *Stromata* I.2.

The Instructor (*Paedagogos*) is a larger work appearing in three volumes and gives practical instruction about the Christian way of life. It is wide-ranging and addresses moral and social issues which Christian beginners are likely to encounter. They include table manners, eating, drinking and managing a home. There is plenty of advice on communication between the sexes; a whole chapter is given over to footwear and considerable length is devoted to the use of perfumes and ointments. It is soon apparent that Clement had little truck with the austerity measures of the Stoics. He has a very positive stance towards material pleasures which he asserts are to be enjoyed in a wholesome manner. Clement's aim is to demonstrate that Christianity transcends other religions. *The Rich Young Ruler* was an important tract to reassure the cultured wealthy pupils at his Christian school that Jesus did not condemn wealth but only the wrong attitude to it.

Clement's significance
Clement was well aware that several of the basic tenets of Gnosticism were anti-Christian, and he intentionally set out to ensure that the Christian Church was free from their influence. There is an anti-Gnostic emphasis which runs through much of his writing. Unlike the Gnostics, Clement has a very positive outlook towards the material world and the pleasures of life, including sexual relationships in marriage. Significantly, he also says that "to be unmarried is a gift of God". Unlike the Gnostics, he did not see the New Testament writings as being world-denying.[83] The apostles, he reminds us, were married and even Paul, he thinks, was quite possibly married.[84] Clement appears somewhat disparaging of second marriages. He does not regard them as sinful but thinks they may hinder those concerned in their progress towards perfection.

Clement's anti-Gnostic stance is visible in his Christology. In *Stromateis* (*c*.203) he wrote: "But in the case of our Saviour . . . he ate, not because of bodily needs, since his body was supported by holy power, but so that his companions might not entertain a false notion about him, as in fact certain men did later, namely that he has been manifested

---

[83] Clement, *Stromata* III.79.
[84] Clement, *Stromata* IV.53.

only in appearance."[85] Because the Gnostics believed the God of the Old Testament was the creator of the material world which is contaminated by evil, they discounted it altogether. However, Clement sought to defend it by allegorizing the stories in order to find the core truth they contained. Those texts in which God was said to do evil he viewed as an earlier revelation of God.

A second major significance of Clement's writing was his positive use of philosophy. In contrast to Tertullian's negative views, he sought to synthesize Greek philosophy with Christian thought. In the first part of *Stromateis*, he took issue with those who considered philosophy to be a waste of time and demonic in its origin. In his view, philosophy is of divine origin since all truth is one and comes from God.[86] Clement does, however, admit that philosophy has been distorted by the traditions of men and led to strange notions and beliefs as seen in the strange esoteric systems put out by the Gnostics. That said, this is no good reason against philosophy in general. Philosophy highlights truth and increases knowledge. There is good and evil in all things including philosophy. Philosophy, Clement points out, has been the means of leading the Greeks to some knowledge of God. This knowledge reaches its finality in the revelation of God in Christ. In the following passage from *Stromateis*, Clement articulates some of the benefits of philosophy:

> Philosophy was necessary to the Greeks for righteousness, until the coming of the Lord: and even now it is useful for the development of true religion, as a kind of discipline for those who arrive at faith by way of demonstration ... God is the source of all good; either directly, as in the Old and New Testaments, or indirectly, as in the case of philosophy. But it may even be that philosophy was given to the Greeks directly; for it was a 'schoolmaster' to bring Hellenism to Christ, as the Law was for the Hebrews. Thus philosophy was a preparation, paving the way to perfection by Christ.[87]

---

[85] Clement, *Stromata* VI.9.
[86] Clement, *Stromata* I.9.
[87] Clement, *Stromata* I.5.

Besides being an aid to bring the Greeks to faith in Christ, philosophy as Clement saw it was very necessary for the Gnostics. It was "a preparatory discipline for the Gnostic". Clement also valued philosophy because it can increase in men and women the ability to think rationally and logically when they are engaged in debate with those who are not Christians. Philosophy is also valuable because it helps us think through and process the issues which we encounter in our daily lives.

Third, in his writings Clement put strong emphasis on Christian lifestyle. We could almost say that Clement is the theologian of everyday living. He lays great stress on behaviour and there are lengthy sections in his writings which deal with personal and social ethics. His emphasis in this regard was particularly relevant. This was an era during which the Christian churches were experiencing intermittent periods of hostility and brutal persecution. It was vital that Christians should be able to commend their faith and their Lord by the quality of their living.

Clement regards manners and lifestyle as a vital aspect of Christian living. He set high store on the need for self-discipline if the believers were going to reflect the image and likeness of Christ. This self-discipline is a compound of three elements: restraint, self-sufficiency and impassibility. Each of these elements are like ascending steps of a ladder of Christian maturity. This wide-ranging scope of Clement's theology stands out very clearly in the pages of *The Instructor*, which he wrote about 198. In Book 2, Chapter 1, he addresses the issue of "eating" and begins by reminding his readers that we must not be ruled by our appetites:

> But we who seek the heavenly bread must rule the belly, which is beneath heaven, and much more the things which are agreeable to it, which 'God shall destroy' says the apostle, justly execrating gluttonous desires.[88]

Clement has much practical advice on the subject of eating including this injunction:

---

[88] Clement, *The Instructor* 2.1.

> We must guard against speaking anything while eating; for the voice becomes disagreeable and inarticulate when it is confined by full jaws; and the tongue, pressed by food and impeded in its natural energy, gives forth a compressed utterance. Nor is it suitable to eat and drink at the same time.[89]

A little later, in Chapter 7, he has strong words against "frequent spitting, violent clearing of the throat, and wiping one's nose at an entertainment". We are not, he continues, "to copy oxen and asses, whose manger and dunghill are together".[90] He advises on oils, ointments and hair dyes, urging "that sweet scents are a bait which draws into sensual lust".[91] He has much to say about clothes, stressing that "in fashioning our clothes we must keep clear of all strangeness . . . for neither is it seemly for clothes to be above the knee . . . nor is it becoming for any part of a woman to be exposed".[92] Regarding jewellery, women should "adopt simplicity".[93] Clement was much concerned about the way in which people bathed both in their homes and at the public baths. He gave strong warnings against the latter: "The public baths", he wrote, "are opened promiscuously to men and women; and there they strip for licentious indulgence . . . as if their modesty had been wasted in the bath." He also goaded those who misused their home bath and "strip off when there are people in the house . . . . as if exposing themselves for sale".[94] Among other issues, Clement urged young men and young women to keep away from the festivals "for things to which their ears are unaccustomed, and unseemly sights, inflame the mind, while faith within them is still wavering".[95]

---

[89] Clement, *The Instructor* 2.1.
[90] Clement, *The Instructor* 2.7.
[91] Clement, *The Instructor* 2.8.
[92] Clement, *The Instructor* 2.8.
[93] Clement, *The Instructor* 2.5.
[94] Clement, *The Instructor* 2.5.
[95] Clement, *The Instructor* 2.7.

Clement's doctrine

Clement is not a systematic theologian, but he does make statements on many of the basic doctrines. He roots all that he says in the apostolic Scriptures, accepting all of the books which later formed the New Testament, with the exception of James, 2 Peter and the Letters of John.

God

In his doctrine of God, he speaks of God as "the formless and nameless", though we give him names such as "Creator", "Lord", "Father" or "Good". He has a very high majestic view of God as infinite and inexpressible.[96] The word "Almighty" cannot adequately indicate his power. God, he wrote:

> cannot be comprehended by knowledge ... It remains that the unknown be apprehended by the divine grace and the word proceeding from him ... Although God is beyond all human comprehension yet he has made himself known to man in the cosmic logos who is Christ. Jesus is the Logos or word of the Father. He is the one who makes God fully known to men.[97]

Clement has a high Christology and speaks of the Son as "most closely joined to the Almighty" and "the greatest pre-eminence which orders all things according to the Father's will, and guides everything aright". In *Stromata* 4, he stresses that the Father does not exist without the Son for "Father" immediately implies "Father of a Son" and that "the Son is the true teacher about the Father". Therefore "in order that we may come to know the Father, we must believe in the Son, because the Son of God is our teacher".[98] Although Clement was perfectly orthodox in his expression of the Son's equality with the Father throughout all time, his Christology comes close to being semi-docetic. Jesus, he asserted at

---

[96] Clement, *Stromata* 5.12.
[97] Clement, *Stromata* 5.12.
[98] Clement, *Stromata* 4.17.

one point "had a human soul like ours but it was exempt from carnal desires".[99]

Clement doesn't deal with the Holy Spirit in any detailed way and makes only passing allusions to the Trinity without any attempt at an explanation. In *Paedogogus* 1, he exclaims: "O wonderful mystery! The Father of all things is one; the Word of all things is one; the Holy Spirit is one and the same everywhere."[100] Regarding the creation, Clement followed Philo in asserting that the six days in Genesis were figurative and not to be taken literally.

Human beings

In respect of the creation of human beings, Clement was unorthodox in that he did not accept that the newborn child inherited pollution from his parents. How can a child which has not yet performed any action have fallen under Adam's curse? When David says, "I was conceived in sins and lawlessness when my mother bore me, he refers to Eve as his mother. But Eve was the mother of all living, and if he was conceived in sin in this sense still he is not himself in sin, nor is he himself sin."[101] Generally speaking, Clement had a fairly optimistic view of the nature of man and came close to asserting a form of universalism.[102] He put forward the view that those who were not brought to a knowledge of God in this life may well have the opportunity at some later point, as was the case of those imprisoned spirits to whom Jesus went and spoke after his resurrection.[103]

Glimpses of early church life

In his various writings, Clement gives us glimpses of church life. He has a strong doctrine of the Catholic Church.[104] It is the "only church" on account of its faithfulness to the apostolic tradition. Those who have left

---

[99] Clement, *Stromata* 4.17.

[100] Clement, *The Instructor* 1.6.

[101] Clement, *Stromata* 7.2.

[102] Universalism asserts that ultimately everyone will find forgiveness and salvation.

[103] See 1 Peter 3:19.

[104] Clement, *Stromata* 7.16.

it will find themselves in assemblies devised by human beings. Clement is also fully aware that there are those who are outwardly part of the Church's life but not "cleaving to the Lord".

In terms of the Church's ministry, popular teaching was beginning in some places to regard the office of presbyter as a continuation of the Old Testament priesthood, but Clement rejected this idea regarding the true priest as one anointed like a prophet with the Holy Spirit. Baptism is a means of "cleansing the filth of our sins" and "a gift of grace".[105] The Eucharist that Clement refers to is always Passover in style and in the context of a shared meal or agape or love feast. Clement described one such in the *Paedagogus* with the husband, wife, children and household slaves gathering round the domestic board (table). For Clement, the Eucharist was a means of grace and nourishment which is received through eating and drinking the bread and wine.[106] Clement's eucharistic language appears somewhat ambiguous with him sometimes speaking of the elements as "hallowed food" and at other times as "nourishment for the soul".[107]

In summary, we can assert with confidence that Clement was a prominent orthodox theologian who in some ways paved the way for Athanasius. All his theology was thoroughly rooted in the Old Testament and the apostolic writings. His teaching had a major impact in rebutting Gnosticism and emphasizing that the Christian faith has to be lived out in the whole of life.

Origen

Origen was a great Christian teacher and theologian who in some ways has never been surpassed. He was a man of the Spirit, a great biblical exegete, a mystic and preacher and some say a heretic. Origenes Adamantius was born about the year 185 and came from a Christian

---

[105] Clement, *The Instructor* 1.6.
[106] Clement, *The Instructor* 2.1.
[107] Clement, *The Instructor* 1.6.

home. His father Leonides was martyred during the persecution[108] and Origen had a strong desire to follow him, but the historian Eusebius recorded that his mother saved the day when "she hid his clothing and compelled him to stay at home"![109] He taught in Alexandria when peace returned and was appointed head of the Catechetical School by Bishop Demetrius in succession to Clement.[110] He adopted an ascetical lifestyle with fasting, vigils and voluntary poverty. According to Eusebius, he mutilated himself, interpreting Matthew 19:12 in a literal sense.[111] He travelled a good deal and even visited Rome where he heard a sermon by Hippolytus. In 215, when trouble broke out in Alexandria in connection with the visit of the Emperor Caracalla (Emperor 198–217), he took refuge in Palestine where he was asked to preach by the bishops of Caesarea and Aelia. As he was only a layman, this was held to be a breach of discipline and his bishop Demetrius deprived him of his position. Origen left Alexandria and took up residence at Caesarea in 231 where he founded a school and devoted himself to preaching and study. In 250, he was imprisoned during the Decian persecution and subjected to torture which he survived for only a short period. He died about the year 254.

Alexandria, where Origen was brought up and received a thoroughly Christian education, was one of the Roman Empire's great centres of learning. It was there that he was a pupil of the neo-Platonic philosopher Ammonius Saccas. Origen's early grounding in philosophy and biblical knowledge formed the basis of his theology. Like his predecessor Clement, Origen regarded philosophy as a preparatory guide to Christian faith.

Origen's significance

Origen's works

Origen taught himself Hebrew so that he could produce his own more accurate Greek text of the Old Testament and compare it with other

---

[108] Eusebius, *History of the Church* VI.1.
[109] Eusebius, *History of the Church* VI.2.
[110] Eusebius, *History of the Church* VI.3.
[111] Eusebius, *History of the Church* VI.8.

versions. Over a period of 25 years, Origen produced a huge volume known as *The Hexapla*, so called because it contained six parallel columns with a different version of the Scripture in each. He was probably therefore one of the earliest pioneers of lower criticism, the science of producing the most accurate texts. Sadly, *The Hexapla* appears to have been destroyed during the persecution in which Origen himself died. In addition, Origen wrote commentaries on all the books of the Bible.

Origen taught that "Scripture is like a man in that it is composed of body, soul and spirit". Scripture, he taught, can be interpreted in three ways. The "body" of Scripture is the literal and most straightforward meaning of the text and is comprehensible even to the simple. The "soul" was the moral meaning and clear to all believers when it was pointed out to them. The "spirit" was the spiritual or allegorical meaning of the text.

Origen developed the allegorical method of interpreting Scripture for two reasons, one positive and one negative. The "positive" use of allegory enabled readers to gain further knowledge from a passage. So, for example, the waterpots at the beginning of John's Gospel are a symbol or allegory of the Old Covenant.[112] Paul's reference to not muzzling the ox that treads the corn becomes a reference to caring for the needs of people.[113] This enabled Origen to overcome moral issues such as polygamy, the wiping out of Canaan with vengeance, inhuman behaviour, the harsh treatment of slaves and children being punished for the sins of their parents. These were to be regarded as pure allegory.

Apologetics

As has already been noted, Origen was a prominent apologist who produced his apology entitled *Against Celsus* in 248. It's in the form of a dialogue with Celsus, a Greek philosopher and opponent of Christianity. Origen's method is to quote substantial paragraphs from his opponent's writings and then to answer them either directly or with a counter argument. Celsus, it should be said, was one of the intellectual elite who had begun to recognize that Christianity was having a significant impact in the Roman Empire. Celsus for example attacked the stories of Moses as

---

[112] Origen, *On First Principles* 4.2.5.
[113] Origen, *On First Principles* 4.2.6.

fanciful and put down Jesus as a sorcerer. Origen took up his points one by one. J. G. Davies wrote that Origen "revealed himself as an apologist of no mean stature".[114]

Origen the churchman

Origen was a strong churchman who believed that the doctrines and laws of Christ could only be found within the Catholic Church. For him there was no faith outside the one Catholic Church. He wrote: "If anyone wishes to be saved . . . let him come to this house where the blood of Christ is for a sign of redemption . . . Let no-one therefore persuade himself or deceive himself; outside the church, no-one is saved."[115]

Theological writings

Origen's third important area of influence was his theological writing. His main theological work he entitled *First Principles*. It was written between 220–30 and is unique in that it was the first systematic Christian theology. Only fragments of the Greek text remain, but the Latin translation by Rufinus (*c*.344–411) has been wholly preserved. There are four books dealing with the doctrines of God, the World, Freedom and Revelation. Origen endorsed all the accepted Christian doctrines but speculated on issues of indifference. He wrote: "The teaching of the church, handed down in unbroken succession from the apostles, is still preserved and continues to exist in the churches up to the present day, we maintain that only that is to be believed as the truth which in no way conflicts with the tradition of the church and the apostles."[116]

Doctrine of God

Origen refers to God as "light" and "Spirit", and "in him is no darkness".[117] He is also omniscient, omnipresent, unchanging and incomprehensible. One of the texts he draws on was Romans 11:33: "How unsearchable are his judgements and his ways past finding out." God is also the Creator:

---

[114] J. G. Davies, *The Early Christian Church* (New York: Anchor, 1967), p. 165.
[115] Origen, *In Iesu Nave homiliae*.
[116] Origen, *On First Principles* I.1.2.
[117] Origen, *On First Principles* I.1.1.

"He made out of nothing the things which he willed."[118] He wrote: "When God in the beginning created all things which he wished to create, that is, natural beings, the only cause he had for creating was his own nature, that is his goodness."[119]

Doctrine of the Son

Origen agrees with the later creedal formulae that Jesus the Son is one substance with the Father. He is also the first theologian to have produced the doctrine of eternal generation. This means that God the Father did not bring the Son into evidence at one point in time, but has always been generating him from eternity. Origen wrote: "His only begotten Son who was indeed born indeed of him . . . is yet without beginning."[120] This overcomes the problem of making the Son less than God because he would otherwise be thought of as a created being. That said, Origen opens himself up to the charge of subordinationism, that is making the Son less or subordinate to God the Father. He refers to Jesus the Logos as "a second God". 'Only the Father is "primal goodness". The Saviour is the image of God but not goodness itself. Origen defended his view on this point by quoting Jesus' words that "the Father who sent me is greater than I" and "do not call me good; no-one is good save God alone". Origen illustrated his perceived distinction between God the Father and the Son with reference to prayer. "Prayer", he asserted, "is never to be offered to any derivative being, not even to Christ himself, but solely to God of the whole universe, the Father to whom the Son prayed."[121]

Origen also believed that Christ's human nature existed before the incarnation. His reasoning for this was his belief that God created all the souls and there was one special one for Christ. This one soul "burned with love for Justice".[122] All other souls were misguided and fell away as

---

[118] Origen, *On First Principles* II.1.4.
[119] Origen, *On First Principles* II.9.6.
[120] Origen, *On First Principles* I.2.2.
[121] Origen, *On Prayer* 14–16.
[122] Origen, *On First Principles* II.6.3.

a result from the Logos. This one unique unfallen soul as a result of its unfallenness eventually became inseparably united with him.[123]

Central to Origen's Christology is Jesus' atonement through the cross. "Christ is a great high priest who has offered himself as the sacrifice once offered not only on behalf of men but also for every rational being."[124] "For Jesus alone", Origen asserted in his *Against Celsus*, "has been able, by his great power, to take to himself the burden of the sin of all and to carry it on the cross on which he hung, apart from God on behalf of all."[125]

The Holy Spirit

Origen stressed the "tremendous majesty" of the Holy Spirit,[126] basing his assertion on the fact that blasphemy against the Spirit has no forgiveness. Origen is clear that the Holy Spirit is uncreated and fully God.[127] He is also particularly impressed with the importance of the Holy Spirit in people's lives. His presence came only to believers through the laying on of the apostles' hands.[128] The Holy Spirit is active in people's lives, enabling them to be holy and exercise the gifts which he bestows on them.[129]

The Trinity

In *On First Principles*, Origen moves from his consideration of the Holy Spirit to consider the Trinity. He stresses the distinctiveness of the Father, Son and the Holy Spirit. He used the Greek word *hypostasis*, which corresponds to Tertullian's use of *persona*, to indicate this. He is clear that the Father is immaterial, writing that "God therefore must not be thought to be any kind of body, nor exist in a body, but to be simple intellectual existence". He goes on to speak of the Son's divinity yet again hints at his inferiority to the Father. The Son may be called God but not in the sense

---

[123] Origen, *On First Principles* II.6.4.
[124] Origen, *Commentary on John* 1.40.
[125] Origen, *Against Celsus* 4.28.
[126] Origen, *On First Principles* I.3.2
[127] Origen, *On First Principles* I.3.3.
[128] Origen, *On First Principles* I.3.7.
[129] Origen, *On First Principles* I.3.8.

that Jesus spoke of the Father as the only God in John 17:3. The Holy Spirit is a person and blows where he wills (John 3:8–9) and distributes gifts where he wills (1 Corinthians 12:11). When Origen speaks of all three persons together, he comes close to subordinationism. In another place, in a fragment quoted by Jerome from the Greek fragment of *On First Principles*, Origen declares that:

> The Son ... is less than the Father ... still inferior is the Holy Spirit ... so that in this way, the power of the Father is greater than the Son, but the Son is more than that of the Holy Spirit.[130]

Baptism and Eucharist

Origen held firmly to the doctrine of original sin, which states that every human being was born with a sinful human nature. "Everyone", he wrote, "who enters the world is said to be affected by a kind of contamination,[131] because they were born in the loins of Adam."[132] It was for this reason, he said, although without any conclusive evidence, that the apostles baptized babies. That said, he warns against thinking that the Holy Spirit is automatically given at baptism.[133] "It is not all who are baptized who are washed so as to obtain salvation. We who have received the grace of baptism in the name of Christ, have been washed, but I know not who has been washed into salvation."[134]

Regarding the Eucharist, Origen urges that "all who take part in the divine mysteries" do so "carefully and reverently".[135] He reminds his readers that even though the elements of bread and wine have been "sanctified through the word of God and prayer", this does not of itself sanctify the recipient,[136] since everything depends on "partaking the

---

[130] Origen, *On First Principles* I.3.5 from the Greek fragment quoted by Jerome.
[131] Origen, *Homily on Leviticus* 12.4.
[132] Origen, *Commentary on the Letter to Romans* 5.4.
[133] Origen, *Homily on Numbers* 3.1.
[134] Origen, *Homily on Ezekiel* 6.5.
[135] Origen, *Homily on Exodus* 13.3.
[136] Origen, *Homily on Matthew* 11.14.

bread with a pure mind and clear conscience according to the proportion of faith".[137]

Origen mentions that in the case of "the more serious offences" the opportunity for penitence is granted only once, "but those more common offences which we frequently incur always admit of penitence and are redeemed continually".[138]

Resurrection

Regarding the resurrection, Origen deviated from the orthodox view that the earthly body is resurrected. He believed in a spiritual resurrection writing that "by the command of God the body which was earthly and animal will be replaced by a spiritual body, such as may be able to dwell in heaven". Even "those of lower worth" and "the contemptible" will be bestowed in this way according to the deserts of their lives.[139]

Final estate

Origen appears to have been a universalist, believing that ultimately everything will be restored to its original pure and spiritual state. The souls of those who have committed sins on earth will be purified after death while good souls will go straight to Paradise. So the resurrection body will be a spiritual body. We cannot begin to imagine "what will be the purity, fineness and glory of that body compared with our present bodies".[140] In the final consummation which follows, Origen asserts that "each being will undergo the punishment which his sins have merited". He then declares: "speaking very cautiously and diffidently, rather by way of discussion than coming to definite conclusions . . . that the goodness of God will restore the whole creation to unity in the end, through Christ, when his enemies have been subdued and overcome".[141]

---

[137] Origen, *Homily on Matthew* 11.14.
[138] Origen, *Homily on Leviticus* 15.
[139] Origen, *On First Principles* II.10.3.
[140] Origen, *On First Principles* III.6.4.
[141] Origen, *On First Principles* I.6.1–4.

Anti-Origenism

Probably no-one would have thought Origen to have been unorthodox in his teaching had it not been for the Arian controversy which beset the Church a century later. Briefly, Arius, a parish priest also based in Alexandria, taught that Jesus was only like God the Father but not the same as God the Father. Arian theologians found echoes of their teaching in Origen's subordinationist Trinity. Towards the close of the fourth century, when Arianism was almost at an end, Epiphanius (c.315–404), Bishop of Salamis, was determined to put an end to Origen's teaching and influence for good. In the spring of 394, he issued a public attack on Origen's views focusing on his Trinitarian subordination, his assertion of the pre-existence of souls, denial of the resurrection of the flesh, his excessive allegorization of the Paradise story so that there was no historical substance in it. Finally, the fifth great General Ecumenical Council, which met at Constantinople in 553, pronounced against Origenism with 15 anathemas. The main accusations included the pre-existence[142] and transmigration of souls,[143] the pre-existence of Jesus' soul,[144] Christ to be crucified again for the demons,[145] universalism,[146] the sun, moon and stars having reasonable bodies,[147] the power of God limited in creation,[148] punishment as temporary,[149] Trinitarian subordination,[150] the subordination of the Son,[151] and angels not created in categories.

It is clear from this that Origen did teach a number of doctrines which after his time came to be regarded as unorthodox. Nevertheless, he remains one of the great thinkers and teachers of the early Christian Church. He was always intent on passing on the teaching and writings

---

[142] Origen, *On First Principles* II.9.2.
[143] Origen, *On First Principles* I.8.4.
[144] Origen, *On First Principles* II.6.3.
[145] Origen, *On First Principles* IV.3.13.
[146] Origen, *On First Principles* I.6.1 and II.10.3.
[147] Origen, *On First Principles* I.7.3.
[148] Origen, *On First Principles* II.9.1.
[149] Origen, *On First Principles* II.10.3.
[150] Origen, *On First Principles* I.3.5.
[151] Origen, *On First Principles* III.5.6.

of the apostles and all his teaching was rooted in them. He was a distinguished defender of the faith, a biblical theologian whose life, courage and work strengthened the life of the early Catholic Church and enabled it to thrust the gospel forward in the Roman Empire.

Conclusion

As we survey the work and lives of these significant theologians, we cannot fail to realize that without their leadership, biblical knowledge, theological scholarship and writing the Christian Church would have fragmented in a world of philosophical confusion and sectarianism. As it turned out the four theologians we have considered along with others, too many to include in the confines of this chapter, guided the Church forward, enabling it to more than conquer the threat of persecution from without and the disagreements and false teaching from within. Each of these four theologians gave their lives to carrying forward the apostolic faith "once for all entrusted to the saints".[152]

---

[152] Jude 3 (NRSV).

9

The Emperor is converted! Constantine and the Christianization of the Empire

In the entrance of St John Lateran, the Cathedral of Rome, there is a statue of the Emperor Constantine the Great. Its massive size symbolizes everything we know about him. He was a powerful soldier, strong authoritarian leader and a skilful politician. The fifth-century bishop and theologian Theodoret described him as "remarkable for his lofty stature and worthy of admiration for personal beauty".[1] His conversion to Christ in 312, on the eve of the Battle of Milvian Bridge on the outskirts of Rome, must rank as one of the most significant events of European history.

Constantine had been appointed one of four assistant Caesars by Emperor Galerius in 306 to rule the Western section of the Empire which included Britain. When Galerius died in 311, there was an immediate struggle for power between the four assistants. It ended with Licinius becoming master in the East and Constantine master in the West.

In the West, Maxentius felt threatened and took up residence in Rome stationing a large army to protect it. In response, Constantine set out from the British Isles to the Imperial City with a much smaller army but gathering more support as he went. Eventually, he crossed Italy and stationed his forces near the walls of the Imperial City. Maxentius, instead of remaining within the security of the city, followed the advice of the Sibylline oracle and came to fight with the River Tiber behind him. Militarily it was a disaster for Maxentius, who was killed, and his troops, many of whom were driven back and drowned in the river.

---

[1] Theodoret, *Ecclesiastical History* I.6.

Accounts of Constantine's conversion

According to Eusebius' account which, he alleged to have received from Constantine himself before he marched into Italy, he had seen a vision of the cross in the sky. In a dream before the battle at Milvian Bridge, he was commanded to mark his soldiers' shields with the monogram of Christ, XP, the letters being *chi* and *rho*, the first two Greek letters for the word Christ. There are three significant accounts of the vision which may well have been embellished to some extent. Eusebius, writing in 337 in his *Life of Constantine,* related that the Emperor told him and swore to the truth of his words, that just after midday he had seen a luminous cross in the sky above the sun, inscribed with the words "by this conquer". During the night that followed, Christ had appeared to him, directing him to make a standard with the cross to carry into battle as a means of securing victory.[2] In his earlier *History of the Church*, published in 326, there is no mention of a cross in the sky but reference is made to the fact that Constantine was "calling in prayer to God in heaven and to His Word, Jesus Christ himself, the Saviour of all, to come to his aid".[3] Lactantius, who wrote in 318, recorded that, just prior to the battle of Milvian Bridge, "Constantine was directed in a dream to cause the heavenly sign to be delineated on the shields of his soldiers".[4] They complied, putting a cross with the top of the upright bent into a Greek letter P (Greek capital R). Much later, at the beginning of the fifth century, Sozomen recorded that the Emperor saw in the vision of the night the sight of the cross shining in heaven and called for Christian priests to explain it to him.[5] In summary, all three of the earlier accounts record that Constantine had some kind of personal encounter with Christ before the battle had begun. Various scholars have raised questions about the phenomenon in the sky. A. H. Jones suggested that what Constantine saw "was a rare but well-attested form

---

[2] Eusebius, *History of the Church* IX.9.
[3] Eusebius, *History of the Church* IX.11.
[4] Lactantius, *Liber de Mortibus Persecutorum* XLIV.
[5] Sozomen, *Ecclesiastical History* I.3.

of the 'halo Phenomenon'".[6] Others have simply regarded the cross in the sky as a mythical embellishment. The reliability of both Eusebius and Lactantius have been questioned on the ground that both were trusted members of Constantine's staff and close to him. However, despite these challenges the fact remains that when the senate approved the dedication of the triumphal monument in Rome in 315 it was dedicated not to Constantine's imperial greatness but to the Godhead.

Evidence of Constantine's conversion

Toleration

Leaving aside these differing accounts of Constantine's conversion, there is plenty of evidence to substantiate its genuineness, the first and most obvious being the *Edict of Milan* which became law in 313. This document came about as a result of a meeting between Constantine and Licinius (263–325), who still held the rank of assistant Caesar and ruled over the Eastern section of the Empire. Sozomen recorded that "all those who, on account of their confession of Christ had been sent to banishment . . . in the mines, public works, the harems or linen factories, should be restored to liberty".[7] The edict guaranteed freedom of worship to everyone; no-one was to be prevented from either practising or embracing the Christian faith and that all property of the Christian corporation that had been confiscated during the persecution should be restored. Eusebius gives more details of how the edict worked out in practice:

> Christians and all others now had liberty to follow whatever form of worship they chose. With regard to places of worship where earlier it was their habit to meet we now decree that if it should appear that any persons have bought these places either from our treasury, or from some other source, they must restore them to

---

[6] A. H. M. Jones, *Constantine and the Conversion of Europe* (London: Macmillan, 1948), p. 96.

[7] Sozomen, *Ecclesiastical History* I.8.

these same Christians without payment and without demand of compensation, and there must be no negligence or hesitation.[8]

Constantine held out the hand of friendship to the Novatian Bishop Acesius as well as to the Montanists.[9] Also included in the toleration were the Manichaeans who denied that Christ existed in the flesh.[10] There is evidence that after his victory at Milvian Bridge Constantine did not engage in pagan sacrifice. Nor did he make the usual traditional procession to the Capitol in Rome or offer the usual homage and thanksgiving to Jupiter, the chief of Roman gods.[11] In so doing, Jedin asserted, Constantine was proclaiming that he owed his victory to another God.[12]

Monuments of tribute to Christ
His Triumphal Arch, which was erected alongside the Colosseum in 315, doesn't have an inscription to the Sun god. Constantine is represented as entering the city in triumph, but the inscription is relatively low-key, simply ascribing his victory to an "inspiration of divinity".[13] A statue of Constantine was erected in the forum at Rome, and he directed that a Christian monogram be placed in his hand. Eusebius recorded the inscription: "By this saving sign, the true proof of courage, I saved your city from the yoke of the tyrant and set her free; furthermore I freed the Senate and People of Rome and restore them in their ancient renown and splendour."[14]

Constantine's legislation
Constantine issued more humane legislation. As early as 314, he forbade the infliction of capital punishment upon any person unless they had

---

[8] Eusebius, *History of the Church* X.5.1.
[9] Socrates, *Ecclesiastical History* I.10.
[10] Socrates, *Ecclesiastical History* I.22.
[11] Eusebius, *History of the Church* IX.7.
[12] H. Jedin, *From the Apostolic Community to Constantine*, Vol. 1 (London: Burns & Oates, 1980), p. 413.
[13] Jedin, *From the Apostolic Community to Constantine*, p. 414.
[14] Eusebius, *History of the Church* IX.7.

either confessed their crime, or the testimony of the accusers was unanimous. It was forbidden to brand slaves and criminals. Debtors to the state treasury were no longer to be scourged.

Constantine ordered more humane treatment of slaves. The crucifixion and the breaking of the legs of slaves was abolished in 315, and in the following year Constantine allowed slaves to be freed in Christian churches. Later, in 334, a law was passed which prohibited the families of slaves to be divided when estates changed hands. This was a major step forward when slaves in the Roman Empire had been so clearly and obviously frequent victims of torture and hatred. Constantine also abolished combats between gladiators.[15]

Constantine introduced childcare in 315, a law being passed in that year that parents who were too poor to support their children should receive support from the state treasury. However, it should be noted that in 322 the sale of children, which had been forbidden by Diocletian, was legalized and children mistreated by their parents could be rescued by a compassionate relative.[16]

Constantine removed the legislation attached to celibacy and strengthened the sanctity of marriage. Ancient Roman law had placed a heavy burden of taxation on the unmarried and childless. Constantine removed these disadvantages. He also determined to strengthen the marriage bond by the introduction of harsh legislation against the sins of unfaithfulness. Servants who were found to have been party to seduction were to have boiling lead poured down their throats. Both guilty parties were to be punished by death.

Constantine and the Church

Constantine made the Christian Church a privileged institution, a fact which Eusebius catalogues in some detail. In Book IX of *The History of the Church*, he records the re-establishment of the Empire's churches:

---

[15] Socrates, *Ecclesiastical History* I.18.
[16] The sale of children was not a total evil. Families who had too many children to feed or provide for could sell them to people who were able to care for them. The money received could then help provide for the remaining family members.

> Above all for us who had fixed our hopes on the Christ of God there was unspeakable happiness ... as we saw that every place which a little while before had been reduced to dust ... was now coming back to life; and that cathedrals were again rising from their foundations high into the air ... [17]

Constantine's policies were designed to raise the Church to a privileged institution. His aim was to gradually make the clergy of the churches take the places of the heathen priests. One of the ways he sought to do this was by making it a corporation capable of receiving legacies.[18] Constantine also made it clear that it was only the Catholic Church to whom these privileges were being extended. In another document dated 313 addressed to Caecilian, Bishop of Carthage (d. c.343), Constantine resolved that "Since we have been pleased with all provinces namely, Africa, Numidia and Mauritania, certain named ministers of the Lawful and most Holy Catholic Church should receive some contribution towards their expenses."[19] He continued, "I have sent letters to Marcus, the eminent finance officer of Africa, informing him that he must arrange a transfer to your steadfastness 3,000 folles in cash."[20] Theodoret recorded that Constantine "wrote to the governors of the provinces, directing that provision-money should be given in every city to virgins and widows".[21]

Constantine improved and raised the status of the clergy. He refers to them as "priests" (Greek *hiereus*, the equivalent of the Latin *sacerdos*) as opposed to presbyters (elders). Eusebius wrote with enthusiasm of "dedication festivals in the cities and consecrations of newly built places of worship", and "convocations of bishops and gathering of representatives from distant lands".[22] "Yes," he wrote, "our leaders performed ceremonies with full pomp, and ordained priests the sacraments and majestic rites of the Church, here with the singing of psalms and intoning of the prayers

---

[17] Eusebius, *History of the Church* IX.18.
[18] Eusebius, *History of the Church* IX.36.
[19] Eusebius, *History of the Church* X.6.
[20] It is not clear how much money this equates to.
[21] Theodoret, *Ecclesiastical History* I.10.
[22] Eusebius, *History of the Church* X.3.

given us from God."[23] Eusebius, who was himself Bishop of Caesarea, was enthusiastic about vestments and recorded his delight that at festivals celebrating the building of churches there were "priests clothed with the sacred vestments, the heavenly crown of glory, and the divine unction of the Holy Spirit".[24]

Constantine did more still to improve the status of the clergy. In 313, they were exempted from the unpopular office of "decurion" which required the collecting of taxes. This later led to abuse on the part of some who joined the ranks of clergy to escape this hateful task. Eusebius cited Constantine's Injunction to Anulinus, Proconsular Governor of Africa, in which he gave the following instruction:

> It is my wish that those within the province entrusted to you, in the Catholic Church ... who are usually called clerics be completely exempt from public duties, that they be not drawn away from the services due to Divinity ... For it seems that, when they render the greatest homage to the Divinity, then the greatest benefits befall the common weal.[25]

Constantine increased the power and status of bishops, especially those in large cities whom he allowed to wear purple which was the Emperor's colour. That said he also "rebuked a number of bishops in Palestine in no measured terms because they neglected their duty".[26] Prominent bishops were allowed to carry a crozier or pastoral staff, the insignia of a provincial governor. It was this growing authority of bishops which gradually led to the custom of their being given the exclusive right to call down the Holy Spirit on those who had been baptized. Formerly this was done by those who did the baptizing immediately the candidates came up out of the water. A little later in time, Jerome complained that this development "is done rather for the glory of the bishop than for any pressure of necessity".

---

[23] Eusebius, *History of the Church* X.3.
[24] Eusebius, *History of the Church* X.4.
[25] Eusebius, *History of the Church* X.7.
[26] Sozomen, *Ecclesiastical History* II.4.

Jerome also noted that "it was unfortunate that those who live in isolated farms and villages have to wait for a bishop to come".[27]

In 321, Constantine legislated that Sundays were to be a public holiday.[28] From this date, Christians were free from work and able to worship, Sozomen writing that "God should be served with prayers and supplications because on this day Christ rose from the dead".[29] It was also proscribed that "all judges, city-people and craftsmen shall rest on the venerable day of the sun".[30] Also from this date the law courts were to remain closed except for the purpose of freeing slaves.[31] Sunday labour was deprecated except where it was essential on farms. In both the East and the West, the Christians tried to replace the astrological names of the days of the week by numerical connotations. In the Greek East, they succeeded, but in the less Christian West the planetary names could not be eliminated.

Constantine, working together with Licinius, also passed legislation in 319 and 320 which suppressed soothsayers and divination.[32] Friendship with men of this profession must be ended, even if they were longstanding relationships. Anyone inviting a soothsayer into their home was to be deprived of their goods and banished to an island.[33] In 325, Constantine abolished the training of condemned men as gladiators.[34]

Church building
Constantine was a great promoter of church buildings. Some of those he sponsored and promoted in the great cities of the Empire were particularly impressive and doubtless intended to convey the authority and importance of the newly accepted Catholic Church. Sozomen, who

---

[27] Jerome, *Dialogue Against Lucifer* 7.
[28] Eusebius, *Life of Constantine* IX.18.
[29] Sozomen, *Ecclesiastical History* I.8.
[30] *Codex Justinianus* 3.13.3.
[31] Eusebius, *Life of Constantine* IX.18.
[32] *Codex Theodosianus* 9.16.1.
[33] *Codex Theodosianus* 9.16.1.
[34] N. Guistozzi, *The Colosseum* (Venice: Mandori Printing Spa, 2002), section entitled Games.

it should be said appears to have been hugely impressed by Constantine, noted there were "the most beautiful temples to God in every place".[35] Large basilicas were erected at sites of major importance in Jesus' life and ministry. These included basilicas at the burial places of Peter and Paul in Rome and in the Holy Land at Bethlehem[36] and the Holy Sepulchre. In 326, Constantine's last visit to Rome was marked by family disputes which prompted him to build "a new Rome" in the East of the Empire at Byzantium. It was named Constantinople (Greek for Constantine's City). There he built the first Church of Holy Wisdom (Hagia Sophia).[37] Constantine then gave his Rome house to the bishops of Rome as an episcopal residence.

After he became sole ruler of the Empire, Constantine brought Helena, his own mother, to faith in Christ. He gave her the rank of first lady in the Empire, a position which she fulfilled with dedication. In his *Life of Constantine*, Eusebius recorded: "Without delay she dedicated two churches to God whom she adored, one at the grotto which had been the scene of the Saviour's birth; the other on the Mount of his Ascension."[38] Helena also journeyed to the sites of Jesus' birth and ministry and organized the building of the Church of the Holy Sepulchre over the alleged burial place of Jesus.[39]

Constantine was familiar with the apostolic writings and held daily services in his palace where they were read. Eusebius relates that "Constantine took the sacred Scriptures into his hands, and devoted himself to the study of these divinely inspired oracles; after which he would offer up regular prayers with all members of his imperial court".[40] Constantine made the production of copies of biblical books a priority ordering Eusebius, Bishop of Caesarea, "to get written on fine parchment, fifty volumes, easily legible and handy for use".[41]

---

[35] Sozomen, *Ecclesiastical History* II.3.
[36] Eusebius, *Life of Constantine* IX.51.
[37] Eusebius, *Life of Constantine* IX.58.
[38] Eusebius, *Life of Constantine* IX.15.
[39] Theodoret, *Ecclesiastical History* I.17.
[40] Eusebius, *Life of Constantine* IX.17.
[41] Theodoret, *Ecclesiastical History* I.15; see also Socrates, *Ecclesiastical History* I.9.

Other activities

Constantine continued to engrave his coins with the sun, but after 319 his coins also bore either a cross or the monogram of Christ.[42] Constantine was a frequent letter writer, and from those he wrote after 313 it is clear that he regarded himself and wrote of himself as a fully committed Christian. He makes mention of Christ as Saviour and writes of his faith in God to keep him safe. He concluded an imperial letter making grants of money to the churches with the words: "May the divine power of the great God keep you safe for many years."

Conclusions

Constantine was undoubtedly a powerful Emperor, soldier and ruler, but he is not easy to assess. He undoubtedly had a major impact on the history of Europe and beyond. He could, if the situation demanded it, be brutal. Such was the case when Licinius, though he had become his brother-in-law, rebelled against his authority and began persecuting Christians in the Eastern Empire.[43] Later he even declared open war against Constantine who in the end was forced to have him killed.[44] He also ordered the death of his wife Fausta when it became clear that she had falsely claimed that Crispus, his illegitimate son, had tried to kill her.

There were other negative aspects which can be levelled against Constantine. As a result of his powerful influence, Christianity came to be associated with the rich and the powerful. Wealth, as we know from medieval history, corrupted many of the great monastic houses. Under Constantine, the Christian faith became increasingly intellectual rather than pastoral. This was seen in many of the episcopal appointments which Constantine authorized. Constantine changed the Catholic Church from a persecuted and scattered minority to a privileged religion.

This had the effect of creating nominal Christian faith. People were suddenly awakened to the fact that if they wanted to get on in Roman

---

[42] Eusebius, *Life of Constantine* IX.15.
[43] Eusebius, *History of the Church* X.8.9 and X.8.17.
[44] Eusebius, *History of the Church* X.9.7.

society, they needed to be seen on the side of the Christians, which at the very least meant some form of presence at Sunday Christian worship and having their children baptized. In short, Christianity under Constantine became formal and institutionalized.

Yet, even given the fact that much of what we know about Constantine comes from the pens of those who were either in his service or his keen supporters, there is much good that still stands out with clarity. In 320, Constantine composed a speech in Latin entitled *Oration to the Saints*. In it he attributed his good fortune to the protection of Christ:

> Be it my special province to glorify Christ, as well as by the actions of my life, as by that thanksgiving which is due to him for the manifold and signal blessings he has bestowed.[45]

He clearly brought an end to the brutal persecutions which Christians had suffered almost continuously for nearly 300 years. He favoured and privileged the Catholic Church but nevertheless granted toleration to all religious groups. He constantly sought to keep the Church in a state of unity as was demonstrated by his calling together the Council of Nicaea in 325, where he made the time and effort to understand the theological issues and bring about a decision, albeit one which needed continuing debate thereafter. He even did his best to sort out more localized disputes such as that between Bishop Caecilian of Carthage and his nearby Catholic episcopal colleagues.[46] He brought respect for Christian values and caused them to impact all aspects of home and family life. Under Constantine's rule, Christianity improved the moral quality of life in the Empire. Slavery was reduced and slaves' treatment considerably improved, marriage was strengthened, and education hugely expanded with many monastic houses leading to the foundation of universities. In all such matters, Constantine paid obvious note to wise and Christian advisers. Prominent among them was Hosius, Bishop of Cordova,[47] who

---

[45] C. Freeman, *A New History of Early Christianity* (Yale: Yale University Press, 2009), p. 228.
[46] Eusebius, *History of the Church* X.5.
[47] Eusebius, *History of the Church* X.7.1.

helped Constantine settle the Donatist Schism in Carthage in favour of Caecilian, the Catholic bishop in 316 and a major theological adviser[48] at the Council of Nicaea in 325.

As well as living out his faith in the public arena Constantine clearly needed to be the shrewdest of politicians. He well knew that the Christian faith had spread across his Empire and realized it was the best cement to hold its life in stability and peace. It was therefore political sense that he do everything in his power to keep in unity. Under his rule, "the tribes on both sides of the Rhine were Christianized, as were the Celts and the Gauls".[49] Sozomen recorded that it was said that the Iberians, a large and warlike barbarian nation, had confessed Christ during Constantine's reign.[50]

Constantine postponed his baptism until shortly before his death just after Easter in 337. He died in the city of Nicomedia having been baptized by the bishop of that city.[51] It's difficult to know his reasons for his delaying the sacrament. One suggested reason is that some feared that killing people on the battlefield might be the sin which could not be forgiven. Following his death, Constantine's funeral took place in a ceremony of great pomp in Constantinople at the Church of the Apostles.[52]

There can be no doubting that Constantine's conversion and subsequent leadership provided an enormous step forward for the Christian Church. In a very real sense, the churches had become "more than conquerors". Christians were now free to worship in public and live out their faith without fear. Constantine's laws had established many Christian values. The challenge now was to ensure that Christianity remained a religion of the heart and didn't become overly intellectualized or a nominal badge for those who wanted to make a good life for themselves in a new-look Empire.

---

[48] See "The Case of Caecilian and the Donatists" in *Cresconium* 3.82, in H. Bettenson (ed.), *Documents of the Christian Church*, 2nd edn (Oxford: Oxford University Press, 1967), p. 18.
[49] Sozomen, *Ecclesiastical History* II.6.
[50] Sozomen, *Ecclesiastical History* II.7.
[51] Eusebius, *Life of Constantine* IX.62.
[52] Eusebius, *Life of Constantine* IX.52 and 53.

1 0

Athanasius versus the world: The defeat of Arianism and the establishment of the Nicaean faith that Jesus is fully God

The background to Arianism

About the year 315, Arius (250–336), who was the priest of the Catholic Church in Alexandria, began to teach a doctrine which later took its name from him. It sparked a controversy and a debate which impacted the Church and its life for the greater part of the fourth century.

The background and context of his teaching was a large Jewish population in Alexandria who were totally and absolutely committed to monotheism, their basic creed being "The Lord our God, the Lord is one" (Deuteronomy 6:4). This meant that both Jewish and Gentile Christians in the city were very careful not to speak of Jesus as a second God. At the same time, Christians did not want to lose sight of the fact that Jesus the Son was and is distinct from the Father. Indeed, they were worried that the churches might fall back into Monarchianism which taught that the Son was simply an emanation which was projected out from the Father for a time and was then drawn back into the Godhead. Monarchianism was nevertheless attractive to those who came from a Jewish background because it preserved the oneness of God.

Arius, who was the priest of the congregation in the parish of Beaucalis, was mindful of this theological background. He, like them, knew that in the Old Testament scriptures "God is one" and is "high and lifted up", as Isaiah saw in his great vision in the Jerusalem temple. At the same time, however, he wanted the people in his church to know that God was also alongside them in their life journeys as friend, guide and helper. In short, he began to react against the teaching of a remote and distant God and began to stress the nearness and role of Jesus as the mediator. This was of course a very important aspect of his pastoral ministry because many of his church members were dockyard labourers and manual workers who needed to know that they had a Lord who understood the strains, struggles and demands of the port and seafaring life. Unfortunately for Arius, he ended up teaching and preaching a Jesus who was rather less than God and at the same time was not fully human. To many of his congregation and fellow clergy it seemed that he was preaching two gods.

The essence of Arianism

Doctrine of God

Arius' teaching was clearly unorthodox on several counts. Arius' doctrine of God was of a being who was so far above the affairs of this world that it was impossible for him to become totally man. In fact, it was apparent that Arius believed that only the Father was "the genuine God". As far as Arius was concerned, God was God and he could not change in nature and that would be necessary if he was to communicate with human beings. He argued that if God could change, he would be weak and fallible and clearly not divine. Alister McGrath expressed the view that Arius believed that it was philosophically impossible for God to physically become a human being.[1] Arius denied the Trinitarian nature of God because he refused to accept that the Father and the Son were of the same essence or substance. "God", according to Arius, "is incommunicable otherwise we would have to admit that he is composed of elements susceptible to division and changes".[2]

Arius' Jesus was largely human but not fully God

Arius declared that the Son is a creature, who, like all other creatures, derived his existence from God. He could feel love, hurt, pain, anger,

---

[1] Alister McGrath, *Christian Theology: An Introduction* (Oxford: Blackwell, 2011), p. 276.
[2] Theodoret, *Ecclesiastical History* I.3.

frustration, hunger, grief, compassion and all the range of human emotions. He could breathe, eat, drink and get tired in the way common to all human beings. Arius believed that Jesus gradually matured as a mortal human being. In fact, he went further and stated that "the Son outranks all other creatures, while sharing their essentially created and begotten nature".[3] In a song entitled *Thalia*, a Greek word meaning "banquet", he named the Son "Logos" and "Wisdom". In his *Confession of Faith*, which he wrote in a deliberately vague manner in order to impress upon the Emperor Constantine that he was orthodox in his beliefs, he even went so far as to speak of the Son as the agent "through whom all things were made". This might at first sight sound fine, but Arius did not believe in the eternity of Jesus the Son. If Jesus was not eternally Son, God could not be eternally Father. But Arius constantly asserted that there was a time when God existed alone. He then created the Son out of nothing, as is suggested in Colossians 1:15, which states that Jesus is "the firstborn over all creation" and Romans 8:29 which says that Jesus is "the firstborn among many brothers and sisters".

Arius did not believe in the eternity of Jesus. He was clear that "the Son had a beginning"[4] and that "prior to his generation he did not exist"[5] and that "there was when he was not".[6] In this assertion, Arius made skilful use of biblical passages. For example, he quoted "God created me" from the Book of Proverbs which he took to be a Messianic text. He also made use of Jesus' words in John's Gospel 14:28, where he said, "The Father is greater than I."[7]

Arius expressed most of these truths in the following lines of his *Thalia*:

> God was not always Father; but there was when God was alone and was not yet Father; afterward he became a Father. The Son

---

[3] McGrath, *Christian Theology: An Introduction*, p. 276.
[4] This was one of the allegations made against him by Epiphanius in *Heresies* 69.6.
[5] Athanasius, *Concerning Synods* 16.
[6] Athanasius, *Against Arians* 1.6.
[7] Athanasius, *Against Arians* 1.2.

was not always; for since all things are created and have been made, so also the Logos of God himself came into existence from nothing and there was a time when He was not; and that before He came into existence He was not; but He also had a beginning and was created.[8]

In summary, Arius' view was that Jesus the Son was a created being and therefore less than God. He reasoned that if a son is a son, he must be created by a father. Jesus was therefore a created being albeit "the firstborn of all creation" and by definition "less than God". Arius was totally opposed to any attempt to make Jesus the Son equal to the Father or "of the same substance of the Father". Arius was not even willing to say that Jesus the Son was a hidden property within the Father who proceeded from him at a later date. Arius was also adamant that as a created being Jesus could falter and change. Arius went even further and declared that Jesus had no communion with the Father or direct knowledge of him. Arius summarized his position to Eusebius, Bishop of Nicomedia, in the following words:

> We say and believe and have taught, and do teach, that the son is not unbegotten [without beginning] .... we say that the son has a beginning, but that God is without beginning ... and likewise we say that ... He is neither part of God, nor any substance with [God].[9]

In summary, Arius denied the co-eternity, co-equality and consubstantiality of the Son with the Father. His Jesus was clearly less than God but more than a man. Being less than God, Arius' Jesus was therefore held to be incapable of bestowing God's forgiveness and salvation. For as Jesus declared in the Gospel: "Who can forgive sins but God?" By the same token, by asserting Jesus had certain divine qualities, he could not be totally human and could not therefore sympathize with human beings in their struggles against temptation, pain, suffering and hurt.

---

[8] Arius, *Thalia*.
[9] Arius, *Letter to Eusebius* in Theodoret, *Ecclesiastical History* I.4.

The stages of Arianism

The controversy and debates over Arianism extended over the greater part of the fourth century. For this reason, it is easier to study it in its significant stages; the first being from the beginnings down to the Council of Nicaea.

The beginning of Arianism to the Council of Nicaea, 318–25
Constantine was deeply grieved at the divisions over Arius' teaching among the bishops and clergy. He therefore convened a major gathering of Church leaders from across the Empire, hoping that a way of reconciliation could be found.[10] Bishop Alexander (250–326) of Alexandria, who had been in office since 313, had opposed Arius on the ground that he had reduced "Jesus the Word" to a "demi-God" (demi meaning "half") and that he had denied his true divinity and made him out to be a creature. Alexander was supported by the recently converted Emperor and succeeded in having Arius' teaching condemned at a local Synod. However, Alexander unfortunately fell into the opposite extreme and maintained that Jesus the Word (*logos*) existed side by side with the Father as a second entirely similar God of equal standing and working in harmony but having no substantial relationship. He was expressing what was in essence ditheism or belief in two gods. Alexander stated his view in a communication to the Bishop of Constantinople:

> We believe, as the Apostolic Church teaches, in one unbegotten Father, who of His being has no cause, immutable and invariable, and who subsists always in one state of being ... and in one Lord Jesus Christ, the only begotten ... of the Father. ... We have learned that the Son is immutable and unchangeable, all sufficient and perfect, like the Father, lacking only in his unbegottenness, He is the exact and precisely similar image of His Father ... And in accordance with this we believe the Son always existed with the Father.[11]

---

[10] Sozomen, *Ecclesiastical History* I.7.
[11] Theodoret, *Ecclesiastical History* I.3.

It took a little time, but eventually in 321 Bishop Alexander called together a council and deposed Arius who was banished to Caesarea where he soon made friends with Bishop Eusebius who enjoyed a close relationship with Emperor Constantine. But Arius was not easy to put down and people of influence soon began to throw in their lot behind him, among them the Bishops of Caesarea and Nicomedia, neither of whom were entirely happy with according Jesus "equal status" with the Father and "genuine godhead". At a more grassroots level, many, including some Alexandrian clergy, were also taken with Arius' *Thalia*, verses of which had been set to dance music. Some of its memorable verses were particularly captivating. Such included "God was not always Father", "once God was alone but afterwards God became a father", "the Son was not always, God was alone" and "the Word is not very God".[12]

In 324, following the death of Licinius, the Emperor of the East, Constantine became the sole ruler of the Empire with the strong hope that Christianity would become the cement that would hold it together. He had recently been successful in resolving issues among the Donatists of the North African provinces and in December 324 decided to convene a Synod at Antioch to resolve the Arian question. The delegates who gathered were unanimous in their condemnation of Arius, taking the view that if Jesus is not God the heart of Christianity is lost because there could no longer be any incarnation or redemption.

The Synod of Antioch paved the way to a far bigger conference which Constantine decided to organize in the following year at Nicaea, a city about 30 miles from the capital Nicomedia. The Council of Nicaea represents the beginning of the second major stage of the Arian controversy.

The Council of Nicaea and the condemnation of Arius

The Council of Nicaea became recognized as the first great ecumenical council on account of the large number of attendees which, according to Eusebius, included 250 bishops most of whom were Greek.[13] Only

---

[12] Arius, *Thalia*.

[13] For the "Nicene" Creed, see Bettenson, *Documents of the Christian Church*, pp. 25-6. See also Socrates, *Ecclesiastical History* I.8.

five came from the West, including Hosius (*c*.256–359), who had been created Bishop of Cordova about the year 295. Many who came to the conference were reported to still carry the marks of beatings and torture at the hands of the persecutors.

Athanasius (295–373) was the leading orthodox theologian. At the time of the council, he was a young church leader in the dockyard area of Alexandria. Between 318 and 320, he had written an important book entitled *Discourse on the Incarnation*. In it, he explained how the redemption of fallen human nature could only be achieved by one who was perfectly God. One who only had the status of a demi or half God, as proposed by Arius, could not accomplish the task.

Athanasius' publication revealed several important differences between Athanasius and Arius. First, it became clear that Arius regarded the Logos as an impersonal force coming from the Father. It was therefore hard for him to conceive how the Logos or Word could become a person in the manner of the Prologue to the Gospel of John. Second, it became clear that Arius regarded "begotten", as in Jesus being God's "only begotten Son", as meaning he was a created being. Athanasius regarded the word "begotten" as meaning exactly the opposite of "created". This was later beautifully captured by a line in the Christmas carol 'O Come all Ye Faithful' that Jesus was "very God begotten, not created". Third, Arius and Athanasius differed on the nature of salvation. Arius saw it in more intellectual terms as a kind of mental assent or enlightenment. Athanasius on the other hand stressed that salvation is a matter of the heart with Christ's presence in the believer. He also made the point that it was from God that the human race had rebelled and only one who is fully God can restore that relationship. Constantine, as Sozomen pointed out, "deemed the dissension in the church as more dangerous than any other evil".[14] In this, we catch a glimpse of Constantine the politician wanting to hold the Empire, as well as the Church, together in unity.

With this in the background and long debates between the assembled bishops and delegates, the Council finally made the decision that the Greek word *homoousios,* meaning "the same substance", defined Jesus' relationship as being of the same substance as the Father. The Emperor

---

[14] Sozomen, *Ecclesiastical History* I.19.

Constantine supported the term possibly because he had great trust in the guidance of his Western Church adviser Bishop Hosius of Cordova. It was also a term with which the Latin West was comfortable because Tertullian had earlier written of the Trinity as three persons of the same substance (*homoousios*). The Council attached a number of anathemas (curses) to their published minutes, one of which was "The Holy Catholic and Apostolic Church anathematizes those who say, 'There was when He was not.'"[15]

However, in the days following the Council's decision, it became clear that a number of the bishops had signed their agreement in support of *homoousios* out of deference to the Emperor, but in reality they were not altogether happy with the term. For them, it appeared to be re-opening the door to Monarchianism which blurred all distinctions between the Father, Son and Spirit. Instead they substituted the term *homoiousios* which means "like" as opposed to "same". That said, the Council condemned Arius and produced an anti-Arian creed, the Creed of Nicaea, which explicitly stated Jesus was "true God from true God, begotten not made, of one substance (*homoousios*) with the Father". Confusingly, this was not the so-called Nicene Creed which was later established by the Council of Constantinople in 381. The Council also ended the Creed with anathemas (curses) on all those who continued to express Arian views.

Most of those who left Nicaea probably did so imagining the last word on this issue had been spoken. Oddly, far from ending debate, it provoked an ongoing struggle which lasted almost to the end of the century and beyond. The period from Nicaea to the Council of Rimini in 359 represents a third stage in the controversy in which Arianism appeared to have gained the ascendancy.

The spread of Arianism from Nicaea to Rimini

It soon became apparent that there were several reasons why the Council of Nicaea failed to put an end to Arius' teaching. Most obvious was the fact that Arianism presented itself as a straightforward basic religion— God was one not two! Arius was able to sell himself as the defender of

---

[15] Socrates, *Ecclesiastical History* I.8.

monotheism against the polytheistic pagan religions. A son comes after a father and must be lesser in status. Arius also claimed the high ground by making good use of biblical words and terms such as "son", "made", "firstborn" and "creature". Arius managed to get invited to the Court and soon endeared himself to the good and the great with his cleverly worded discourses. But it was not just the rich who took to him, even the common people entered into the debate. Two dockhands at Alexandria were heard in dispute. The first said: "There was when he was not." The other replied: "There was not when he was not!"

Leaving aside Arius' debating and communication skills, the fact was the Creed of Nicaea was open to more than one interpretation. *Homo* could mean "same", as in the general "manness" shared by a group of men, or "exact sameness", as in the case of identical twins. Many Arians continued to strongly oppose this latter view because of their worries about the danger of Monarchianism.

A further reason for the failure of Nicaea was the fact that Arius not only appeared at court but came to have an increasing influence on the Emperor Constantine and Eusebius (*d. c.*341) the Bishop of Nicomedia, the capital city of the Eastern Empire. Theodoret gives the text of Arius' letter to Eusebius in which he summed up his position "that the Son has a beginning, but that God is without beginning".[16] Added to this, several influential opponents of Arius found themselves excluded from the public debate for differing reasons. Eustacius (*d.*360), Bishop of Antioch and a rigorous opponent of Arianism, was banished for speaking disrespectfully against the Emperor's mother Helena. Athanasius, who had become Bishop of Alexandria in 328, was sent into exile for allegedly dealing roughly with the Meletians, a schismatic group who regarded the Catholic Church as overly lenient with those who denied their faith during the persecutions. Rumours were also put about that he had threatened to call a dock strike at Alexandria.[17] Then Marcellus (*d. c.*374), Bishop of Ancyra, a dedicated supporter of Nicaea, was banished by Constantine for failing to accept his invitation to the dedication of his new Church of the Holy Sepulchre at Jerusalem in 335.

---

[16] Theodoret, *Ecclesiastical History* I.4.
[17] Theodoret, *Ecclesiastical History* II.8.

The key factor in the rising influence of Arianism lay in the hands of the Emperor Constantine. Strangely he, who had been the greatest advocate of the *homoousion* clause and the Nicaean settlement, gradually had a change of heart. In particular, he came under the influence of Eusebius, Bishop of Nicomedia, and Valens, the Bishop of Mursa (Osijek in modern Croatia). Both men emerged as powerful Arian leaders, Valens attending every Synod from 330 to about 370.[18] Always the politician, Constantine may well have come to feel that siding with the Arians offered greater possibilities of a united Empire than the Nicaeans.

Then, at a critical moment in 335, Constantine called a Synod at Tyre which Athanasius failed to attend, as a result of which he was banished to the Rhine frontier.[19] Following the Synod, Constantine directed all the delegates to Jerusalem where they re-admitted Arius into communion on the ground that he had recanted and now acknowledged the truth.[20] Constantine's sister Constantia and Helena his mother had both become strongly Arian in their sympathies. To cap it all, when Constantine became seriously ill and knew he was going to die,[21] he declared "that the confession of Nicaea was attested by God and asked to be baptized".[22]

Constantine was immediately succeeded by his son Constantius (317–61), who in 350 eventually became the sole ruler of the Empire. He then decided that the right moment had arrived to bring the West to accept the Arian understanding of Jesus' divinity. As things turned out, this was relatively easy since many of the Western bishops were no longer clear or united in their understanding of the issues. However, it should be said that by this time the Arians had also become diverse in their views. The Semi-Arians held to the view that the Son was "like" (*homoiousios*) the Father. In contrast, the Extreme Arians led by Eudoxius (*d*.370),

---

[18] Socrates, *Ecclesiastical History* I.27.
[19] It is significant that Athanasius was exiled from Alexandria and recalled five times. Socrates, *Ecclesiastical History* I.28.
[20] Socrates, *Ecclesiastical History* I.27.
[21] Socrates, *Ecclesiastical History* I.39.
[22] Socrates, *Ecclesiastical History* I.39.

Bishop of Antioch, asserted that the essence of the Son was "unlike" (*anamoiousios*) the Father.[23]

Nevertheless, in 359, Constantius decided the time was still right to hold a major Council at Rimini. In the debate, the Western bishops were persuaded by Valens, Bishop of Mursa and one of their own number, to cast their votes with the Arians. This caused Jerome, a little later, to write that "the world groaned to find itself Arian".[24] The Council agreed to do away with the term *ousia* (essence) in all future discussions and declared that "the Son is like the Father in all things, as the holy Scriptures teach".[25] When Athanasius, who was in exile, heard this decision of Rimini, he declared in the words of the prophet Jeremiah, "They have forsaken me the fountain of living waters and hewed out for themselves broken cisterns which can hold no water."[26] The Council of Rimini represents the high-water mark of Arianism. It was one of the most widespread erroneous teachings which the Catholic Church has faced. Bede related that Arianism had even taken root in the British Isles and described it as "a pestilential heresy that poured into this island".[27] The Emperor Constantius had hoped that the formular agreed by the Council of Rimini that Jesus is "like the Father in all things" would end the dispute for good but it was not to be. After his death in 361, the tide began to turn back in favour of the Nicaean position and this proved to be the fourth and final stage. It did not happen quickly and nor was Arianism completely defeated. The Nicaeans were stronger in the West but in parts of the East the Arians remained active and indeed even brutally persecuted those who didn't share their views.[28]

---

[23] Socrates, *Ecclesiastical History* I.5.

[24] Jerome, *Dialogue Against Lucifer*, 19 in Bettenson, *Documents of the Christian Church*, p. 44.

[25] See Bettenson, *Documents of the Christian Church*, p. 43.

[26] Theodoret, *Ecclesiastical History* II.18.

[27] Bede, *Ecclesiastical History of the English People* I.8.

[28] Socrates, *Ecclesiastical History* II.27.

The defeat of Arianism and the triumph of the Nicene formula, 361–381

Several factors contributed to the swing away from Arianism towards what became the established Nicaean orthodoxy. Constantius was succeeded as Emperor by his brother Julian (331–63) who was a pagan but allowed all the exiled churchmen to return to their home towns and spheres of work. This brought Athanasius back into the action, and he was joyfully received in Alexandria[29] and was able to bring the Nicaeans together. He had used his exile to write a major work entitled *Four Discourses Against the Arians*. In it, he dealt with all of the Arians' favourite texts and explained the essential unity between God the Father and Jesus the Son. Throughout Athanasius worked for peace and reconciliation. Being careful not to use the word *homoousios*, he sought to win over the Semi-Arians who still maintained that Jesus was like the Father. Instead, he used their watch word *homoiousios*. He became aware that many Arians were much closer to his views than he had previously realized.

In *Four Discourses Against the Arians*, Athanasius made four important arguments. First, if Jesus was less than God, then to worship him would be blasphemous. Second, if Jesus was not eternally Son, then God could not be eternally Father. Third, if Jesus wasn't divine then he would not be able to unite us with God in the way that baptism symbolizes. Fourth, he went on to make the point that the Holy Spirit can only unite us to the divine Son if he too is divine. On his return to Alexandria in 362, Athanasius immediately called a Synod which "asserted the divinity of the Holy Spirit and comprehended him in the consubstantial Trinity".[30] Athanasius eventually died in 373 with the task of asserting the Nicaean faith almost complete. He had fought a life-long battle to defend its biblical truth against fierce and widespread opposition. The words *Athanasius contra mundum* (Athanasius against the world) were in truth a reality. His persevering struggle for biblical orthodoxy played a major role in enabling the Catholic Church to "conquer" the opponents of apostolic Christianity. It is hard to overestimate the contribution of Athanasius'

---

[29] Socrates, *Ecclesiastical History* II.2.
[30] Socrates, *Ecclesiastical History* III.7.

deep personal orthodox Christian faith, debating skills and theological knowledge.

Just eight years after Athanasius' death, the Emperor Valens, who had held office from 364–78, died fighting the Goths at the battle of Adrianople and the situation changed almost overnight. He had, in the words of Socrates, "cruelly persecuted those who would not embrace Arianism".[31] His successor as sole Emperor of East and West was Theodosius the Great (347–95). He had been nurtured in the Nicaean faith[32] and on taking office immediately made it known that this was to be the only recognized faith within the Empire. So in 381, he summoned a large ecumenical council to Constantinople. They re-affirmed the Nicaean key word *homoousios*, meaning that the Son is identical in substance with the Father. They also ratified the Nicaean Creed, taking on board Basil of Caesarea's proposal that it should include the words that "the Holy Spirit is worshipped and glorified together with the Father and the Son". The council also made Constantinople the second See of the Empire.[33] Theodosius also ruled that "the title of 'Catholic Church' should henceforth be exclusively confined to those who rendered equal homage to the three persons of the Trinity".[34] Arianism was not yet totally defeated, but after 381 it gradually declined, until by the end of the fifth century it was left with only a few scattered groups largely located among the Teutonic tribes.

Conclusion

The contemporary relevance of Arianism is hard to escape. Much preaching and indeed spirituality seem to suggest or assume that the Father and the Son are two separate beings in a way not dissimilar from the views held by Arius. Jesus is frequently presented as a secondary God

---

[31] Socrates, *Ecclesiastical History* IV.17. For more on Valens' persecutions see Socrates, *Ecclesiastical History* IV.24.
[32] Sozomen, *Ecclesiastical History* VI.12.
[33] Sozomen, *Ecclesiastical History* VI.12.
[34] Sozomen, *Ecclesiastical History* VI.12.

sent to earth to achieve salvation whilst the Father is seated in a distant transcendental heavenly realm. The Arian controversy is a compelling reminder that God is a Trinity.

In his later years of struggling to uphold the Nicaean faith, Athanasius had found allies in three episcopal scholars who lived and worked in Cappadocia. The chapter which follows examines the powerful impact of their faith, life and in particular their contribution to the doctrine of the Trinity.

1 1
Wise men from the East: The Cappadocian Fathers and their caring Trinitarian faith and spirituality

Background

By the middle of the fourth century, the relationship between the Father and the Son had been largely agreed and settled. The focus of attention then moved on to the relationship of the Father to the Spirit and the Son to the Spirit. The Cappadocian Fathers, especially Basil of Caesarea, defended the deity of the Spirit so vehemently and in such persuasive terms that it led in turn to renewed attempts to explain and define the Trinity.

The Cappadocian Fathers

The Cappadocian Fathers are so called because they all came from the Roman province of Cappadocia in the centre of modern Turkey. Basil (c.329–79) was Bishop of Caesarea and his brother Gregory (c.335–95) was Bishop of Nyssa in Cappadocia. Their friend Gregory (c.329–89) of Nazianzus was ordained priest under pressure about the year 362. Then, about ten years later, possibly in 372, he was consecrated Bishop of Sasima, a very small see in Cappadocia, though he remained in Nazianzus. In 381, he was appointed Bishop of Constantinople but resigned before the end of the year and returned to Nazianzus. He was a powerful preacher. All three Cappadocians were strong orthodox Christians who had powerfully, thoughtfully and intellectually supported

Athanasius and the Nicene faith. The theological focus of attention now moved on to consider the deity of the Holy Spirit and the doctrine of the Trinity to which the three men gave much attention and articulated in a consistent and convincing manner. Their dioceses were close together and situated in the middle of the province of Cappadocia and this made meeting and discussion relatively easy.

This chapter begins with an examination of Basil of Caesarea's teaching on the deity of the Holy Spirit and then considers some of the metaphors which the Cappadocians used to explain the Trinity. The Cappadocians were not only significant theologians; they were men of faith, deep spirituality and pastoral care. This chapter therefore ends with a focus on these aspects of their lives.

Basil of Caesarea and the deity of the Holy Spirit

In several ways, Basil stands out as the leading figure of the trio. It was he who in his book *On the Spirit* argued convincingly for the deity of the Holy Spirit. Once this was agreed the way was open to define the Trinity. In Chapter 16 of *On the Spirit*, Basil asserted "that in all things the Holy Spirit is inseparable and wholly incapable of being parted from the Father and the Son". He cites as an example the apostle Peter's words to Ananias: "How is it that you have agreed to tempt the Spirit of the Lord? You have not lied unto men but unto God." This quotation from Acts 5:3–4, he asserted, demonstrates "that sins against the Holy Spirit and against God are the same; thus in every operation the Spirit is closely conjoined and inseparable from, the Father and the Son".[1]

The Father as the source or fountainhead from whom the Spirit flows
The Cappadocians put forward the idea of God the Father being the fountainhead or source of divinity. Their thinking was that the Father imparts his being to the other two Persons. So, Gregory of Nyssa could speak of "one and the same Person (*prosopon*) of the Father, out of whom the Son is begotten and the Spirit proceeds".

---

[1] Basil, *On the Spirit* 16.37.

The problem for the Cappadocians and the Eastern theologians was this. If the Holy Spirit proceeds from the Father and the Son, as the Nicene Creed of 381 declared, it made the Spirit appear to be the junior partner of the three and in consequence less than the Father and the Son. Gregory of Nazianzus was adamant that what is said about one member of the Godhead must be said of all of them. He wrote of the Spirit as follows in his Fifth Theological Oration:

> For our part we have such confidence in the Godhead of the Spirit that, rash though some may find it, we shall begin our theological exposition by applying identical expression to the Three. So, "He was the true light that enlightens every man coming into the world"—yes, the Father. "He was the true light that enlightens every man coming into the world"—yes, the Son. "He was the true light that enlightens every man coming into the world"—yes, the Comforter. These are three subjects and three verbs—he was, he was, and he was. But a single reality was.[2]

The Holy Spirit is eternal

Gregory made the assertion in the same work that if there was never a time when the Son did not exist that same must be said of the Holy Spirit:

> If there was a "when" when the Son did not exist, there was a "when" when the Holy Spirit did not exist. If one existed from the beginning, so did all three. If you cast one down, I make bold to tell you not to exalt the other two. What use is an incomplete deity?[3]

Gregory used a touch of irony against his theological opponents, saying that if the Son bestows the Spirit rather than the Father "God apparently has a grandson, and what could be odder than that"![4]

---

[2] Gregory of Nazianzus, *Fifth Theological Oration: On the Holy Spirit* 31.3.
[3] Gregory of Nazianzus, *Fifth Theological Oration: On the Holy Spirit* 31.4.
[4] Gregory of Nazianzus, *Fifth Theological Oration: On the Holy Spirit* 31.7.

The Spirit works with the Lord in distributing spiritual gifts

Basil then gives us some examples of the Holy Spirit operating together with the Lord in the distribution of spiritual gifts in 1 Corinthians 12. In verse 4, he points out that "There are different kinds of gifts but the same Spirit." Then he continues in verse 5, "There are different kinds of service but the same Lord", adding in verse 6, "There are different kinds of working but the same God works all of them in all people." Basil carefully points out that because the Spirit is mentioned before the Father in this passage that we are to regard the Spirit as greater in rank.[5]

Further reasons for asserting the divinity of the Holy Spirit

Basil added a host of additional and important reasons for asserting the deity of the Holy Spirit. The Spirit was present in every aspect of the life, death and resurrection of Jesus and in the birth of his church.[6] Then in Chapter 16.48 Basil reminds us of "the Spirit's unapproachable power", and that he is called "Holy", is called "good", "bestows good gifts", is "truth and righteousness", is "another comforter", "the Spirit of Wisdom" and "the Spirit of God", and finally, "He existed; He Pre-existed; He co-existed".[7]

Basil of course was not the only Cappadocian who argued for the deity of the Spirit; Gregory of Nazianzus in *On the Holy Spirit* stressed that "it is the Spirit in whom we worship, and in whom we pray. For the Scripture says, God is a Spirit, and they that worship must worship him in Spirit and in truth." This led him to conclude that "Therefore to adore or to pray to the Spirit seems to me to be simply Himself offering prayer or adoration to Himself."[8]

---

[5] Basil, *On the Spirit* 16.39.
[6] Basil, *On the Spirit* 16.39–40.
[7] Basil, *On the Spirit* 16.48.
[8] Gregory of Nazianzus, *Fifth Theological Oration: On the Holy Spirit* 11.

The Cappadocian Fathers and the Trinity

With Basil having so clearly and convincingly established the deity of the Holy Spirit, the way was then open to define the nature of the Trinity or to be precise, the relationship between the Father, Son and Holy Spirit. In his *The Third Theological Oration on the Son*, written between 379 and 381, Gregory of Nazianzus, speaking of the Trinity wrote, "I know not how this could be expressed in terms altogether excluding visible things."[9] Unsurprisingly, the Cappadocians therefore used a variety of metaphors and images in their attempts to define and explain the Trinity. All of the images demonstrate how the three persons were distinct but all combined or shared in every quality and activity.

Their shared holiness and designation as comforter

In 380, Gregory of Nyssa challenged the Arian Bishop of Cyzicus in Mysia. In *Against Eunomius*, he made the point that Father, Son and Holy Spirit are all given the appellation "Holy".[10] "The Lord our God is Holy" and Jesus likewise is ascribed as Holy. In the same way the Father, Son and Holy Spirit are all spoken of as "Comforter". The Father is "the God of all Comfort" and Jesus spoke of the Holy Spirit as "another comforter" implying that "he too is the comforter".[11] Gregory expressed this in the following sentence:

> But I have been taught that this very name [comforter] is also applied by the inspired Scripture to Father, Son and Holy Spirit alike. For the Son gives the name 'Comforter' equally to Himself and to the Holy Spirit; and the Father, where He is said to work comfort, surely claims as His own the name 'comforter'.[12]

---

[9] Gregory of Nazianzus, *Third Theological Oration: On the Son* 3.
[10] Gregory of Nyssa, *Against Eunomius* II.14.
[11] Gregory of Nyssa, *Against Eunomius* II.14.
[12] Gregory of Nyssa, *Against Eunomius* II.14.

Their shared moral perfection

At the close of section 15 of *Against Eunomius*, Gregory of Nyssa underlined the fact that "the inspired Scripture teaches us to affirm . . . the terms 'good', and 'wise' and 'incorruptible' and 'immortal' and all such lofty conceptions and names to Godhead".[13] In a later paragraph, Gregory presses the point home as follows: "If one may discern alike in Father, Son and Holy Spirit the properties of being incorruptible, immutable, of admitting no evil, of being good, right, guiding, of working all in all the like attributes, how is it possible by identity in these respects to infer any difference in kind?"[14]

Their shared role in the creation

In *On the Spirit*, Basil considered the cooperation of the Father, Son and Holy Spirit in the creation. He sees them as co-creators. The Father is the original (as in origin) cause; the Son is the creative cause; and the Spirit is the perfecting cause. "So", he concludes, "the ministering spirits subsist by the will of the Father, are brought into being by the operation of the Son, and perfected by the presence of the Spirit."[15] Basil also wrote of the Father who creates by his sole will, who wills through his Son and the Spirit who wills to make perfect. He sums up this point as follows: "You are therefore to perceive three, the Lord who gives the order, the Word who creates, and the Spirit who confirms."[16]

Their shared role in perfecting holiness

The Cappadocians made the point that the unity of the three persons of the Godhead was seen in their role in perfecting holiness. Basil put forward the illustration of cooperation with the Father, Son and Holy Spirit all working to perfect holiness. In this matter, there is no difference between them. He compared the ministry of Father, Son and Spirit in sanctification to a branding iron in the fire.[17] The branding iron, the

---

[13] Gregory of Nyssa, *Against Eunomius* II.15.
[14] Gregory of Nyssa, *Against Eunomius* II.15.
[15] Basil, *On the Spirit* 16.37.
[16] Basil, *On the Spirit* 16.37.
[17] Basil, *On the Spirit* 16.38.

material and the fire are conceived together and yet are distinct. Basil was also taken with the fact that the Seraphim cry "Holy, Holy, Holy". "How could they do this were they not taught of the Spirit how often true religion requires them to lift up their voice in ascription of glory?"[18]

Their shared activity in gifts and ministries

The Cappadocians made the point that the unity and the distinctives of persons of the Trinity were demonstrated by their shared activity in gifts and ministries. Gregory of Nyssa made this clear in his Treatise to Eustathius entitled *On the Holy Trinity, and the Godhead of the Holy Spirit* (written in 380):

> We understand that the operation of the Father, the Son, and the Holy Spirit is one, differing or varying in nothing, the oneness of their nature must needs be inferred from the identity of their operation. The Father, the Son, and the Holy Spirit alike give sanctification, and life, and light, and comfort, and all similar graces. And let no one attribute the power of sanctification in an especial sense to the Spirit, when he hears the Saviour in the Gospel saying to the Father "Father sanctify them in Thy name". So too all the other gifts are wrought in those who are worthy alike by the Father, the Son and the Holy Spirit: every grace and power, guidance, life, comfort, the change to immortality, the passage to liberty, and every other boon that exists which descends to us.[19]

In this passage, Gregory of Nyssa draws our attention to the shared roles of Father, Son and Holy Spirit in ministering grace and sanctification, but he includes other gifts and indeed "every other boon that exists which descends to us"!

---

[18] Basil, *On the Spirit* 16.38.

[19] Gregory of Nyssa, *On the Holy Trinity, and the Godhead of the Holy Spirit*, Nicene Fathers, 328.

Their shared connumeration as Father, Son and Holy Spirit

Basil rejected the views of those who made use of subnumeration to argue that the Holy Spirit is less than the Father and in the case of some, less than the Father and the Son. The fact is, he stated, that we speak of Peter, Paul and John in subnumeration terms as first, second and third, but this does not mean they are not equally men or that any one of them is above the others or that they are a hierarchy. The same is true of the Father, Son and Holy Spirit. Speaking of the Holy Spirit as the "third person" does not permit us to take the view that he is less in status than either the Father or the Son. This is because all three are of exactly the same essence. In *On the Spirit* Chapter 17, Basil concluded as follows: "We assert that connumeration is appropriate to subjects of equal dignity, and subnumeration to those which vary in the direction of inferiority."[20]

Gregory of Nyssa was also clear that number is indicative merely of the quantity of things, giving no clue as to their real nature.[21] Basil was adamant that if we use the number of the deity, we must use it "reverently". He pointed out that while each person is designated one, they cannot be added together. The reason for this is that the divine nature which they share is simple and indivisible.

Their communal fellowship

The Cappadocians emphasized that Father, Son and Spirit share in constant fellowship with one another. They used the Greek word *perichoresis* to express this. *Perichoresis* is also found in the Latin word *circumcessio*, meaning "mutual interpenetration" in English. It refers to the way in which three distinct persons can share in the life of each other. *Perichoresis* denoted "a community of being". As has been noted in Chapter 7, modalism taught that God existed or revealed himself in three modes of being. First, he existed as the Father who created the world and then as the Son who redeemed it and finally as the Spirit who completed it following his ascension into heaven. In contrast to modalism, the Cappadocians used *perichoresis* to assert that each of the

---

[20] Basil, *On the Spirit* 17.42.
[21] Gregory of Nyssa, *Against Eunomius* 2.17.

three persons, Father, Son and Holy Spirit, were involved together at every point.

The advantage of this way of looking at the Trinity is that it demonstrated that God exists at the same time in all three modes of being—Father, Son and Holy Spirit. So, for example, Basil of Caesarea wrote:

> Everything that the Father is, is seen in the Son, and everything that the Son is belongs to the Father. The Son in his entirety abides in the Father, and in return possesses the Father in entirety in Himself. Thus, the hypostasis of the Son is, so to speak, the form and presentation by which the Father is known, and the Father's hypostasis is recognized in the form of the Son.[22]

In this statement, the Godhead can be said to exist undivided in divided persons. Basil, it should be emphasized, stuck firmly to *homoousios* (same substance), because it strongly underlined "a community of essence (*ousia*) but distinction (*hypostasis*)". For Basil, the Trinity was a union of divine nature shared by Father, Son and Holy Spirit.

Their shared eternity

In paragraph 3 of his *Third Oration on the Son*, Gregory of Nazianzus posed the question, "When did the Father, Son and Holy Spirit come into being?" He then gives the answer as follows, "And when did the Father come into being? There never was a time when He was not. And the same is true of the Son and the Holy Spirit. Ask me again, and again I will answer you, When was the Son begotten? When the Father was not begotten. And when did the Holy Spirit proceed? When the Son was, not proceeding but begotten beyond the sphere of time, and above the grasp of reason."[23] Gregory of Nazianzus then asked the poignant question, "How then are they not alike unorignate, if they are coeternal? Because they are from Him, though not after Him. For that which is unoriginate

---

[22] Basil of Caesarea, Letter 38 to his Brother, para 8..
[23] Gregory of Nazianzus, *Third Theological Oration: On the Son* 29.3.

is eternal."[24] Gregory concludes stating, "If God is not from the beginning he is in the same rank with myself, even though a little before me . . . If He is in the same rank with myself, how can He join me with Godhead?"[25]

Their shared name but distinct attributes
In his Book II of *Against Eunomius*, Gregory of Nyssa presents the Trinity as having only one name but with three attributes. In para 2, he writes as follows:

> In regard to essence He is one, wherefore the Lord ordained that we should look to one Name: but in regard to the attributes indicative of the Persons, our belief in Him is distinguished into belief in the Father, the Son and the Holy Spirit; He is divided without separation, and united without confusion. For when we hear the title "Father" we apprehend the meaning to be this, that the name is not understood with reference to itself alone, but also by its special significations indicated the relationship to the Son. For the term "Father" would have no meaning apart by itself, if "Son" were not connected by the utterance of the word "Father". When then we learnt the name "Father" we were taught at the same time, the self-same title, faith also in the Son.[26]

Gregory then goes on to assert that the deity cannot change. "It is by its nature", he stated, "permanently and immutably the same." So, we cannot speak of the Father without implying the Son. He continues, "He who is very Father was named Father by the Word."[27]

Having established the distinctiveness and yet inseparability of Father and Son, Gregory introduced their indissoluble link with the Holy Spirit. "We conceive there is no gap between the anointed Christ and His anointing, between the King and His sovereignty, between Wisdom and the Spirit of Wisdom, between Truth and the Spirit of Truth, between

---

[24] Gregory of Nazianzus, *Third Theological Oration: On the Son* 29.3.
[25] Gregory of Nazianzus, *Third Theological Oration: On the Son* 29.4.
[26] Gregory of Nyssa, *Against Eunomius* II.2.
[27] Gregory of Nyssa, *Against Eunomius* II.2.

Power and the Spirit of Power ... " So, from all eternity, there is in the Father and Son the Holy Spirit who is the Spirit of Truth, Counsel "and all else the Son is called". For this reason, Gregory asserted, the disciples came to speak of the name (singular) of the Father, Son and Holy Spirit, a union in three distinctions. In Book II.4 of *Against Eunomius*, Gregory goes on to emphasize that "the Gospels which are read continuously from ancient times do not tell us we should believe and baptize into 'the one and only true God'... but in the name [singular] of the Father and of the Son and of the Holy Spirit." He concludes that true faith "comprehends the name of the Father and of the Son and of the Holy Ghost".[28]

Again, in the same section of Book II.4, Gregory of Nyssa stresses that asserting our faith and trust in "one" God does not indicate that the Father is alone. Rather it includes the Son with the Father, since the Lord said, "I and My Father are one".[29] Thus, the name "God" belongs equally to the beginning in which the Word was, and to the Word who was in the beginning. In a later paragraph, Gregory makes the same point. "Without the Son", he writes, the Father has neither existence nor name, any more than the Powerful without Power, or the Wise without Wisdom. For Christ is "the Power of God and the Wisdom of God".[30]

Their universality and particularity

The Cappadocians also sought to explain how one substance could simultaneously be present in three persons by the analogy of the universal and the particular. Basil wrote that *ousia* (substance) and *hypostasis* (distinctives), are differentiated exactly as universal and particular are. So, for example an individual man represents the universal man but has certain characteristics which mark him off from other men.[31] For Basil, these particularizing characteristics are "paternity", "sonship" and "sanctifying power". Gregory of Nazianzus defined them as "ingenerateness", "generateness" and "mission".[32]

---

[28] Gregory of Nyssa, *Against Eunomius* II.4.
[29] Gregory of Nyssa, *Against Eunomius* II.4.
[30] Gregory of Nyssa, *Against Eunomius* II.4.
[31] Basil, *Letter* 38.2.
[32] Gregory of Nazianzus, *Oration* 25.16.

Summary of the Cappadocian Fathers' Trinitarian theology

In their speaking and writing about the Trinity, the Cappadocians used their terms with great carefulness and consistency. They always used *ousia* (meaning substance or essence) when they were talking about what was constant and the same in the Godhead. And they always used *hypostasis* (that which stands out) for what was distinctive or different between the Father, the Son and the Holy Spirit. In several cases, they avoided using the term "person", since it was often taken by their opponents to imply three people, three gods or tritheism. Thus, they sometimes spoke of three "individualities", "distinctives", or "realities".

In the following quotation, Gregory of Nazianzus uses the term "individuality" to highlight the differences of Father, Son and Holy Spirit:

> When I speak of God ... There are three *individualities* or hypostases, or, if you prefer, persons. Why argue about names when words amount to the same meaning? There is one substance (i.e.) Deity. For God is divided without division, if I may put it like that, and united in division. The Godhead is one in three and three in one. The Godhead has its being in the three, or to be more precise, the Godhead is three ... We must neither heretically fuse God together into one [Monarchianism] nor chop him up into inequality [Arianism].[33]

In another piece, Gregory used the metaphor of "three suns" joined to each other to illustrate three undivided, three separate persons:

> To us there is one God, for the Godhead is One and all that proceeds from Him is referred to as One, though we believe in Three Persons. For one is not more and another less God; nor is One before and another after; nor are they divided in will or parted in power; nor can you find here any of the qualities of divisible things; but the Godhead is, to speak concisely,

---

[33] Gregory of Nazianzus, *Third Theological Oration: On the Son* 11.

undivided in separate persons; and there is one mingling of Light, as it were of three suns joined to each other. When we look at the Godhead, or the First Cause, or the Monarchia, that which we conceive is One; but when we look at the Persons in whom the Godhead dwells, and at Those Who timelessly and with equal glory have their Being from the First Cause—there are Three whom we worship.[34]

Gregory of Nazianzus used another illustration to make the same point. Peter, James and John were three individuals but were all called humans because they all shared a single common humanity. In the same way, the Father, Son and Holy Spirit are three individuals with their own distinctives, but they are all called divine because they all share a common divinity. All these metaphors and illustrations which the Cappadocian Fathers used helped the Catholic Church to grasp that Father, Son and Holy Spirit share the same underlying divine essence and equality while at the same time retaining their distinct characteristics.

Cappadocian faith, spirituality and pastoral care

All three Cappadocians were men of the Holy Spirit and their deep spirituality included practical caring for the poor. Basil set up food banks for the poor in his diocese. At the same time, he pioneered an ascetic life which eventually led to him founding a monastic community at Annisa. He recommended a secluded and remote habitation which he believed would keep the soul from distraction. His monastic community was one of the first to focus on medicine, healing and healing prayer. Basil also founded a hospice which was especially for the poor and the lepers. He had a heart for evangelism, and he held missions in both Pontus and Cappadocia which brought many to faith. Gregory of Nazianzus, while not dishonouring marriage, also gave a high place to virginity. Gregory of Nyssa, scholars believe, was quite possibly married. Whilst their asceticism probably kept them from the temptations of money and

---

[34] Gregory of Nazianzus, *Third Theological Oration: Of the Son* 14.

sex, they demonstrated a vulnerability when it came to power. Basil was certainly an ambitious prelate. Gregory of Nyssa was a strong opponent of slavery on the basis that "God would not reduce the human race to slavery ... since he Himself had come to bring freedom".

Cappadocian spirituality

Basil spent time in Athens where he became challenged by the state of the city's culture and society. This led him to investigate the ascetic lifestyle of the Egyptian hermits and monastic communities.[35] He wrote:

> I marvelled at their steadfast sufferings. I was amazed at the vigour of their prayers, at how they gained mastery over sleep, being bowed down by no necessity of nature, ever persevering, exalted and unshackled the purpose of their soul in hunger and thirst, in coldness and nakedness, not concerning themselves with the body.[36]

Soon after his return from the city probably in 357, Basil started his own community close to the River Iris at Annisa in Pontus. There he pioneered a lifestyle which focused on prayer, Scripture reading and meditation, and social care in the community.

Annisa formed the basis of the monastery which Basil later developed and organized when he became Bishop of Caesarea. He was spurred into action by a major famine in 369. His community had an urban focus offering care for the poor and the sick. On the edge of the city, Basil set up a hospice, part hospital for the sick, part shelter for the poor, and part feeding station for the starving.[37] Basil proved himself an effective fund raiser for the hospice and attracted grants from the Emperor Valens for developing a large complex of new buildings.[38] He believed that the rich

---

[35] J. McGuckin, *Saint Gregory of Nazianzus: An Intellectual Biography* (Crestwood, NY: St Vladimir's Seminary Press, 2001), p. 76.

[36] Basil of Caesarea, *Letter* 223.2, cited in Frend, *The Early Church*, p. 194.

[37] P. Whitworth, *Three Wise Men from the East* (Durham: Sacristy Press, 2015), p. 130.

[38] Whitworth, *Three Wise Men from the East*, p. 130.

ought to contribute to the needs of the poor and has sometimes been claimed as a forerunner of socialism.

Gregory of Nazianzus, who was also drawn to monasticism, visited Annisa but struggled at the rigours of Basil's regime. He wrote: "We do not dishonour marriage because we give a higher value to virginity."[39] Indeed the married could also be "pure and unmingled with filthy lusts".[40]

Gregory of Nyssa, Basil's brother, wrote books which focused on the spiritual journey including *On Virginity* (368), *The Life of Moses* (390–5), and a treatise entitled *On Perfection*. He was drawn to the monastic ideal but bemoaned that he could not fully enter into it since he was debarred from marriage.[41] In *On Virginity*, he listed the benefits of a well-balanced marriage "in every way most happy".[42]

Whilst asceticism may have helped Basil and Gregory of Nazianzus to control the temptations of money and sex, they showed vulnerability over episcopal appointments. Basil enlisted the support of others in gaining his own appointment as Bishop of Caesarea.[43] He then strengthened his own position as Metropolitan of Cappadocia which included Pontus, Galatia, Bithynia and Greater and Lesser Armenia, by appointing his brother to the See of Nyssa (*c.*371)[44] and his friend Gregory of Nazianzus to the See of Sasima in 372.[45] In 379, he was summoned to Constantinople where his eloquent preaching in the Church of the Resurrection was powerfully effective in support of the Nicaean faith. During the Council of Constantinople, he was appointed Bishop of Constantinople but resigned before the end of the year, appalled at the intrigues of the bishops and the ways of the councils. The event marked a change in the

---

[39] C. G. Browne and J. E. Swallow, *Select Orations of Saint Gregory Nazianzen* (Buffalo, NY: Christian Literature Publishing Co., 1894), p. 729.

[40] Browne and Swallow, *Select Orations*, p. 790.

[41] Whitworth, *Three Wise Men from the East*, p. 149.

[42] Gregory of Nyssa, *On Virginity* 2, cited in Whitworth, *Three Wise Men from the East*, p. 149.

[43] McGuckin, *Saint Gregory of Nazianzus*, p. 101.

[44] McGuckin, *Saint Gregory of Nazianzus*, p. 189.

[45] F. J. Foakes-Jackson, *The History of the Christian Church to* AD *461* (London: George Allen & Unwin Ltd, 1909), p. 385.

office of a bishop. No longer was he just a spiritual leader; he was a public one who liaised with the authorities of the Roman Empire. Some now wore purple, the Roman Emperor's colour.

The three Cappadocians were the Eastern champions of *homoousios* and pioneers and promoters of monasticism. They established the deity of the Holy Spirit and articulated the doctrine of the Trinity in a convincing manner. That said, no eulogy for these Christian leaders would be just or complete without reference to Macrina (*c*.330–79). She was the sister of Basil and Gregory of Nyssa and had stood firm in her faith during a local persecution. It was her zeal, stronger faith and example which impacted and inspired the two of them to become influential bishops. Gregory, in his *Life of St Macrina,* remembered her as a child being devoted to the Scriptures. Sometime later when Basil had returned home from his studies Macrina rebuked him because "he was monstrously conceited about his skill in rhetoric".[46] Macrina's father had organized for her to marry her fiancé, but he died shortly before the wedding was due to take place. This led to her resolve never to leave her mother and to commit herself to a single life. Daughter and mother soon moved to one of their family's rural estates in Pontus and established a community of virgins who came from both aristocratic, servant and commoner backgrounds. All members were free and slaves had the same rights and obligations as everyone else. Gregory recorded that his sister "never did turn away people who sought her help nor did she seek out benefactors".[47] Macrina is a significant figure in monastic history in that she set the standard for being a holy early Christian woman.[48]

---

[46] Gregory of Nyssa, *Life of St Macrina*. The Life of St Macrina is written in the form of a letter. There are no numbered paragraphs in the short text.
[47] Gregory of Nyssa, *Life of St Macrina*.
[48] Peter Brown, *The Body and Society* (New York: Columbia University Press, 1988), p. 272.

1 2

From Constantinople to Chalcedon: The struggle to assert that Jesus is both fully God and fully human

The greater part of the fourth century, as we have seen in the two previous chapters, was the major struggle the Catholic Church had in asserting that Jesus is the same (*homoousios*) substance as the Father. Following the declarations of the Council of Constantinople in 381, the Church finally became confident of Jesus being fully God. However, in the years which followed and on into the fifth century, a further issue emerged. This was concerned with the precise nature of Jesus' humanity, and its relationship with his divinity. In short, how could Jesus be both fully God and fully human in one being? This proved to be another extended debate which was largely ended in 451 with the pronouncements of the Council of Chalcedon.

Apollinarius

The first theologian to raise serious questions about Jesus' humanity was Apollinarius (*c.*310–*c.*390). The son of a grammarian of Beirut in Syria, he became Bishop of Laodicea about the year 360. His ecclesiastical responsibilities appear to have been relatively small, and this gave him plenty of time to study and write though most of his extensive writings have been lost. He was a close friend of both Athanasius and Basil of Cappadocia. He was therefore understandably a very strong opponent of Arianism and determined to assert the full deity and sinlessness of the Son. In his endeavours to achieve this, Apollinarius taught that Jesus was altogether totally God but not fully human. According to Gregory of Nazianzus, the Apollinarian heresy began about the year 352. His problem was he could not accept that Jesus had a fallible rational human mind. Jesus' body, emotions and feelings were those of an ordinary living man but "the divine energy fulfils the role of the human mind".[1] Jesus' will was, he argued, solely that of the Logos, the Word of God. In a letter written to the bishops at Diocaesarea, Apollinarius set out the leading features of his Christology:

> We confess that the Word of God has not descended upon a holy man, which was what happened in the case of the prophets. Rather the word himself has become flesh without having assumed a human mind which is enslaved to filthy thoughts—but exists as an immutable and heavenly divine mind.[2]

At one point, according to Theodoret, Apollinarius was even alleged to have taught "that the Holy Virgin Mary had come down from heaven with God the Word".[3] Sozomen wrote in similar vein that Apollinarius' Jesus "brought with Him His own flesh which he had already possessed in heaven ... and was destitute of intellect (Greek *nous*) but that the deity of the only begotten Son fulfilled the nature of intellect".[4] J. N. D. Kelly encapsulated Apollinarius' solution to this problem stating that the Word "was performing the functions usually exercised by the will and the intellect ... the Word was the sole life of the God-man infusing vital energy and movement into Him even at the purely physical and biological level". Kelly added that Apollinarius found support in texts such as Jesus was "found as a man" and was "in the likeness of men".[5]

Apollinarius was evidently mistakenly thinking of the incarnation as a union of two persons: "God joined with a man, one complete being

---

[1] Fragment 2 in Kelly, *Early Christian Doctrines*, p. 292.
[2] Alister McGrath, *Historical Theology: An Introduction to the History of Christian Thought* (Oxford: Blackwell, 1998), p. 53.
[3] Theodoret, *Ecclesiastical History* V.3.
[4] Sozomen, *Ecclesiastical History* VI.26.
[5] Kelly, *Early Christian Doctrines*, p. 292.

with another complete being".[6] He therefore argued it was not possible for any person to be motivated by two separate wills. In Fragment 150, he wrote: "It is impossible in one and the same subject that two wills can be together, who will what is opposed to each; for each works what is willed by it according to its own proper and personal motives."[7] Put another way, the divine will would will one thing and the human will another thing. Apollinarius was clear that he could have no confidence in a Jesus who was controlled by a fallible human mind. His view was that Jesus had human flesh, but his will was solely divine. In straightforward terms, Jesus was a human without but divine within. He expressed it as follows in a letter to the Emperor Jovian:

> We do not speak of two natures in one Son, of which one is to be worshipped and one is not, but of only one nature of the Logos of God, which became flesh and with His flesh is to be worshipped with one worship; and we confess not two sons; one who is truly God's Son and to be worshipped and another the man who is of Mary and is not to be worshipped.[8]

A number of theologians strongly disagreed with Apollinarius' teaching. Among them were the aged Athanasius and Gregory of Nazianzus who attacked his views in a letter to Cledonius. In brief, his argument was if a man is to be totally redeemed then the redeemer must himself be totally man. The following lines make Gregory's argument explicit: "But, says someone, the godhead was sufficient in place of the human intellect. What, then, is this to me? For the godhead with flesh alone is not man, nor with the soul alone, nor with both apart from mind, which is the most essential part of man."[9] Gregory was asserting that if Jesus was to redeem anyone it must be on the basis of like for like. If he was to redeem our

---

[6] Fragment 81 in Lietzmann, *The Founding of the Church Universal*, p. 224.
[7] Fragment 150 in Lietzmann, *The Founding of the Church Universal*, p. 247.
[8] Apollinarius, *Letter to Emperor Jovian*, in Ayer, *A Source Book for Ancient Church History*, p. 405.
[9] Gregory, *Letter 1 to Cledonius*, in Ayer, *A Source Book for Ancient Church History*, p. 497.

flesh before God, he himself must be flesh and similarly with the human mind and spirit, he must himself be human mind and spirit.

Apollinarius' teachings were condemned at Synods held at Alexandria, Rome and Antioch and finally by the Council of Constantinople in 381. The Synodical wording has been preserved by Theodoret (423–57) Bishop of Cyrrhus, in his *Ecclesiastical History*: "Similarly they openly condemn the innovation of Apollinarius in the phrase 'And we preserve the doctrine of the incarnation of the Lord, holding that the flesh is neither soulless, nor mindless, nor imperfect.'"[10] The Council also inserted into the Creed after the words born of the Virgin Mary, the words "and was made man".

Nestorius

Nestorius (386–451) was a native of Germanicia in Syria. In his early days, he was attached to a monastery as a theological teacher. In 428, he was appointed Archbishop of Constantinople by the Emperor Theodosius II, a position he held until 431. He at once proclaimed himself as a zealous upholder of orthodoxy. And following the emphasis of the Antioch School of Theology he at once laid stress on the real manhood of Jesus. This was particularly important because following the defeat of Arianism there was a growing move in some churches to sit light on the humanity of Jesus. Nestorius and his followers, so his opponents claimed, stressed Jesus' manhood to such an extent that he was two separate personalities: a living conscious human personality and an equally divine one. He expressed it in the following lines:

> With one name, Christ, we designate at the same time two natures ... The essential characteristics in the nature of the divinity and in the humanity are from all eternity distinguished.[11]

---

[10] Theodoret, *Ecclesiastical History* V.8.
[11] *The Fragments of Nestorius* 196, in Ayer, *A Source Book for Ancient Church History*, p. 501.

He made the same point in another place, stating that:

> God the word is also named Christ because He has always existed in conjunction with Christ. And it is impossible for God the Word to do anything without the humanity for all is planned upon an intimate conjunction, not on the deification of the humanity.[12]

In these lines, Nestorius is standing up against the view of Apollinarius who, as we have just noted, maintained the humanity was absorbed by the deity of Jesus. Importantly Nestorius also appears to have believed in the eternal humanity of Jesus rather than the orthodox view which asserted only the eternity of the Son and with the humanity beginning at the incarnation.

Because Nestorius put so much emphasis on the humanity of Jesus, his opponents who belonged to the Alexandrian group of theologians decided to give him a test. They all followed Athanasius and set great emphasis on the deity of Jesus so they asked him, "Would he be willing to give Jesus' mother Mary the title *theotokos*, a Greek word meaning 'God- bearer'?" In other words, did he believe Jesus was divine from the moment of his birth? Nestorius pondered over the word for some time and finally gave a guarded yes if it was in conjunction with *anthropotokos* meaning "man-bearer". A little later, he went even further, stating that he preferred *Christotokos* meaning "Christ bearer". This term, he felt, stressed the conjunction of the two natures human and divine in the one person of Christ.

In making this distinction, Nestorius was clear that Mary was the mother of Jesus but not the mother of the divine personality. "Christ", he declared, "was still two persons", *prosopa* being the word he used. He appeared to have been confusing "nature" with "person". Yes, Jesus had two natures, a human and a divine, but he was still only one person. Nestorius, it should be said, was a little uneasy about calling Mary "the mother of God", because, as he pointed out, when the Scriptures speak of salvation, they stress the humanity of Jesus rather than the divinity. He

---

[12] *The Fragments of Nestorius* 275, in Ayer, *A Source Book for Ancient Church History*, p. 502.

was also concerned about the use of "God-bearer", because it appeared to make her into a kind of goddess.

In this struggle, Nestorius' chief opponent was Cyril (*d*.444), who had become Patriarch of Alexandria in 412. He began by setting out the orthodox view that the Logos was the eternal Son of God who took human nature to himself in the womb of the Virgin Mary who for this reason is rightly titled *theotokos* or "God-bearer". The deity and the humanity are united, he said, but can only be distinguished theoretically.

Nestorius revealed his strongly contrasting views, stating, "I could not call a baby two or three months old 'God.'"[13] In opposition, Cyril aimed to show two important things. First, the unchangeable nature of Christ, but in doing so he stated that it was impossible for him to sin. In this, he ran counter to the orthodox view that "Jesus was able not to sin rather than not able to sin". Second, Cyril asserted that the incarnation was not the taking of a human personality by the Word but the complete assumption of humanity itself.

Cyril was very quick off the mark in his condemnation of Nestorius and before long both men were appealing to Celestine, the Bishop of Rome, for help. Celestine responded with a letter in support of Cyril which he then forwarded to Nestorius and added 12 anathemas of his own.[14]

In 430, Cyril called a council at Alexandria at which he set out the teaching of Nestorius as he perceived it followed by his response. The first canon issued by the council stated: "If anyone shall not confess that the Emmanuel is in truth God, and that therefore the Virgin is '*theotokos*', in as much as, according to the flesh, she bore the word of God made flesh; let him be anathema." The ninth anathema stated:

> If anyone shall not confess that the flesh of the Lord is life-giving, and belongs to the Word of God the Father as his very own, but shall pretend that it belongs to another... and... has served only as a dwelling for the Divinity... let him be anathema.[15]

---

[13] Theodoret, *Ecclesiastical History* VII.34.
[14] "The Anathemas of Cyril of Alexandria", in Cyril, *Letter 17*.
[15] "The Anathemas of Cyril of Alexandria", in Cyril, *Letter 17*.

During the following year, 431, Nestorius was summoned by the Emperor Theodosius II (Emperor from 402–50)[16] to the Council of Ephesus. But as he saw it Bishop Cyril's anathemas were a repetition of Apollinarius' teachings, and he felt sure that they would be rejected. As things turned out, he was mistaken and on 22 June his views were condemned with a declaration that Jesus was:

> Perfect God and perfect man consisting of a rational soul and body, of one substance with the Father in his Godhead, of one substance with us in his manhood, so that there is a union of two natures; on which ground we confess Christ to be one and Mary to be the Mother of God.[17]

It should be said that opinion is divided as to precisely what it was that Nestorius taught. He has been accused of teaching not only two natures but also two different persons in Christ. But on the other hand, it remains a fact that he constantly stressed Jesus' oneness. This may well have been because of his constant fear of Monophysitism[18] tendencies which were looming on the horizon.

Eutychianism

What Nestorius appears to have feared came to pass in the teaching and writings of a monk named Eutyches (378–454). He was the Archimandrite (head) of a monastery in Constantinople. Nestorius emphasized the distinction between the two natures, the human and the divine, to a point where he appeared to believe there were two separate beings inside the one Jesus. In stark contrast, Eutyches took a completely opposite view and blurred the distinction. He taught that the humanity

---

[16] The Emperor Theodosius II (401–450) was proclaimed Augustus in his infancy.

[17] "The Declaration of the Council of Ephesus", August 431 quoted in full in Kelly, *Early Christian Doctrines*, pp. 328–9.

[18] The belief that Jesus only had a divine will but no human will.

of Jesus was gradually completely absorbed by the deity so that in the end he was solely divine. Jesus, according to Eutyches, had a human body but no human will or emotions. This belief came to be known as "Monophysitism" meaning one nature.

A Synod was held at Constantinople in 448, at which he was asked "Do you or do you not confess that our Lord, who is of the virgin, is . . . of two natures after the incarnation?" In response, he replied: "I confess that our Lord *was* of two natures before the union but after the union one nature." From this statement, it would appear that Eutyches believed Jesus to have had a human nature prior to the incarnation only to be swallowed up thereafter. To illustrate the point, he used the illustration of a drop of honey being swallowed up in the sea. The difficulty of Eutyches' teaching was that it denied the real humanity of Jesus. If he wasn't fully human, how would he be able to atone for human sin?

On 28 July, the Emperor Theodosius II died and was succeeded as Emperor of the East by Marcian (392–457), who was a strong member of the Antiochene party which emphasized the humanity of Jesus. He very soon called together a council which met in Chalcedon in 451 which was conveniently close to Constantinople where the Emperor resided. Eutyches' views were denounced by the Council who produced a very full statement on the two natures which has remained a basic doctrine of mainstream Christianity ever since.

The Council statement begins with the words "The Holy, great, and ecumenical synod assembled by the grace of God and the command of our most religious and Christian Emperors Marcian and Valentinian . . . has decreed as follows."[19] There is first of all extended reference to the creed and council of Nicaea and the subsequent problems raised by Nestorius and Eutyches.[20] This is then followed by the Chalcedonian definition of the two natures of Jesus:

---

[19] *The Council of Chalcedon* A.D. 451, in Ayer, *A Source Book for Ancient Church History*, p. 517.

[20] *The Council of Chalcedon* A.D. 451, in Ayer, *A Source Book for Ancient Church History*, pp. 518–19.

> Following the Holy Fathers, we all with one voice teach men to confess that the Son and our Lord Jesus Christ is one and the same, that He is perfect in godhead and perfect in manhood, truly God and truly man, of a reasonable soul and body, consubstantial with the Father as touching His godhead, and consubstantial with us in His manhood, in all things like unto us, without sin; begotten of his Father before all worlds according to His godhead; but in these last days for us and for our salvation of the Virgin Mary, the Theotokos, according to his manhood, one and the same Christ, Son, Lord, only begotten Son, in two natures, unconfusedly, immutably, indivisibly, inseparably; the distinction of natures being preserved and concurring in one person and hypostasis, not separated or divided into two persons, but one and the same Son and Only begotten, God the Word, the Lord Jesus Christ, as prophets from the beginning have spoken concerning Him, and as the Lord Jesus Christ himself has taught us, and as the creed of the Fathers has delivered us.[21]

The leading theologian at Chalcedon was Pope Leo "the Great", who held office from 441–61. He wrote an extended piece in which he covered everything he held to be apostolic biblical teaching concerning the two natures of Jesus' person. His document became known as the *Tome of Leo*, a tome being an official papal letter.[22]

According to Chalcedon the two natures of Christ, the human and the divine, are not to be thought of as confused or thought of as mixed up with each other like the ingredients of a cake. The two natures both exist in Jesus in such a way that neither are diminished by the other. In other words, the divine isn't watered down by mixing with the human in the way that yellow paint mixed with blue becomes green. Equally, the human isn't absorbed or swallowed up into the divine. The two natures, according to the Chalcedon definition, are separate and distinct from one another but not to the point where they become two separate persons.

---

[21] *The Council of Chalcedon* A.D. 451, in Ayer, *A Source Book for Ancient Church History*, pp. 519–20.

[22] See Bettenson, *Documents of the Christian Church*, pp. 48–51.

The Council of Chalcedon did not bring matters to a complete end. There was still an ongoing debate in the late fifth and sixth centuries. The strongest opposition came from the Coptic Church in Egypt which, together with the Ethiopian Orthodox Church, still retain a Monophysite Christology maintaining that Jesus has only a divine nature as taught by Eutyches. There are still also a small number of Nestorian churches in Iraq, Syria, India and parts of North and South America. That said the great majority of the Western churches retained full confidence in the Chalcedonian definition. There can indeed be no doubt that it was a significant step forward that enabled the Catholic Church and many thousands of individual Christians to become more confident in their faith. The Canon and the events leading up to it was, and remains, hugely important to the present day as a core understanding of the two natures of Christ.

13

The call of the desert: Monastic communities, hospitality, faith and scholarship

Following his conversion the Emperor Constantine declared religious freedom for all but made Christianity a privileged religion. This gradually caused the Church to begin to grow lax and to be infiltrated with worldly standards. The process was accelerated considerably after 381 when the Emperor Theodosius made Christianity the official religion of the Roman Empire. By the end of the fourth century, there was a growing awareness that you needed to be a Christian to make progress in life. The result was that increasing numbers were becoming Christians in name only.

Yet, even before Constantine's conversion, there were periods when persecution eased and Christians became half-hearted in their commitment. As early as the second decade of the third century, Callixtus, who was Bishop of Rome from 217–22, preached a sermon on this issue in which he described the Church as being like the Ark and taking in both the clean and the unclean. Because of situations like this, there were calls for a greater rigour and purity on the part of the churches. Only by an improved standard would it be possible for there to be effective Christian mission and evangelism. Clement of Rome made such a plea in the following passage of his *Letter to the Corinthians*:

> Take care then, my friends, lest if we fail to conduct ourselves worthily of Him and to do what is good and acceptable to Him ... Let us keep in mind the nearness of his presence, remembering

that not a single one of our thoughts or reasoning can ever be hidden from Him.[1]

Clearly there were two groups in many of the early Christian churches even in the decades before Constantine's conversion. There were those whose faith was nominal, but there were others who were serious in their commitment and trust in Christ and who refused to worship the gods of the Roman pantheon. Among those who were wholehearted believers there were growing numbers who were drawn to the desert as a place where they could grow in faith away from distractions of the Empire.

Influences on early Christian monasticism

The word "monk" comes from the Greek word *monos*, meaning alone. The movement to be alone was not solely Christian in origin. It was visible in the tradition of the Old Testament Rechabites and the life of the prophet Elijah. It was also evident in the Essene and Qumran communities and the life and ministry of John the Baptist. These and several other factors gave a more immediate impetus to Christian monasticism; most obvious were the teaching of Jesus and the need for refuge in times of persecution.

In Matthew 19:21, Jesus challenged a rich young man of the danger of being attached to his wealth: "If you want to be perfect, go, sell your possessions and give to the poor, and you will have treasure in heaven." This saying prompted many in the early days of Christianity to take vows of poverty. There is no evidence that Jesus ever married, but we know from Paul's First Letter to the Corinthians that his disciples and Peter took their wives with them on missionary journeys.[2] That said, Jesus is recorded in Matthew 19:12 as saying, "For there are eunuchs who were born that way, and there are eunuchs who have been made eunuchs by others—and there are those who choose to live like eunuchs for the sake of the kingdom of heaven."

---

[1] Clement, *Letter to the Corinthians* 21.
[2] 1 Corinthians 9:5.

It is also clear that dualistic philosophy impacted the thinking of people in large cities such as Alexandria, Memphis and Thebes. The Greek philosopher Plato's (c.427–348 BC) mantra "the body is the prison house of the soul" was widely believed and caused individuals to suppress the desires of their flesh or at the very least keep it in check. The Alexandrian Christian leader Origen was among those who took matters to their extreme and castrated themselves. Others, like Jerome (347–420), became almost fanatically attached to celibacy and virginity. He was one of the fourth-century pioneers of monasticism and went into seclusion in Bethlehem largely in an attempt to overcome sensual impulses. However, like many of the early Desert Fathers, he found himself unable to overcome his lustful thoughts and desires. His temptations were later well portrayed by the Italian Renaissance painter Giorgio Vasari's painting *The Temptations of St Jerome* with its portrayal of Venus, the Goddess of love, accompanied by cupids.

The persecutions also contributed to the growth of monasticism. During the brutal treatment of Christians in the second and third centuries, many fled into the deserts for safety and as a means of protecting copies of the Scriptures and other sacred books, treasures and artifacts. The rigorous persecution of groups of Christians by the Emperor Decius resulted in the emergence of communities known as "anchorites", the term coming from a Greek word meaning "to withdraw". Some of those who eventually came to a full monastic life did so by this process, Jerome recording that Paul of Thebes (230–341) was among them. Sometimes described as the first Christian hermit, he is reputed to have died at the age of 111.

During the persecutions instigated by the Emperor Diocletian in the years immediately following 300, there was a further expansion of monastic communities. For some, it has been said, the monastic ideal became a substitute for martyrdom. Athanasius experienced several periods of exile during which he sought refuge in monastic communities. He became firm friends with Anthony who was to become a very influential figure in the monastic movement. Indeed, in his later years Athanasius wrote a *Life of Anthony* in 362.

For a variety of reasons, monasticism took early root in particular centres. Egypt offered all-year-round good weather which made living in the open and camping considerably easier. Added to this, areas where dualistic philosophy was strong proved to be fertile ground for the spread of monastic communities.

Centres of early Christian monasticism

Egypt

Alexandria, with rigorous Christian leaders such as Clement, Origen and Athanasius, proved to be a stimulus to monastic communities which sprang up in a number of places along the Nile valley. One of the great initiators of monasticism was Anthony (251–356). He came from the village of Comas in the middle of Egypt. When only 18 years old, he responded to Jesus' words "go and sell all that you have". He began his ascetic existence on the outskirts of his home village. Amongst many things, he gave priority time to prayer and studied parts of Scripture in depth. In his later years, he lived in a cave tomb and then a disused castle near the Red Sea. That said, Sozomen described him as "exceedingly meek and philanthropic; prudent and manly; cheerful in conversation and friendship".[3] Apart from two visits to Alexandria, he remained in solitude throughout his very long life. He appeared in the city in 311 to strengthen the persecuted Christians. During the Arian controversy, Anthony and his monks remained staunch supporters of orthodoxy. Because of his sanctity of life, many came to him to seek his advice and guidance. J. G. Davies wrote of him: "There can be no doubt that the example of his life made monastic life attractive to many who were disposed by circumstances to turn their back on the world."[4]

Athanasius portrayed Anthony as a Christian who experienced the rigours of an intense spiritual battle. He often found the pull of the temptations he experienced to be very strong. Athanasius wrote that Anthony sometimes felt himself "beset by devils and all manner of frightful shapes" during which his remarkably strong spiritual life sustained him. Anthony was a monk who practised his spiritual gifts.

---

[3] Sozomen, *Ecclesiastical History* I.13.
[4] Davies, *The Early Christian Church*, p. 245.

For example, Athanasius described how Anthony was crossing the desert on one occasion with some of his monks. When their water supply had run dry, Anthony knelt down and prayed and water flowed out from the rocks.[5] In another place, a court official named Fronto came to visit Anthony. He was terribly diseased. Anthony told him to depart and how he would be healed. Immediately, Fronto set off and he was healed.[6] In Section 59, it is clear that Anthony had the gift of knowledge. He saw a vision of two men on the desert road, one of whom had just died and the other was still alive. The abbot told his monks to run to him on the road back to Egypt with a pitcher of water. They found the man and the water they had brought saved him. In Section 63, there is an interesting account of how Anthony perceived an evil spirit on account of a very unpleasant smell. In Section 80, Athanasius recounted how Anthony delivered people from demons by calling on Jesus and signing them several times with the sign of the cross.

Athanasius presents Anthony as a saintly-living wise man with a strong commitment to Nicaean orthodoxy. He is also portrayed as a wise and distinguished teacher whose advice was sought by many people. In Section 81, Athanasius quotes the text of some of the letters Anthony received from the Emperor Constantine and his sons Constantius and Constans.[7] The century following Anthony's death was a significant time for Egyptian monasticism. It was the age of the hermits who became known as "the fathers of the desert". The Egyptian Macarius (c.348–466), a disciple of Anthony, established a community at Scete. His monks had no common discipline but established their own rule of life.[8]

Shenoute (c.348–466) was another isolate who kept rigorous standards in his own life. In his later years, he became head of the White Monastery where a strict rule was observed. It combined communal living with periods of isolation in the desert region in specially prepared cells. Those joining had to recite a covenant which had to be adhered to literally: "I vow to go into this Holy place . . . I will not defile my body in any way,

---

[5] Athanasius, *The Life of Anthony* 54.
[6] Athanasius, *The Life of Anthony* 57.
[7] See Sozomen, *Ecclesiastical History* I.13.
[8] Davies, *The Early Christian Church*, p. 246.

I will not steal; I will not bear false witness; I will not lie; I will not do anything deceitfully secretly. If I transgress what I have vowed, I will see the kingdom of heaven, but will not enter it."[9]

Socrates recorded that the monasteries in Egypt were ruled over by devout superintendents, among them Pambo, Heraclides and Macarius.[10] He also singled out Dioscorus, Ammonius and Eusebius who were "distinguished both for the sanctity of their lives and their erudition".[11] Mention should have been made of Amma Syncletica (c.270–c.350) of Alexandria. She was born of wealthy parents but after their death sold her inheritance and left the city with her younger sister. She became the abbess of a community of women and was recognized as a wise woman who didn't overvalue chastity which she regarded as a potential source of pride. She did, however, assert that "a strong soul is strengthened by freely accepting poverty".[12] *The Life of Syncletica* was originally thought to have come from the pen of Athanasius though recent opinion regards this as unlikely since the book wasn't published until 450 which was more than 70 years after his death.

Africa

Bordering around Egypt was the rest of the vast African continent. Their northern provinces proved to be another ideal seedbed for monastic living. Perhaps the most significant African monk was Pachomius (292–346). In his early life, he was a soldier and during his time serving with the military he became adept in organization and management. One day, he heard what he took to be the voice of God saying: "Stay here and build a monastery and many will come to you in order to be monks." He was obedient to the call and established a rule which was held to be moderate compared with others. It included work, a degree of

---

[9] Besa, *Life of Shenoute* 9–12, in David N. Bell, *Besa: The Life of Shenoute*, Cistercian Studies Series, Vol. 73 (Kalamazoo, MI: Cistercian Publications, 1983).

[10] Socrates, *Ecclesiastical History* IV.23.

[11] Socrates, *Ecclesiastical History* IV.23.

[12] Benedicta Ward, *The Desert Fathers: Sayings of the Early Christian Monks* (London: Penguin Books, 2003), p. 56.

abstinence and obedience to the one in charge of each monastic house who was called "abbot", which is Syriac for "father". His communities marked the beginning of more ordered and structured monastic living.[13] Sozomen recorded that the community on the island of Tabenna in which Pachomius lived consisted of about 1,300.[14] Close by, his sister Mary established a similar community of women with Pachomius acting as visitor and providing a rule. By the time of his death in 346, Pachomius was directing 11 monasteries, nine for men and two for women with an estimated total of over a thousand individuals.[15]

Asia

In the latter part of the fourth century, a number of monasteries were founded in the province of Cappadocia in Asia Minor. Part of the reason for this may have been the links with Athanasius who was exiled there and who had close links with the Cappadocian Fathers Basil of Caesarea, Gregory of Nazianzus and Gregory of Nyssa. Basil had made a careful study of Egyptian monasticism[16] and formed a community at Pontus which centred on both the needs of the monks and the local community. He encouraged prayer, study of the Scriptures and care for the sick and needy. His communities were well governed, and the monks kept constantly at work and prayer.[17] Basil's *Shorter Rule* gives details of the life of his communities. There was common dress and property, frequent prayer and four Eucharists were held each week. The rule recognized episcopal control over daily life.[18] Although those who joined were invited to take vows of chastity, poverty and obedience, in general Basil's rule steered clear of extreme rigour and asceticism. Basil encouraged the pursuit of prayer, study of the Scriptures, agriculture and nursing. Over the centuries which followed, monasteries developed a long tradition

---

[13] Frend, *The Early Church*, p. 192.
[14] Sozomen, *Ecclesiastical History* III.14.
[15] Davies, *The Early Christian Church*, p. 320.
[16] Davies, *The Early Christian Church*, p. 221.
[17] Foakes-Jackson, *The History of the Christian Church to* AD *461*, p. 587.
[18] W. K. Lowther-Clarke, *St Basil the Great: A Study in Monasticism* (Cambridge: Cambridge University Press, 1913), p. 195.

of caring for the sick. Many ancient hospitals had their foundations in monastic communities.

Another quaint and perhaps fanatical Asian monk was Simon Stylites (390–460). Born in Syria, he became well known for his sanctity and purity of life. People came from all over the surrounding countryside to seek his guidance, help and advice on a whole range of questions. The church historian Theodoret (c.393–c.458) relates that he had such a constant stream of visitors that he constructed and lived on a pillar about a yard high in order to have the opportunity for some peace and quiet. He stayed on top of it for about 30 years; 32 years was the time he gave. He is reputed to have gradually increased the height of his pillar until it eventually reached 74 feet above the ground. Other individuals who were impressed with Simon's godly living and prayer set up their own versions of his practice. Some who constructed pillars became known as stylites, *styles* meaning a pillar. Others lived in the tops of trees and became known as "dendrites", the word coming from *dendros*, meaning tree. These individuals represent the extreme edge of monasticism, but they were respected for their serious pursuit of the Christian faith and spirituality.

Europe

Frances Young pointed out that in 339 Athanasius, Bishop of Alexandria, fled to the West from the Arian bishops and for a period went to Rome. It was while he was there that he introduced monastic ideals to the Western Church.[19] His writing, and his *Life of Anthony* in particular, conveyed the Egyptian monastic system in a palatable way. Jerome (340–420) studied in Rome where he was baptized and came to embrace the monastic ideal. About the year 374, he settled as a hermit for four years at Chalcis in the Syrian desert. For the early part of his life, he lived in the cave in Jerusalem where Jesus was alleged to have been buried. Then, in 382, Jerome moved to Rome where he acted as secretary to Bishop Damasus (c.304–84) for two years. He finally left the Imperial City about the year 385, eventually settling in Bethlehem where he translated the Greek

---

[19] Frances M. Young, *From Nicaea to Chalcedon: A Guide to the Literature and its Background*, 1st edn (London: SCM Press, 1983), p. 67.

Bible into the Latin or Vulgate version. Under his influence, several communities for men and women were established in the Jerusalem area. During his last years in Rome, Jerome came to have a strong influence over Roman society, most notably instructing and becoming a spiritual director to a number of upper-class women. One of their number, Paula (347–404), a lady of noble birth, followed Jerome and after visiting the hermits of the Egyptian deserts settled in Jerusalem where she founded three convents, one of which was for monks and nuns. Paula and her daughter Eustochium both had a good knowledge of Hebrew, better according to Jerome than his, and it is likely that they contributed to his translation. Paula gave her wealth to charity for the benefit of the poor, the needy and the sick. Jerome wrote of her in one of his longest letters: "What poor man, as he lay dying, was not wrapped in blankets given by her."[20] Jerome also wrote of her: "If each of my limbs were to be gifted with a human voice, I could still do no justice to the virtues of the holy and venerable Paula."[21] Paula must rank as a person of considerable significance in the emergence of monasticism.

Another eminent Roman woman who came under Jerome's influence was Marcella (325–411). Wealthy and pious, she was widowed after just seven months of marriage. Her palace on the Aventine Hill became a centre of Christian influence. She assembled groups of devout Christian women to live ascetic lives and to study the Scriptures in Hebrew and Greek. Jerome described her as "the glory of her native Rome".[22] "I will praise her", he wrote, "for nothing but the virtue which is her own ... she has sought the true nobility of poverty and lowliness."[23] She suffered severe injuries from which she died when the Goths invaded and captured Rome in 410.

Martin of Tours (316–97) is generally held to be the founder of monasticism in the West. In his early years, he served as a cavalry officer in the Roman army. He came to faith in Christ through the preaching of Hilary (c.315–c.367), who was Bishop of Poitiers from about the year

---

[20] Jerome, *Letter 108 to Eustochium* 5.
[21] Jerome, *Letter 108 to Eustochium* 1.
[22] Jerome, *Letter 127 to Principia* 1.
[23] Jerome, *Letter 127 to Principia* 1.

353. He adhered strongly to the apostolic faith.[24] Tradition asserts that while billeted with the Roman army in Gaul Martin encountered a poor beggar who was suffering in the cold. Out of compassion he cut off half of his cloak and gave it to the unfortunate man. As Martin slept during the following night, he thought he saw Jesus wearing the half of his cloak which he had given to the beggar.[25] With the passing of time, Bishop Hilary made a gift of some land at Marmoutier on which he was able to build a monastery at Ligugé. The monastery, which was begun in 361, became a centre for five other Gallic communities each with their own church and system of pastoral care. Martin made regular visits to them in the summer months.[26] Each community held everything in common and met together each day to share a simple meal. There was strong emphasis on healing,[27] while the younger men focused on transcribing the Scriptures.[28] Martin became a powerful Christian leader, preaching, healing and casting out demons. Sulpicius Severus (362–425), one of his disciples, who completed his *Life of Martin* in 397, wrote that it was inevitable that he should be called to wider service. This moment came in 371 when he was consecrated Bishop of Tours.[29]

Augustine (354–430), not to be confused with Augustine the Roman monk who brought the Christian faith to England in 597, was Bishop of Hippo in North Africa. He too came to have a major influence on the expansion of monasticism across Europe.[30] About the year 400, he wrote *On the Work of Monks*, in which he urged that monks should earn their living by manual labour. As a young man, Augustine was known for his lascivious behaviour and he once prayed, "Lord, give me chastity but not just yet!" He produced a fairly straightforward rule for his monks that

---

[24] C. Donaldson, *Martin of Tours: Parish Priest, Mystic and Exorcist* (London: Kegan Paul, 1985), p. 64.
[25] Donaldson, *Martin of Tours*, pp. 26–7.
[26] Davies, *The Early Christian Church*, p. 249.
[27] Donaldson, *Martin of Tours*, p. 100.
[28] Donaldson, *Martin of Tours*, p. 81.
[29] Donaldson, *Martin of Tours*, pp. 67 and 70.
[30] See Davies, *The Early Christian Church*, p. 247.

included having all things in common, appointed times of prayer, plain dress and obedience to a superior.

John Cassian (360–435) was a monk who lived and worked in Jerusalem. Little is known of his early life, but he was ordained a priest in 405. In 415, he founded a community for women at Marseille and an Abbey at St Victor where he remained as abbot. His most influential work was entitled *Institutes of Monastic Life*, which he compiled between 420 and 429. His book *The Conferences* outlined a strict rule of self-denial in daily living which apparently proved to be too rigorous for some of the younger brothers.

Benedict (480–547) was born at Nursia in Italy and founded a monastery at Monte Cassino. Sometimes referred to as the "Father of Western Monasticism", he wrote the rule which became the established norm for monastic living throughout much of Europe. It marked the end of monks withdrawing on their own in a solitary manner. *The Rule of Benedict* was written about the year 530 and was not overly long, being about 12,000 words. Strictly speaking, Benedict is a little outside the focus of this book, but the fact is he was much impacted by the monastic ideals of Pachomius and Basil of Caesarea.[31] Benedicta Ward has pointed out that the Rule of Benedict explicitly refers to the sayings of the Desert Fathers.[32] Its main element was the practice of obedience. It was written so that those who follow it may "by labour of obedience" return to God "whom they have abandoned by sloth and disobedience". The rule explains there are various categories of obedience. There is obedience of the heart and body to the spiritual counsel extracted from the Gospels. There is obedience to the rule and there is obedience to the abbot.

The rule lay particular emphasis on the quality of obedience. It is "obedience without delay". Whatever is being done must be dropped at once. True obedience is instant and without fear, dawdling or lukewarmness. The rule also includes poverty and the monks were to

---

[31] Lavinia Byrne, *The Life and Wisdom of Benedict* (London: Hodder & Stoughton, 1998), p. 5.
[32] Ward, *The Desert Fathers*, p. xx.

have nothing which they could call their own.³³ The structure of the Benedictine monastic life was built around the daily round of prayers which is based on two biblical pillars: Psalm 119:62, "at midnight I rise to give you thanks" and Psalm 119:164 "seven times a day I praise you."³⁴ The Benedictine rule was not altogether strict. Rule 40 states that "one pint of wine a day is enough for each monk" and the prior is to take care in all things lest satiety or drunkenness creep in.³⁵ Rule 55 prescribed "for bedding, a mattress, a woollen blanket, a woollen under-blanket and a pillow shall suffice".

Monks and their theology

The Church historian Socrates explained that there was one major disagreement between some of the early monastic communities as to whether God has a body. Those who followed Theophilus (*c.*345–412) believed that such was the case and were called "Anthropomorphitae".³⁶ That said, a large number of monks followed in the steps of Anthony and strongly endorsed the Nicaean faith.³⁷ Sozomen recorded that "Anthony's firmness in defending the doctrines of the Nicaean Council were extremely displeasing to the Arians".³⁸

Throughout the first five Christian centuries, there were many godly women who gave wise and exemplary leadership in monastic communities; too many to record in the confines of this chapter. In conclusion, we may note Pulcheria and Olympias. Aelia Pulcheria (399–453) was an Eastern Roman princess who advised her brother, the Emperor Theodosius II, during his minority years.³⁹ She became Empress in 414 and in the same year took a vow of virginity, allegedly

---

[33] *The Rule of Benedict*, p. 33.
[34] *The Rule of Benedict*, p. 15.
[35] *The Rule of Benedict*, p. 40.
[36] Socrates, *Ecclesiastical History* VI.7.
[37] See also Davies, *The Early Christian Church*, p. 321.
[38] Sozomen, *Ecclesiastical History* III.15.
[39] Sozomen, *Ecclesiastical History* IX.1.

to escape being married.[40] However, she impressed the court by her demeanour and wise decisions. She and her sisters turned the imperial palace into a kind of nunnery into which they invited a select group of women. Together they founded several hospitals and a number of churches. Pulcheria is also credited for being one of the founders of the University of Constantinople in 425. She gave her brother a good grounding in theology which enabled him to play a valuable role at the Council of Ephesus in 431. She also attended the Council of Chalcedon in 451, where she was loudly acclaimed by the assembled bishops.

Olympias (c.361–408) was also a wealthy heiress, a citizen of Constantinople and later in her life a friend of Bishop John Chrysostom. A person of influence, she lived under the watchful eye of the Emperor. Her husband died shortly after her marriage, and she immediately took up a celibate lifestyle. She lived in seclusion with a community of more than 200 consecrated women which was based around her house. Olympias offered her services to Archbishop Nectarius (archbishop from 381; d.397), who ordained her as a deacon, even though she was well below the permitted canonical age. During the time of his successor John Chrysostom (c.347–407), Olympias began to devote her giving to the poor and needy rather than to the support of the clergy. Her willingness to accept other women provided a safe haven for many vulnerable women. Her last years were spent in Nicomedia where she died in 408 after a long illness.

An assessment of early monasticism

Clearly there were a number of reasons which prompted people to embark on monastic life. Some believed that friendship and worship of God should include elements of hardship and perhaps even in some cases self-punishment. Monasticism provided a way of avoiding the pull of materialism. For others, monasticism represented a test of their sincerity and commitment to Christ. There were also those who felt that a methodical approach to life was the most obvious way to live.

---

[40] Sozomen, *Ecclesiastical History* IX.1.

Monasteries also provided a refuge from persecution and a securer way of life in a world and Empire in which moral values were degenerating and even collapsing altogether.

The challenges of austerity
Inevitably there were some dysfunctional aspects which stemmed from monastic community life. There were times when monastic communities got into turbulent arguments and needed control. This eventually led to the Council of Chalcedon passing Canon 4 which subjected all monasteries to episcopal control.[41] Some communities appear to have lost the capacity to enjoy the God-given pleasures of life. There was certainly an overemphasis on celibacy. *The Sayings of the Early Christian Fathers* make it clear that many monks struggled with lust and the constant temptation to leave their cells and seek for worldly company.[42] Most of the early hermits appear not to have come to terms with their own sexuality and indeed overlooked the fact that they had been created for sexual intimacy. Socrates recorded that the Egyptian hermit Ammoun "never saw himself naked, because of being accustomed to say that it became not a monk to see even his own person exposed".[43] Among many examples found in the sayings of the Desert Fathers was that of a brother who asked a hermit: "What can I do? My mind is always thinking about fornication; and does not let me rest even for an hour, and my heart is suffering." After some discussion the hermit said: "This is the way to be strong; when temptations start to speak in your mind, do not answer them but get up, pray, do penance, and say 'Son of God have mercy upon me.'"[44] Many monks appear to have had a somewhat harsh and austere image of Jesus. There was an overemphasis on encouraging people to opt out of the world instead of being communities within the world as Jesus had urged his followers.

The lure of the desert nevertheless proved to be a huge ongoing attraction such that by 300 in the Egyptian city of Oxyrhynchus there

---

[41] Davies, *The Early Christian Church*, p. 321.
[42] See Ward, *The Desert Fathers*, pp. 118–22.
[43] Socrates, *Ecclesiastical History* IV.25.
[44] Ward, *The Desert Fathers*, p. 44, para 32.

were said to be 10,000 monks and 20,000 nuns.[45] Many strengths emerged from monastic living. It promoted holiness of living with dedication to prayer, worship and spiritual life. Large numbers of men and women demonstrated that it was possible to live out the Christian faith in simple, practical ways. The monasteries provided a united voice and standard against moral evil and the general laxity of the post-Constantinian years. Many monasteries became centres of learning, copying books and engaging in theological studies. Bishop Martin of Tours established training for clergy in his monastery at Marmoutier. As we have noted, a number of monks gave powerful theological support to the orthodox Catholic Church. Several prominent universities emerged from monastic communities.

Hospitality and healing

Monasteries became significant centres of welcome and hospitality where the poor and needy were cared for. Socrates informs us that Macarius the Great (c.300–90) was always cheerful to his visitors and "performed so many cures and cast out so many devils, that it would require a distinct treatise to record all that the grace of God enabled him to do".[46] *The Rule of Benedict* required that "all guests were to be received as Christ himself; For He himself had said, 'I was a stranger and you took me in.'"[47] The Cappadocian monastic houses in particular pioneered the importance of nursing and care for the sick.

Monasteries gradually became resource centres for mission and evangelism. The latter aspect appears to have issued largely from their practical care rather than by word of mouth and preaching.

In conclusion, there is no doubt that monasticism was a major influence in shaping European society and indeed other distant corners of the Roman Empire. It also gave strong and vital support to the orthodox Catholic Church's theologians in their struggle to defend the teaching of the apostolic Scriptures, the doctrine of the Trinity and the

---

[45] Norman Russell (tr.), *The Lives of the Desert Fathers* (London: Mowbray, Cistercian Publications, 1981), p. 50 cited in Ward, *The Desert Fathers*, p. xx.

[46] Socrates, *Ecclesiastical History* IV.23.

[47] *The Rule of Benedict*, p. 53.

faith of Nicaea and Chalcedon. The monasteries undoubtedly enabled the early Christians and the Church to "more than conquer" the misleading theologies of Arius, Apollinarius, Nestorius and Eutyches.

The study of the lives of the men and women of the desert is important. They and their monastic communities have left a huge legacy of godly living, spirituality and practical care which continues to resource the contemporary Christian churches. The excessive pace of contemporary life is causing many people to seek the quiet of a desert place or retreat. It was for this reason that Catherine de Hueck Doherty pioneered the development of Poustinias from the Russian word meaning "desert".[48] These are small, quiet and isolated places designed for silence and solitude.[49]

---

[48] Catherine de Hueck Doherty, *Poustinia: Christian Spirituality of the East for Western Man* (Notre Dame, IN: Ave Maria Press, 1983).

[49] Hueck, *Poustinia*, p. 21.

14

The furthest corner of the Empire: Christianity in Britain and Ireland

Before the Romans set foot on British soil at some point in the early part of the first century, the major inhabitants of the land were the Celts who had come originally from the area around the Black Sea. It seems likely that some of the military and administrative personnel who were sent to establish the Roman province of Britannia, possibly as early as 50, were practising Christians who shared their faith with their new neighbours. They evangelized and began to establish church life based on the administrative organization of the Roman Empire with its dioceses and parishes. This fact is clear because in 314, after Christianity became officially recognized throughout the Roman Empire, three British bishops represented the English church at the Council of Arles, with the newly converted Emperor Constantine paying their travelling expenses. Among them were Eborius of York, Restitutus from London and Adlephius from Caerleon (possibly Caerleon-on-Usk).

There is evidence of an early Christianity at Water Newton, west of Peterborough, which was one of the great centres of commerce in Roman Britain. A large haul of plate belonging to a Christian church dating from the late-third to early-fourth centuries was found concealed within the town walls in 1975. This included three bowls with engraved Christian symbols, one of which appears to have been used as a chalice, and 19 other items, most with decorative Christian imagery including the Chi-Rho cross. There is a wine bowl inscribed with the words "I Publius, relying on you, honour your holy sanctuary". At Catterick near Hadrian's Wall, a large stone plunge bath with a Chi-Rho monogram on the outside has been found and it is thought it may possibly have been used for baptisms.[1]

At Hinton St Mary in Dorset, a Roman Villa was excavated in 1964. Among other things a mosaic pavement with an image of a clean young man with a Chi-Rho monogram behind his head was revealed. Archaeologists date it as not later than 350. The mosaic has now been reassembled in the British Museum. At Lullingstone in Kent, a house church has been excavated. It has murals which depict people with their arms outstretched in prayer. At Silchester in Hampshire, the remains of a large church building have been uncovered. It was clearly erected after Constantine's conversion and the Edict of Milan's authorization of official church buildings. It is an impressive structure, 42 feet in length and occupying a central place in the middle of the forum. The erection of this building has been put as about 360. This is based on a coin minted between 348 and 353 found in the floor mortar. In addition to Silchester, substantial official Roman church buildings have been found in Colchester dated about 330, at Tower Hill, London (380), at Lincoln at St Paul-in-Bail, Lancaster and at Uley in Gloucestershire.[2]

There is evidence of Christianity at Corinium (Cirencester), where a Christian cryptogram (*rotas, tenet, arepo, sator*—the letters making Pater Noster x2) has been found. There was clearly a Christian settlement in the Roman town of Verulamium where the martyrdom of Alban took place probably in 303. Bede, who is generally held to be a reputable historian, gives a full account, relating that Alban was a layman who gave shelter to a Christian priest who was fleeing from Roman persecutors. When the soldiers arrived Alban, dressed in the priest's cloak, gave himself up and was cruelly put to death on the hill where the abbey church now stands.[3] In the same chapter, Bede gives the names of two other English martyrs, Aaron and Julius who were citizens of legions which may be

---

[1] F. W. Watson, "Christianity in the Roman army", in R. C. P. Hanson (ed.), *Christianity in Britain 300–700* (Leicester: Leicester University Press, 1968), p. 53.

[2] See Malcolm Todd, *Research in Roman Britain*, Britannia Monograph Series 11 (Gloucester: Alan Sutton Publishing Ltd, 1989).

[3] Bede, *Ecclesiastical History of the English People* I.7.

Lincoln.[4] These fragments of history provide sufficient evidence of the early influence in Britain of the Roman and the later Catholic state church of Constantine and Theodosius.

It wasn't until later in 381 when the Emperor Theodosius made Christianity the official religion of the Roman Empire and the bishops of Rome began to increase their influence in a way which would have significantly impacted Britain and Ireland. In fact, the opportunity for Roman influence on the English Church was short, since in 409–10 Rome was invaded by the Goths and the soldiers who were garrisoned in Britain were called back to defend the heart of the Empire and the Eternal City. Yet, even at this point in time, many English churches were still only loosely attached to the practice of the Roman Church and not fully under the authority of its important bishops.[5] Part of the reason for this was that many churches had been founded by Celtic missionaries from Ireland who had a different non-diocesan structure and whose spirituality and pastoral care was markedly different from the Roman tradition. So from an earlier point there were two, sometimes rival church structures, the Roman and the Celtic. The latter was strongly and deeply impacted by the life, teaching and example of Patrick. It wasn't until 597, which is beyond the scope of the present book, that the missionaries led by Augustine of Rome set foot in England with the aim of re-asserting the influence of the Catholic Church.

In the period between 409 and 451, Irish Celtic missionaries began to expand their particular brand of Christianity in Scotland, England and Wales. Much of its character derived from Patrick. Patrick (*c.*389–461)[6] was the son of a British local official who was also a deacon in the church. While still a teenager, Patrick was captured by pirates from his father's farm, which was probably in what is present-day Glamorgan, and taken to Ireland where he was held captive for six years. He eventually escaped to Gaul where he came into contact with the monastic movement under

---

[4] Bede, *Ecclesiastical History of the English People* I.7.
[5] See also A. B. E. Hood, *St Patrick: His Writings and Muirchu's Life* (London: Phillimore, 1978), pp. 5 and 9.
[6] The main sources for Patrick's life are his *Confession* and his *Letter to Coriticus*.

Martin of Tours. He is generally believed to have studied in the monastery of Lérins, possibly between 412 and 415, shortly after which he followed in his father's footsteps and was made a deacon. He eventually returned to Britain and in 432 Germanus, having consecrated him in that year as bishop to work in Ireland following the death of Bishop Palladius. He went to the court of the High King Laoghaire (*d*.458) at Tara, County Meath, where he gained toleration for Christianity despite strong opposition from the Druids. He preached widely in Connaught, Leinster and Meath where he established numerous churches and a number of monastic communities. Following a visit to Rome in 440, he was consecrated archbishop and returned to Ireland in 444 to establish a church hierarchy and a cathedral church at Armagh, which shortly afterwards became an educational, training and administrative centre for the Irish Church.

Ireland at the time of Patrick was a largely rural society with very few large towns. It had never been part of the Roman Empire, so that the country wasn't organized to fit with the secular Roman administrative system of diocese and parish. Patrick therefore developed a more informal strategy which was based on establishing small monastic communities close to the existing scattered village settlements. Here they lived alongside and served the local people in a system in which the abbot or ruler of the monastic community became the leader rather than a bishop. Priests in the Celtic system could be married men. The distinctive Celtic spirituality which emerged from Patrick's Irish missions was rooted in the rural, the domestic and everyday living.

In AD 432, Patrick wrote the *Book of the Law of Moses (Liber Ex Lege Moisi)*, which later came to be used by the local chieftains. The *Liber* still survives in four tenth- and eleventh-century manuscripts and is a distilled compilation of the Law of Moses. It covers matters of diet and following ceremonial law many Celtic Christians among other things did not eat pork. It also included guidelines about when a woman is unclean, and when a married couple might have sexual relations. Money lending had to be in accordance with Jewish practice and tithes had to be paid to the church in the same way that offerings were made to the Jewish temple. The *Liber* also had a detailed penitential system involving restitution which had to be carried out for breaches of law.

Thus, from the time of Patrick, a large number of Celtic congregations emerged in the British Isles which were largely independent of the Roman Church. They were remarkable for their distinctive spirituality, evangelism, church planting and monastic communities on account of which they grew and expanded rapidly. Significantly, many of the Saxons who invaded Britain following the departure of the Roman armies were themselves converted to Celtic Christianity.

The spread of Celtic Christianity

The Celts spread their brand of Christianity so effectively on account of their many forthright pioneer evangelists. They were men and women of prayer and compassion and a heart for the poor. In addition to Patrick, there were many other able and saintly evangelists and leaders. Among them was Ninian (*c.*360–*c.*432),[7] an English monk who studied under Martin at Marmoutier in France. He was consecrated as a bishop in 394 and came to Britain as a missionary about the year 397. He eventually settled at Whithorn in Galloway, where he founded a monastery which became a training base and from which he and his monks sought to convert their neighbouring Britons and the Picts. Following the example of Jesus whose works incarnated his words, the Celts evangelized with signs and wonders. Patrick wrote: "It is our duty to fish well and diligently, as the Lord urges and teaches us, saying: 'Follow me, and I shall make you fishers of men' (Matthew 4:19) . . . And so it was our bounden duty to spread our nets, so that a vast multitude and throng might be caught for God and there might be clergy everywhere to baptize and exhort a people that was poor and needy."[8]

Doctrine and worship
The Celts were thoroughly immersed in the Scriptures of the Old and New Testament and were avid copyists of the Bible and biblical

---

[7] There are two main sources for Ninian's life: Bede's *Ecclesiastical History* and a more elaborate but less reliable twelfth-century *Life of Ninian* by Ailred.
[8] Patrick, *Confession* 20.

commentaries. Patrick's *Confession* typifies the Celtic devotion to the Scriptures, being full of biblical references. Patrick was emphatic that he sought only to follow what was written in the Scriptures. He wrote: "The words are not mine, but of God and the apostles and prophets who have never lied."[9] In all matters of theology and morality, the Celts were thoroughly grounded in the Scriptures. The rules which were followed in Celtic monastic houses were also based in Scripture. The monk and missionary Aidan of Lindisfarne (*d*.651) taught his monks to meditate on the Scriptures and learn the Psalms as they walked through the countryside of northern Britain. The Celts used many of their songs as a vehicle to teach doctrine and this was particularly helpful as a means of instruction for those who were not able to read.

Although the Celts had a vivid sense of the presence of Jesus, they also thought of God the Father in strong and majestic terms. Indeed, in Patrick's Breastplate, he is described as "the High King of Heaven" and Celtic Christians approached him with a sense of awe and wonder. The Celts had a strong doctrine of the Trinity with a deep sense of the Holy Spirit's presence in their lives. Their pagan background, in which triads featured, may well have helped them to grasp the Trinity more easily than those who encountered Christianity in the Roman Empire. When Patrick was once asked by some Irish princesses to explain the doctrine of the Trinity, he didn't enter into a theological discussion but simply bent down and picked up a shamrock and pointed to its three leaves growing on one stem.[10] The Celtic understanding of the Trinity is clearly articulated in his Breastplate hymn:

> I bind unto myself today
> The strong name of the Trinity
> By invocation of the same
> The three in One and One in Three.

---

[9] L. Hardinge, *The Celtic Church in Britain* (London: SPCK, 1968), pp. 25–9.
[10] Ian Bradley, *The Celtic Way* (London: Darton, Longman & Todd, 1993), p. 44.

Patrick urged that with "faith in the Trinity . . . we ought to spread God's name everywhere confidently and fearlessly".[11]

The Celts seem to have had a high regard for baptism. Celtic bishops were wont to speak of baptism as "the waters of salvation for the forgiveness of sins"[12] and of being "cleansed in the life-giving waters of baptism".[13] Families were baptized on conversion and babies soon after birth. Baptism was in the name of the Trinity and in the flowing water of a river if possible.

The Celts were a sacramental people who knew the immanent presence of the Lord in all aspects of their living. They were able to drink in the presence of God while they worked, walked through the countryside or joined in common meals. The Eucharist was an important part of their sacramental living which they sometimes celebrated in the open air. They valued the Eucharist at special moments in their life. Singing also played an important part in Celtic life and worship. The Celtic Christians loved to sing while they were out walking in the open countryside or while they engaged in manual labour in the monastic community. Singing, particularly antiphonal singing, was central to the monastic worship.

Spirituality

The Celts were people of the Spirit. Patrick, for example, related at the beginning of his Confession that Jesus "poured out on us abundantly His Holy Spirit, the gift and pledge of immortality, who makes those who believe and obey to be sons of God and heirs along with Christ".[14] Patrick related how when he first reached Ireland as a captive, he was able to pray before dawn in all weathers, snow, frost and rain "because the Spirit was fervent within me".[15] On occasion, Patrick was profoundly conscious of the Holy Spirit praying from deep within his own spirit. His description of this experience is not dissimilar from that recounted by people who

---

[11] Patrick, *Confession* 14.
[12] Bede, *Ecclesiastical History of the English People* V.6.
[13] Bede, *Ecclesiastical History of the English People* V.6.
[14] Patrick, *Confession* 4.
[15] Patrick, *Confession* 16.

pray in tongues or who enter a state of constant intercession by praying the Jesus Prayer. Patrick related:

> I saw Him praying within me and I was, as it were, inside my own body and I heard His above me, that is to say above my inner self, and He was praying there powerfully and groaning; and meanwhile I was dumbfounded and astonished and wondered who it could be that was praying with me, but at the end of the prayer He spoke and said, that He was the Spirit ... The Spirit helps the weakness of our prayer, for we do not know what to pray for as we ought; but the Spirit Himself intercedes for us with unspeakable groans which cannot be expressed in words (Romans 8:26) and again: 'The Lord our advocate intercedes for us' (1 John 2:1).[16]

Celtic Christians were people of prayer. They prayed constantly throughout the day often in short one-sentence prayers. As far as the Celtic Christians were concerned, nothing was too small to pray about and no situation too insignificant to bring God into. They knew what George Herbert was later to discover and articulate in his hymn "Teach me, my God and King, in all things Thee to see, and what I do in anything to do it as for Thee". In his *Confession* Patrick related:

> ... after I had come to Ireland I used to feed cattle, and I prayed frequently during the day; the love of God and the fear of Him increased more and more, and faith became stronger, and the Spirit was stirred; so that in one day I said about a hundred prayers, and in the night nearly the same; so that I used to remain in the woods and in the mountains; before daylight I used to rise to prayer, through snow, through frost, through rain and felt no harm; nor was there any slothfulness in me, as I perceive, because the Spirit was then fervent within me.[17]

---

[16] Patrick, *Confession* 25.
[17] Patrick, *Confession* 16.

The result of this was that Celtic Christians had a very vivid sense of the presence of Jesus with them. This sense of God's omnipresence is very marked in Patrick's celebrated Breastplate:

> Christ be with me, Christ within me,
> Christ behind me, Christ before me,
> Christ beside me, Christ to win me,
> Christ to comfort and restore me,
> Christ beneath me, Christ above me,
> Christ in quiet, Christ in danger,
> Christ in hearts of all that love me,
> Christ in mouth of friend and stranger.

An important aspect of Celtic prayers was blessings. These included blessings for special occasions such as baptisms, journeys and death but also prayers said over everyday domestic situations. Ian Bradley noted that among other Celtic prayers were blessings for the house, for taking a bath, for hatching eggs, clipping sheep and tending the loom.[18] Celtic spirituality was a spirituality of the everyday, which caused Bradley to remark that "one of the most important lessons we can learn from the Celts is to reinvest the ordinary with a measure of sanctity, to value again the importance of little things and to find God once more in the trivial round, the common task".[19]

The Celts' spirituality was rooted in the creation for which they had both a great love and a healthy respect. They enjoyed the elements to the full. If God had seen fit to bless the earth with wind and rain, they were happy to walk in it and pray as they did so. They understood that human beings need to have a delicate and close relationship with the natural world around them. They sought to glorify God by valuing and appreciating his creation. They did not, however, confuse God and his creation or see them submerged into one another as certain elements of the New Age movement have done. The Celts did not regard the created world as a living, self-regulating being, which many new agers call "Gaia",

---

[18] Bradley, *The Celtic Way*, p. 49.
[19] Bradley, *The Celtic Way*, p. 39.

the Earth Goddess. The Celts did, however, strongly emphasize God's being immanent or very present in his creation.

It seems that the Celts also took seriously the command to rest as an important part of their spirituality. The Celtic Church kept their Lord's Day or Sabbath as the Jews did from Friday night to Saturday night and then worshipped on Sunday with no restrictions about working or making journeys. Patrick records in his *Letter* that on one occasion when he was resting on the Lord's Day on the seashore by the salt marsh, a short distance from the place known as the Ox's Neck, he was disturbed "by a noisy din coming from pagans who were working on the Lord's Day making a rampart". Patrick remonstrated with them, but they paid no heed. He rebuked their leader, Mudebrod, saying: "However much you work, may it get you nowhere." So it proved during the following night when rough seas destroyed their work.[20]

Art, particularly copying of manuscripts and decorative design, was an important aspect of Celtic spirituality. They delighted in intricate patterns and knots and were famous for their beautifully carved stone crosses. Pagan art forms and culture were transformed for the glory of God.

The prophetic

The Celtic congregations displayed a marked concern to listen to what they took to be the voice and instruction of the Lord and to follow it through in their actions. In his *Confession*, Patrick recounted eight visions which he saw in dreams, all of which were direct messages from God. The most vivid and most important in so far as the direction of his life was concerned was his call to return to Ireland and proclaim the gospel. Patrick described it in terms which resemble the apostle Paul's Macedonian call in Acts 16:9:

> And then I saw, indeed, in the gloom of the night, a man coming as it were from Ireland, Victorinus by name, with innumerable letters, and he gave one of them to me... And while I was reading aloud the beginning of the letter, I myself thought indeed in my mind that I heard the voice of those who were near the wood of

---

[20] Muirchu, *Life of Patrick* 24.

Foclut, which is close by the sea. And they cried out thus as if with one voice, 'We entreat you, holy youth, that you come, and henceforth walk among us'.[21]

At another point in his *Confession*, Patrick tells us that he was frequently warned and guided by prophecy.[22]

Spiritual conflict

The Celtic missionaries were acutely aware that extending God's kingdom was a battle against unseen and sometimes dark forces. Whilst it is true that they have often been praised because they did not destroy the culture of those to whom they preached the Christian message, they certainly did not go along with beliefs and practices they found to be incompatible with orthodox teaching. Indeed they were always at the ready to stand against pagan powers and strongholds. This is nowhere better seen than in Patrick's confrontations with the Druids who were based at their stronghold in Tara. He and his companions incurred the wrath of their king by their presence in the area. As one of the king's henchmen came out to meet Patrick, reviling the name of Jesus and the Trinity as he walked, Patrick called out to the Lord in a loud voice to destroy the man who was indeed, according to Muirchu, smitten and died.[23] Patrick recorded another occasion during his labours in Ireland when he was attacked by the devil, writing in his *Confession*: "I was asleep, and Satan attacked me violently, something which I shall remember as long as I am in this body; and there fell on top of me a huge rock, as it were, and I was completely paralysed." However, after shouting out, aided by Christ and his Spirit, he was set at liberty.[24]

Celtic Christians developed a range of strategies and rituals to invoke God's protective powers against evil and danger. At such moments, some Celts would draw a circle round themselves and their loved ones or using their index fingers they would point and turn round sun-wise

---

[21] Patrick, *Confession* 23.
[22] Patrick, *Confession* 35.
[23] Muirchu, *Life of Patrick* 17.
[24] Patrick, *Confession* 20.

reciting a prayer of protection.[25] The breastplate prayers, of which the one attributed to Patrick is the most well known, seek in a similar way to surround those who pray with the protective clothing of God. This of course has clear scriptural precedent in Ephesians 6:10–18. The verses from Patrick's Breastplate illustrate the wide range of powers which the Celts invoked for protection; the strong name of the Trinity, the life, death and resurrection of Jesus, the angelic hosts, the faith of the confessors and the word of the apostles. It has even been suggested that the pattern known as the Celtic knot was designed and used to ward off the devil's powers.

Monastic houses

A key feature of Celtic Christianity was the importance of monastic houses. A frequent Celtic mission strategy was to ask permission from the local leader if they could live near the local Druid community. They would then build a small monastic settlement, often on the Egyptian model, from which they would serve the neighbourhood who in time would come to embrace the Christian faith. In this way, sometimes whole communities believed and were baptized together with their children. The Celts believed in belonging before believing, and it often was the case that pagans came to faith simply as a result of being served and cared for in very practical ways. The Celts developed the monastery as a hub which could function as a worshipping and caring community, a place for instruction and training and a base from which to reach out into the surrounding community. Much of this vision came from Patrick, the principal apostle of Ireland who encouraged monasticism for both men and women. Indeed, monks who were trained in Ireland began to find their way to both England and Scotland. The central place given to the monastery was ideal in Ireland, which was a country without towns and which had never been part of the Roman Empire. It therefore never had the Roman civil government structure of dioceses into which the post-Constantinian Church so easily fitted.

Because of this absence of towns, the Irish episcopate did not flourish. Irish society was essentially tribal with the extended family as its essential

---

[25] See Bradley, *The Celtic Way*, p. 47.

unit. When a family became Christian, it was natural for it to stay together, and it was from this that the early Irish monastic communities developed. These were of several different types. There were often large numbers of married people, still part of their family unit but attached to the monastery and engaging in agricultural or craftsmanship of one kind or another. This system, which was established by Columba in Iona on the west coast of Scotland, was certainly different from the Roman system where the town at the centre of the local diocese served as the hub from which training and evangelism emanated. This was the place where the bishop had his cathedra or chair and from which the surrounding area was pastored and evangelized. Ian Bradley wrote:

> The Celtic missionaries had a wholly different attitude towards those with whom they were seeking to share the light of Christ. For them evangelism was more a matter of liberating and releasing the divine spark which was already there in every person than imposing a new external creed. They did not see the primal pagan religion of the people as a threat to Christianity or a dangerous heresy to be eliminated. Rather it represented, however imperfectly, a stirring of the spiritual and a reaching to the eternal.[26]

Theology

During the history of Christianity in the period down to 451, there was one major theological controversy which came about through the teaching of Pelagius (355–420), a Welsh monk who was attached to a monastery at Bangor. He was described as a well-educated Romanized Briton. About the year 380, he left Britain's shores and never returned. He was a godly, much-loved, gracious man who was respected wherever he went. He arrived in Rome about 384 and was appalled at the lax state of behaviour. He later journeyed on with his follower and disciple Caelestius to North Africa where he met with Augustine, Bishop of Hippo, who proved to be his major opponent. Pelagius strove to encourage Christians

---

[26] Bradley, *The Celtic Way*, p. 94.

in particular to be the best they could be and to bear witness against corruption, wealth and injustice.

The heart of the matter which concerned Pelagius was the issue of choice and for this reason he wrote a book entitled *The Freedom of the Will*. In it he claimed that to assert that God made men and women with an inbuilt bias to do what is evil and wrong was to denigrate the justice of God. He argued that there must be in every person an unbiased equal power of choosing between good and evil. If there isn't, he argued, there can be no such thing as sin or guilt.

Pelagius' opponent, Augustine, countered stating that man is not free to choose. His view was one of rigid predestination in which we are either governed by grace or sin. Without grace we can only choose evil. In his *On the Gift of Perseverance*, he expressed it as follows:

> Will any man presume to say that God did not foreknow those to whom he would grant belief? And if he foreknew this, then he certainly foreknew his own kindness, with which he vouch saves to deliver us. This, and nothing but this, is predestination of the saints; namely, the foreknowledge and planning of God's kindness, by which they are surely delivered, whoever are delivered. As for the rest, where are they left by God's righteous judgement save in the mass of perdition where they of Tyre and Sidon were left? And they moreover, would have believed, had they seen the miracles of Christ. But it was not granted to them to believe, and therefore the means of believing was denied them.[27]

Pelagius was therefore against anything that might invalidate free will and Augustine opposed to anything that might smack of human merit. Augustine taught that in Adam everyone sinned and that the punishment of that sin was passed down from one generation to another to all in the human race. In response, Pelagius was of the view that Adam's sin did not affect his descendants. In fact, he went further and argued that it was possible for man to live without sin and that some people had even

---

[27] Augustine, *On the Gift of Perseverance* (*De Dono Perseverantiae*) 35.

managed to achieve this. Pelagius was vehement that the only way not to become captivated by sin is by not following in Adam's footsteps.

Later in their disputes, Augustine introduced the issue of infant baptism which was then widely practised in many churches. He asked why was it that infants were baptized with exorcisms in which the devil was either renounced or cast out? This was surely proof that they were infected with sin. As J. N. D. Kelly put it, "He believed that taint was propagated from parent to child by the physical act of generation, or rather as a result of the carnal excitement which accompanied it."[28] Pelagius' response was that infants were baptized not to purge them from original sin but to impart to them higher sanctification through union with Christ.

At this point, we see the clear contrast between Pelagius' and Augustine's experience of the Christian faith. They represent the tension between those who insist that without the divine assistance of special grace it is impossible to please God and those who believe, as Pelagius did, that God's gift of common grace is given to all. Pelagius steadfastly rejected any idea of special grace influencing believers to choose good. There had to be an equal opportunity for everyone to do good. In the final analysis, when it came to salvation, Pelagius was of the view that salvation is accomplished by good works, while for Augustine salvation is by grace alone and it is the gift of God that prevenient grace is given only to the elect that they may embrace it. As far as Augustine was concerned, only the elect can be saved.

The dispute had a very wide impact on the churches of the Empire including those in Britain. It was finally brought to a head and condemned by the Council of Carthage in 411. Pelagius was in Jerusalem at the time and defended himself but was then condemned at the Second Council of Carthage in 418. Pelagius had little inclination to continue the struggle and disappears from history with his last days unknown. Augustine died in 430.

This was not the end of the matter, however, as Pelagianism continued to spread in Britain where it took a stronghold through the teaching of Agricola who receives a passing mention in Book 1 of Bede's *Ecclesiastical*

---

[28] Kelly, *Early Christian Doctrines*, p. 365.

History of the English People. Bede relates that the English bishops became so anxious about the spread of Pelagianism in the English churches that they persuaded two French bishops, Germanus, Bishop of Auxere (418–48) and Lupas of Troyes (427–79), to come to England and help combat the heresy. The controversy continued in Gaul during the fifth century.[29]

Pelagianism never completely died away. Indeed, in the Middle Ages it strongly revived, powerfully influencing the life and theology of the Roman Church whose doctrine of salvation came to be deeply rooted in a system of good works which included attendance at the sacrament of the Mass, fasting, penance, pilgrimage and the adoration of sacred relics. Pelagianism, it should be noted in conclusion, was condemned in the Church of England *Article 9 Of Original or Birth Sin* of the *Articles of Religion*:

> Original sin standeth not in the following of Adam, (as the Pelagians do vainly talk;) but it is the fault and corruption of the Nature of every man, that naturally is ingenedered of the offspring of *Adam*; whereby man is very far gone from original righteousness, and is of his own nature inclined to evil, so that the flesh lusteth always contrary to the Spirit; and therefore in every person born into this world, it deserveth God's wrath and damnation. And this infection of nature doth yet remain, yea in them that are regenerated.

---

[29] Bede, *Ecclesiastical History of the English People* I.17.

1 5

More than conquerors: Churches and the Christians in the mid-fifth century

Neither Christians nor the Church can remain static; both are living entities and are constantly interacting with their surrounding society. Inevitably therefore both will find it necessary to express their faith in cultural terms which the people of their age can appreciate, readily access and understand. So while beliefs about God, salvation and other core apostolic doctrine cannot be changed, they may need to be re-explained and restated using images and metaphors that are appropriate and relevant to each succeeding age and society. In this interaction, the Church will impact the surrounding culture which in turn will shape the Church's worship, beliefs and organization. It may indeed bring about developments in doctrine. In such cases, as was seen in many of the conciliar debates of the third and fourth centuries, the challenge for the Church was, and always will be, to ensure that any such changes are in keeping with the teaching of Jesus and his apostles.

The place of Christian worship—from houses to public buildings

As has already been noted, in New Testament times Christian worship took place almost exclusively in houses. These would most likely have been homes where the head of the family was a Christian.[1] As the Church grew in numbers, larger houses sometimes became the base where

---

[1] See Chapter 1.

slightly larger groups gathered for Sunday worship. Such was the church at Dura Europos in Syria which was a place of worship from about the year 233. It has a baptistery and frescos of the Good Shepherd, the healing of the paralytic, and Peter and Jesus walking on the water. The oldest known church in Rome dates from about 140 and lies beneath the present church of Santa Pudenziana al Viminale on the Esquiline Hill. There are remains of several other early Christian house churches which have been unearthed beneath present-day church buildings in Rome. Among them is the house church of Clement which lies beneath the existing church of San Clemente close to the Colosseum.

During the first three centuries, Christians suffered harsh and bitter treatment at the hands of the persecuting Roman authorities. In consequence, they were forced to worship in secret and away from the public eye. Most Christians gathered in the homes belonging to believers, often before dawn when the rest of the world was sleeping. Finally, after almost three centuries of persecution the Emperor Constantine became a Christian, the first Roman Emperor to do so. He met with Licinius, the Eastern Emperor, and with him issued the *Edict of Milan* in 313 which "guaranteed that Christians and all others should have freedom to follow the kind of religion they favoured without any hindrance". For the first time, public buildings for Christian worship were allowed by Imperial decree.[2] The fourth-century church historian Eusebius wrote of "large churches springing up all over the Empire in important cities". These buildings included basilicas such as St John Lateran in Rome, the Church of the Holy Sepulchre in Bethlehem, and other places of worship at sites where martyrdoms such as those of the apostles Peter and Paul had taken place. Many of the church buildings that were erected in the countryside across the entire Roman Empire were inevitably smaller in size and were patterned on Roman houses. The atrium became the space where people gathered and the eating area with the family table became what was later known as the sanctuary where the Eucharist was shared.

---

[2] *Edict of Milan*, 313 in Lactantius, *On the Death of the Persecutors* 48, in Bettenson, *Documents of the Christian Church*, pp. 15–16.

The style of worship—from informality to structure

Numbers attending home-based worship in most instances must have been small, probably a mere cluster of ten or a dozen people. The atmosphere would have been relaxed, informal and participatory with people sharing personal experience and discussing the meaning and application of the Scripture they had been reading. There would have been breaking of bread, singing and those present invited to share their needs, offer prayers and contribute words of encouragement. If a prepared homily was given, it would probably have been short and interactive.

However, these small home-based churches became a feature of the past during Constantine's rule. The more spacious buildings which soon came to be erected made it possible for larger groups of people to gather for worship and this meant that spontaneity and informal sharing was often no longer practicable. Structure and order were now the order of the day so that things didn't get out of hand. This in turn led to the development of more ordered, detailed and theological liturgies. Prepared homilies would probably not have been widespread or appropriate in house churches, particularly in times of persecution. That said, Hippolytus (*c.*170–*c.*236), a theologian and church leader in Rome, gave details of the liturgy with which he was familiar, and it included a sermon. Tertullian, another early theologian, wrote and published sermons.

Credal statements

As was noted in the first chapter, it is clear that the early churches made use of short statements of faith which were read or spoken out at times of public worship. By the close of the second century, there were a number of sects such as the Gnostics, Montanists and the Monarchians whose teachings challenged the apostolic faith. It therefore became necessary for Christians to know what they believed. Essentials of the faith were written down, circulated and began to feature at Sunday worship and at baptisms and burials. Some of these early statements of the apostolic faith were gradually collected together and became known as *The Rule of Faith*. It is likely that Irenaeus made use of it in *Against Heresies* to distinguish the orthodox apostolic traditions from those to which the heretics were appealing.[3]

With the passing of the years there emerged what became known as *The Apostles' Creed*, so called not because it was dictated by the apostles, but because it reflected apostolic teaching. Like the later creeds which followed it, the Apostles' Creed is Trinitarian in structure with paragraphs addressed to the Father, Son and Holy Spirit. Its actual title is first found about the year 390 in the writings of Ambrose (*c.*339–97), Bishop of Milan,[4] though it must have been in evidence well before that time. Other more developed Trinitarian Creeds emerged in the wake of Arianism. *The Nicaean Creed* was drawn up in 325 at Nicaea in embryo form and included the word *homoousios,* asserting Jesus to be the same substance as the Father. It was officially updated and endorsed by the Council of Constantinople in 381 as *The Nicene Creed* at the behest of the Emperor Theodosius the Great. *The Athanasian Creed,* which differs from the Apostles' Creed and the Nicene Creed, was also used in many of the Western churches. It did not find acceptance in the Eastern churches who could not accept the "filioque clause", *filioque* meaning "and the Son". The Western Church had added the words "and the son" to convey their conviction that the Holy Spirit was sent by both the Father and the Son. The Eastern Church did not accept this as they held that it made the Spirit appear to be less than the Father and the Son. The corporate recitation of the creeds was viewed as far more than a mere statement of orthodoxy, the early churches regarding it as being a spiritual declaration of truth to the pagan world which helped disperse the darkness of error and unbelief.

---

[3] Irenaeus, *Against Heresies* I.9.4.
[4] Ambrose, *Letter 42*, para 5.

Leaders of worship and church life

As was seen in the first chapter, during the earlier years of the first century the apostles oversaw the Church's ministry. Wherever new churches were formed, for the most part they followed the synagogue pattern and appointed presbyters to lead, teach and give pastoral care and deacons to take on the practical and administrative work. All leaders and their roles are to some extent influenced and shaped by the cultures of which they are a part. It comes as no surprise that Edward Schillebeeckx felt compelled to argue that in using the title "presbyter" for its leaders the early churches were drawing on a term which was also used of a civic functionary in the Roman Empire.[5] In his view, the office of elder was modelled on Roman administrators.

Ministries and prophets

During the first two centuries, the ministry of presbyters (elders) and deacons appears to have overlapped or been supplemented by a fivefold ministry of apostles, prophets, pastors, teachers and evangelists, as outlined in Paul's Letter to the Ephesians.[6] There has been some debate as to whether these were ministries or functions which leaders were to perform or whether they were also particular offices. The evidence seems to be both. There were certainly elders who had a prophetic ministry and as well as their leadership role. *The Didache*, an early second-century church manual, gives instructions regarding prophets. "A genuine prophet", it states, "who wishes to make his home with you has a right to a livelihood."[7] That said, warning is also given that "not all who speak in the spirit are prophets, unless they also exhibit the manners and conduct of the Lord".[8] It is by their behaviour that you can tell the impostor from the true. The office of prophet remained an important one almost to the end of the second century, at which point it ceased to have a prominent

---

[5] Edward Schillebeeckx, *The Church with A Human Face* (London: SCM Press, 1985), p. 126.
[6] Ephesians 4:11.
[7] *Didache* 13.
[8] *Didache* 11.

role. This was probably brought about by groups such as the Montanists who specialized in ecstatic prophecies which were held to be from the mouth of God but turned out to be false. Such was true of Montanus who, with his two women co-leaders Prisca and Maximilla, declared that the world would end in 185 with Christ returning at Pepusa.[9]

Deacons

There are references to deacons in the letters of both Clement and Ignatius. Writing about 97, Clement speaks of the apostles appointing deacons.[10] About the year 110, we find mention of bishops and deacons in the letters of Ignatius.[11] He speaks of deacons "as entrusted with the service of Jesus Christ" suggesting that their main ministry was one of practical and pastoral care rather than evangelism, leading in worship and teaching.[12] That said, Justin Martyr, writing at Rome about 150, stated that deacons took consecrated bread and wine to the sick and those in prison. It is evident that some deacons exercised congregational leadership roles and must have presided at the Eucharist. Indeed, the Council of Nicaea in 325 ruled that deacons should no longer be permitted to preside over the Eucharist.[13] This may not have been widely adhered to since the Council of Laodicea meeting in 352 ruled that "Presbytides, as they are called, or female presidents are not to be appointed in the church".[14] Women were clearly still holding leadership roles in the Church of the fifth century; the Council of Chalcedon in 451 ruled on the subject of women deacons: "No woman under forty years of age is to be ordained a Deacon and then only after close scrutiny." It also added a further ruling that "If after receiving ordination and spending some time in the ministry she despises God's grace and gets married, such a person is to be anathematized along

---

[9] Eusebius, *History of the Church* V.16f.
[10] Clement, *First Letter to the Corinthians* 42.
[11] See Ignatius, *Letter to the Trallians* 2; *Letter to the Philippians* 1.
[12] Ignatius, *Letter to the Magnesians* 6.
[13] Chadwick, *The Early Church*, p. 48.
[14] *Council of Laodicea*, Canon XI. See Sally Hogg, *Invisible Women: A History of Women in the Church* (lulu.com, 2011), p. 96.

with her spouse." The Canon clearly indicates that some women were officially ordained to certain roles within the Church.[15]

Presbyters

In New Testament times, "bishop" and "elder" were interchangeable terms. In his Letter to Titus, for example, Paul instructed Titus to appoint "elders" (*presbuteroi*) in every town[16] and then went on to refer to them individually as "the bishop" (*episkopos*).[17] The word "priest", a contraction of the Greek word *presbyteros*, is not used specifically of Christian minsters in the New Testament, though it is applied to the Christian body as a whole.[18] Irenaeus, for example, wrote of "all just men belonging to the sacerdotal order",[19] and Tertullian declared: "Are not all priests? It is written: 'He has also made us a kingdom of priests to God and his Father' ... for where there is no bench of clergy you offer and baptize and are your own sole priest. For where there are three, there is a church, though they be laymen."[20] Origen also asserted that "all Christians are a sacerdotal race".[21] The idea of a priestly ministry emerged later in the third century with the gradual development of a sacrificial understanding of the Eucharist based on the Old Testament ideas of priesthood. The presbyters of the New Testament do not seem to have been referred to as priests (*sacerdotes*) until the time of Cyprian (*d*.258), a Bishop of Carthage, who was a champion of sacerdotalism.[22]

Bishops and priests

During times of intense persecution in the second century, it became necessary for the early churches to have leaders who could answer to

---

[15] This is not referring to deacons or priests. See Hogg, *Invisible Women*, p. 78.
[16] Titus 1:5.
[17] Titus 1:7.
[18] 1 Peter 2:5 and Revelation 5:10.
[19] Irenaeus, *Against Heresies* IV.8.3.
[20] Tertullian, *Exhortation to Chastity* 7. At the time of writing this, Tertullian had joined the Montanists.
[21] Origen, *Letter 8*.
[22] Cyprian, *Letter 61*.

the authorities and act as custodians of the faith. Presbyters and laity therefore elected representatives from their own number to act on their behalf.[23] With the passing of time, these duly appointed leaders became a separate office and ministry which was spoken of as monarchical episcopacy. In this way, bishops and presbyters (later called priests) became two separate orders of ministry. Schillebeeckx suggests that after this distinction between bishop and presbyter occurred, a shift took place in the image and role of the latter. Presbyters now began to be spoken of as "priests". This change in emphasis became clear for all to see in the fourth century.[24] With the passing of time the role of the priest became increasingly formal and authoritarian. About 381, Bishop John Chrysostom (c.347–407) wrote in *On the Priesthood*: "God has given greater power to priests than to natural parents, not only for punishment, but also for help."[25] He also listed other functions of priesthood as "instruction, warning and prayer" and "remitting sins and praying for the sick".[26] Chrysostom also spoke of the priest being like a father. "The priest", he wrote, "should treat those he rules as a father treats very young children."[27] The distinction between clergy and laity didn't become clear until the middle years of the second century. And it wasn't until Constantine's time in the early third century that priests and other clergy began to wear distinctive dress. Dom Gregory Dix asserted that "the earliest mention of specifically religious garments in Christian worship is 330".[28] In later years, particularly after Constantine's conversion, the Church's ministry solidified into what came to be known as the threefold order of Catholic ministry of bishops, priests and deacons.

Strangely, it would appear that in early days presbyters made bishops by election, but in later days bishops came to make presbyters in a ceremony known as ordination. Monarchical bishops grew in importance as they

---

[23] On some occasions, Constantine tried to remove the rights of the people in the appointment of bishops.

[24] Schillebeeckx, *The Church with a Human Face*, p. 140.

[25] John Chrysostom, *On the Priesthood* III.4.

[26] John Chrysostom, *On the Priesthood* III.4.

[27] John Chrysostom, *On the Priesthood* IV.6.

[28] Gregory Dix, *The Shape of the Liturgy* (London: Dacre, 1943), p. 399.

came to be viewed as guardians of the apostolic faith. Tertullian wrote that the churches were able to guarantee their orthodoxy with their lists showing a continuous unbroken line of their bishops going right back "to one of the apostles or one of the apostolic men who, though not an apostle continued with the apostles".[29] Cyprian was of the same opinion which he expressed in stronger terms:

> Our Lord, whose precepts and admonitions we are bound to observe, ordered the high office of bishop and the system of his Church when he speaks in the Gospel and says to Peter, 'You are Peter, etc.' (Matthew 16:18–19) ... Thence age after age has followed bishop in succession, and the office of the episcopate and the system of the Church has been handed down, so that the Church is founded on the bishops and every act of the Church is directed by the same presiding officers.[30]

Cyprian went further in a subsequent letter, writing, "You should know that the bishop is in the Church and the Church is in the bishop, and that if anyone be not with the bishop he is not in the Church."[31] After becoming a Christian, Constantine soon recognized that there were many thousands of Christians all over the Empire, even as far away as Britain, who respected their bishops and Christian leaders. The politician in him soon recognized that they could assist in the running and administration of the Empire. So he raised the status of the bishops of large towns and cities to "Metropolitan" and in some cases to that of senior government officials. Bishops became in effect the Emperor's administrators.

Following Constantine's time as Emperor there was a slow but gradual increase in both the secular and spiritual power of the episcopal office. This was particularly visible in the ministry of Ambrose of Milan (339–97). Elected to office in 374, he has been described as marking "the dawn of an era when a new kind of bishop entered the episcopal ranks,

---

[29] Tertullian, *On Prescription against Heretics* (*De Praescriptione Haereticorum*) 32.
[30] Cyprian, *Letter* 36.1.
[31] Cyprian, *Letter* 68.8.

that recruited from the Roman senatorial aristocracy".[32] In 386, Ambrose's dominance was demonstrated when the Emperor Valentinian, an Arian sympathizer, summoned him to the Imperial Court and demanded the use of the Basilica Portiana on the outskirts of the city for use at Easter by the Arian Bishop Auxentius. In response, Ambrose summoned the people of the city who marched to the church and prevented the Emperor from using it. The utterances of John Chrysostom (c.347–407) demonstrate that the bishops of the Church had moved even further from Jesus' stress on humility and servanthood. He declared: "Prefects and city magistrates do not enjoy such honour as the magistrate of the church; for if he enters the palace, who ranks the highest, or among the matrons, or among the houses of the great? No-one is honoured before him."[33]

Ordinations

Significantly ordination began to emerge and develop in the late second century; the word "ordination" coming from the Latin *ordinarius* meaning a "magistrate". Each local *paroikia* or parish, the smallest administrative unit of the Roman Empire, had its own chosen or elected magistrate. Ordination was simply a ceremony for making a magistrate. The literal meaning of *paroikia* meant the area alongside (*para*) the house (*oikos*); it referred to the magistrate's house. The early Christians began to follow suit and over time established a parallel ceremony for making a presbyter. The earliest known Christian ordination rite is found in *The Apostolic Tradition of Hippolytus*, which is dated about the year 215. In it, prayer is made that each candidate "be given the grace and counsel of the presbyterate, so that he might help and govern the people with a pure heart".[34] Later ordination rites are found in the *Liturgy of Serapion* and *The Apostolic Constitutions*. Cyprian, Bishop of Carthage, wrote a letter about the year 265 to the clergy and people of Spain. It concerned the ordination of two bishops, Sabinus and Felix, in place of Basilides and Martial who had denied their faith in the persecution and been deprived

---

[32] James Steven, *Ambrose of Milan on Baptism: A Study of De Sacramentis and De Mysteriis*, Joint Liturgical Studies 84 (2017), p. 43.

[33] Freeman, *A New History of Early Christianity*, p. 261.

[34] Hippolytus, *Apostolic Tradition*, section entitled Ordination of Presbyters.

of their office. Cyprian asserted that an ordination of a bishop "properly completed cannot be annulled".[35] Increasingly in the post-Constantinian era, the Emperors assumed control of the Church and often took the major role in the appointment of bishops of large towns and cities.

Sacraments

During the course of the first three centuries, the early churches developed their understanding and practice of both baptism and the Eucharist. This was a gradual process in which the outward forms of water, bread and wine gradually became intertwined with the reality they were intended to represent. Thus, baptismal water, instead of simply being an outward sign of the cleansing and forgiveness from sin which flows from the cross of Christ, came to be regarded as the instrument and means of that cleansing. In a similar way, over time, the bread and wine of Holy Communion eventually came to be regarded as the actual body and blood of Christ rather than a representation of his broken body and outpoured blood of the cross.

Baptism

In New Testament times, baptisms often took place almost immediately, or at least very soon after, a person professed faith in Jesus. Thus those who responded to Peter's challenge to commit themselves to Christ on the Day of Pentecost were baptized on that day.[36] The Ethiopian official who was converted as a result of talking with Philip in his chariot was baptized on that very day on his profession that Jesus is the Son of God.[37] Other instances include the immediate baptism of Cornelius' household in Caesarea,[38] the Philippian jailer and his family on the night of their coming to faith,[39] and a group of converts at Ephesus.[40] For the most part, baptism in the first four centuries would have been by immersion. In the

---

[35] Cyprian, *Letter 67*.
[36] Acts 2:41.
[37] Acts 8:38.
[38] Acts 10:48.
[39] Acts 16:33–4.
[40] Acts 19:5.

very early days, the essential requisite for each candidate was repentance from sin and their acknowledgement that Jesus is Lord.[41] In Acts 19, Paul appears to have baptized a small group of believers "in the name of the Lord Jesus".[42] Elsewhere, baptism was in the name of the Father, the Son and the Holy Spirit, as the risen Lord had instructed.[43]

The early-second-century document *The Didache* suggests that both the baptizer and the baptized should fast and others if they can beforehand, and that ideally baptism should be by immersion "in the name of the Trinity" and in "living water". However, if no suitable cold water is in the vicinity it will suffice "to pour water three times on a person's head in the name of the Trinity".[44] A little later, in the middle years of the second century, it is clear that Justin in his *Apology* placed a little more emphasis on the importance of preparation and fasting. He also seems to suggest that regeneration comes about, at least in part, through physical contact with the water. He wrote:

> Those who are convinced and believe that what we teach is true, and undertake to live in accordance with it are brought together. Then after prayer and fasting together for the remission of sins they are taken to a place where there is water and there they are regenerated. For they then receive the washing of water in the name of God, the Father and the Lord of the universe, and our Saviour Jesus Christ, and the Holy Spirit.[45]

From a very early point, baptism was regarded as essential in order to be a member of the church.

As the churches became more organized, they began to recognize the need for a period of instruction before a baptism could take place. The length and content of these probationary periods appears to have varied from place to place. The Spanish Council of Elvira in 306, for example,

---

[41] See, for example, Acts 2:38 and 8:37–8.
[42] Acts 19:5.
[43] Matthew 28:19.
[44] *Didache* 7.
[45] Justin, *Apology* I.61.1.

required a person to remain as a catechumen for a period of two years[46] and the *Apostolic Constitutions* was even more demanding, extending it to three years.[47]

Justin Martyr in his *First Apology*, which is dated between 155 and 160, stated that after a baptism it was the custom to offer prayers for the newly enlightened and for the brethren to greet one another with a kiss of peace.[48] Tertullian, writing about the same time in *De Corona*, mentions that in the churches with which he was familiar those who are to be baptized are first required "to renounce the devil and his pomp, and his angels".[49] They are then "three times immersed, making a somewhat ampler pledge than the Lord has appointed".[50] In *De Baptismo*, Tertullian taught that in the waters of baptism "we are cleansed and prepared for the Holy Spirit".[51] In a similar vein, he wrote "the act of Baptism is carnal, in that we are plunged in the water, but the effect is spiritual, in that we are free from sins".[52] This happens as hands are placed on those who have been baptized "invoking the Holy Spirit through benediction".[53] After this each baptized person is anointed with oil.[54] In another place, Tertullian mentions that Easter and Pentecost were often times when large numbers of people were baptized but he added that "every day is the Lord's, every hour, every time is suitable for Baptism".[55] He also noted that on these larger occasions it was customary for the bishop to anoint the newly baptized with oil and to lay his hand upon them that they might receive the Holy Spirit. The Eucharist followed, and on some occasions the baptized were given a mixture of milk and honey as a sign

---

[46] *The Council of Elvira*, Canon 42.
[47] *Apostolic Constitutions* 8, 47.
[48] Justin, *First Apology* 65-7.
[49] Tertullian, *Of the Crown* 3.
[50] Tertullian, *Of the Crown* 3.
[51] Tertullian, *Of the Crown* 3.
[52] Tertullian, *Concerning Baptism* 7.
[53] Tertullian, *Concerning Baptism* 6.
[54] Tertullian, *Concerning Baptism* 7.
[55] Tertullian, *Concerning Baptism* 19.

they had entered the Promised Land.[56] Most of those who were baptized during the second century would have joined the church as adults. The earliest reference in favour of infant baptism is found in Irenaeus' *Against Heresies* which was written about 180.[57] Cyprian, who was Bishop of Carthage from 248-58, had a high view of the Church and would not admit the validity of any baptismal rite performed outside the Church.[58]

Some of the Easter baptisms which took place in the later fourth century were large and very impressive occasions. On a Thursday before Easter, John Chrysostom (*c*.347-407), the Bishop of Constantinople, was arrested for allegedly having "used words offensive to the Empress".[59] He had already baptized three thousand men and many more were still waiting for their moment to come to enter the baptistery. A fellow bishop who shared Chrysostom's views on public baptism was Ambrose (340-97) who was Bishop of Milan from 374 until his death. He rarely left Milan in Lent, as this was a preparation time for public baptisms which were celebrated not only in Milan but across the Mediterranean area.[60] For Ambrose, baptism focused on the Trinity. To the baptized he declared: "God anointed you, the Lord signed you and the Holy Spirit is lodged in your heart."[61] Ambrose also asserted that in baptism "all guilt is washed away".[62] The baptisteries were usually expansive places where large numbers of people could congregate. Many were often octagonal in shape signifying new birth. Some cathedrals situated their baptisteries just a yard or two outside the main church. Examples include those which can be seen at Pisa and St John Lateran in Rome and Ravenna. On some of these occasions it became customary for the bishop to anoint the newly baptized with oil and to lay his hands on them to receive the Holy Spirit.

---

[56] Tertullian, *Of the Crown* 1.1.
[57] Irenaeus, *Against Heresies* II.22.4.
[58] Cyprian, *Letters 74-75*. See also Socrates, *Ecclesiastical History* VI.15.
[59] S. Neill, *Chrysostom and His Message* (London: Lutterworth Press, 1962), p. 15.
[60] See Ambrose, *On the Holy Spirit* 1.17.
[61] Ambrose, *On the Sacraments* 6.58.
[62] Ambrose, *On the Sacraments* 3.7.

It is clear that the theology and practice of Christian baptism changed a good deal in the first four centuries. Whereas in the first century baptisms often took place at the time of conversion, or very shortly following, it came to be put on hold until those concerned had been prepared and instructed on the basics of the faith. Over time, there was a growing stress on the ritual to the point where the consecrated water was believed to effect the cleansing from sin. Baptism in most instances was followed by anointing with oil and the candidate's first communion.

The Lord's Supper / Eucharist

In the first century, the Lord's Supper was a very frequent, straightforward home-based occasion celebrated in homes and houses in the context of Passover-style meals which were called agapes or "love feasts". Each occasion was kept as near as possible to the practice and ethos of the Last Supper which Jesus had shared with his disciples in the Upper Room. The early Christians in Jerusalem attended public worship, but they continued the practice of sharing bread and wine in their houses.[63] In his First Letter to the Corinthians, Paul gives a glimpse of their communion services which were informal in nature with a shared meal. He and other early church leaders clearly thought of the Lord's Supper in Passover terms. For example, he reminded the Corinthians that "Christ our Passover lamb has been sacrificed"[64] and referred to the communion cup as "cup of blessing" (*eulogias*), the cup of blessing being the third Passover cup.[65]

This practice of having communion in the context of a meal continued in many places up until the end of the second century and in some areas a lot longer. Justin Martyr (c.100–c.165) gave details of the sacrament of the Eucharist, "which Jesus Christ ordained to be offered by Christians in every region of the earth with thanksgiving [the Eucharist] for the bread and the cup".[66] Tertullian (c.160–225) of Carthage wrote of the sacrament of the Eucharist "which the Lord commanded to be taken at meal times and by all". "We take it", he continued, "before daybreak

---

[63] Acts 2:46.
[64] 1 Corinthians 5:7.
[65] 1 Corinthians 10:16 (NRSV).
[66] Justin, *Dialogue with Trypho* 117.

in congregations".[67] The church historian Salminius Sozomen recorded that in a number of cities in Egypt, people met on Sabbath evenings "to partake of the mysteries"[68] after they had dined.[69] Socrates stated that this practice at Alexandria of sharing food before partaking of the mysteries is of great antiquity.[70] In some parts of the Empire, provincial governors who tolerated Christianity allowed public worship and even in some places in their own church buildings. That said, most Christian worship continued to be largely home-based until the conversion of Constantine.

By the beginning of the third century, it appears that the Eucharist was gradually being separated from the agape meal. There are several reasons for this. The most obvious was that the early third century witnessed the beginning of periods of extended and brutal persecution and Christians soon realized they needed to keep a lower profile. A further factor was the growing emphasis being placed on clergy as a separate order from the laity. By the time of Hippolytus (d.236), in many places, "presidency", as it came to be called, was gradually being confined to the clergy. This meant that it was not quite so easy for lay people to organize an agape meal in their own houses. Nevertheless, the Lord's Supper must have taken place very largely in homes owing to the severe and sustained periods of brutal persecution. The emphasis was doubtless still focused on eating and drinking to remember not a deliverance from slavery in Egypt but from the consequences of sin and selfishness. It was of course more than just a vivid remembrance or anamnesis; it was also a receiving or participation in the blessings and benefits of Christ's death.[71]

The conversion of the Emperor Constantine in 312 meant that it was no longer necessary for Christians to worship covertly as there was now freedom of worship for all. Christians were suddenly encouraged by the state to erect their own larger buildings for worship. It is clear that there were some attempts to arrange agapes in the new public buildings, but they were proving to be lacking in good taste and reportedly had lost

---

[67] Tertullian, *Of the Crown* 3.3–4.
[68] The Lord's Supper / Eucharist was often referred to as "the mysteries".
[69] Sozomen, *Ecclesiastical History* VII.19.
[70] Socrates, *Ecclesiastical History* V.22.
[71] 1 Corinthians 10:16.

the sense of the Lord's presence. Significantly, at the end of the fourth century, the Council of Carthage in 397 enacted that no bishop, let alone more junior clergy, "should hold a love feast in a public church building ... and that their flocks should also, as far as possible, be debarred from entertainments of this kind".[72]

During these first three centuries, there were a number of significant changes in the theology, ethos, leadership and practice of the Lord's Supper. The development of Eucharistic doctrine is immediately visible in the prayers which were said in the preparation of the bread and wine and at their distribution. The *Didache,* which is held by most scholars to be an early second-century manual for churches, quotes prayers to be said over the bread and wine. Both are thanksgiving in nature. The prayer for the cup which comes first is as follows: "We thank you, our Father, for the holy vine of David Your Servant, which you made known to us through Jesus your Servant. Glory be to you for ever." The prayer over the bread is parallel in form. Significantly the words are not an exact recitation of the recorded words spoken by Jesus at the Last Supper. Separate prayers for the wine and bread may suggest that there was a meal between the drinking of the wine and the eating of the bread. The main emphasis throughout is one of thanksgiving. There follows an instruction that no-one is to eat or drink the Eucharist but those who are baptized, because the Lord had said: "Give not that which is holy to dogs."[73]

In Justin Martyr's *Apology* and in his *Dialogue with Trypho,* there is a strong emphasis on thanksgiving. In his *Apology* 67, he commented that "the president sends up praise and glory to God the Father of all, through the name of the Son and the Holy Spirit; and gives thanks at length for our being worthy of these things".[74] These strong words of thanksgiving still bear the earlier influence of the Jewish prayer of blessing (*berakah*). We find the same emphasis on thanksgiving in Justin's *Dialogue with Trypho.* In Chapter 41, he writes of "the bread of *thanksgiving,* which

---

[72] Paul Stutzman, *Recovering the Love Feast* (Eugene, OR: Wipf and Stock, 2011), p. 119.

[73] All quotations in the paragraph are taken from *Didache* 9.

[74] Justin, *First Apology* 67.

Jesus Christ our Lord commanded to be offered for a memorial of the passion".[75]

In the writings of Irenaeus (c.120–202), we encounter the first hints of a moment of consecration brought about by a prayer of thanksgiving. In *Against Heresies* 4, he wrote that "Bread the produce of the earth receiving the epiclesis of God is no longer common bread but the eucharist".[76] And again in the following chapter: "The elements receiving the word of God become the eucharist."[77] A little later, about the year 217, in his *Apostolic Tradition*, Hippolytus wrote:

> We offer You the bread and the cup, making eucharist to You because You have bidden us to stand before You and minister as priests to You ... We pray that You would send Your Holy Spirit upon the oblation of Your Holy Church and would grant to all Your Saints who partake to be united [to You].[78]

The Eucharist of Hippolytus gives a strong feeling that things have changed with his introduction of an *anaphora* or offering up the bread and cup and the *epiclesis* or calling down the Holy Spirit on to the bread and wine.

The fourth century witnessed a number of important developments in church life. The Western Church adopted Latin as its liturgical language, and this had the immediate effect of creating a distinction between Eastern and Western Eucharistic liturgies. Within areas differentiated by language a number of distinctive liturgies were produced. In the West, these included Roman, Milanese, African, Spanish, Gallican and Celtic. There were also considerable variations in the East exemplified in Greek, Coptic, Palestinian and Syrian liturgies.

In *The Sacramentary of Serapion*, by Bishop of Thmuis in the Nile delta, we get a glimpse of the Egyptian liturgies about the year 350. His

---

[75] Justin, *Dialogue with Trypho* 41.
[76] Irenaeus, *Against Heresies* IV.18.5.
[77] Irenaeus, *Against Heresies* V.2.13.
[78] Hippolytus, *Apostolic Tradition* I.4.11.

prayer said over the bread and wine clearly indicates a belief that they change in nature:

> O God of truth, let Your holy word come upon this bread that the bread may become the Body of the Word, and upon this cup that the cup may become the Blood of Truth; and make all who partake to receive the medicine of life, for the healing of every sickness and the strengthening of all advancement and virtue.[79]

The significance of Serapion's prayer is that it explicitly asks that the bread may *become* the body of the Word and the cup "the blood of truth". Serapion paved the way for believing there is a moment of consecration. This became explicit in the writings and teaching of Cyril (*c*.313–86), who became Bishop of Jerusalem about the year 350. In a *Catechetical Lecture* which included teaching on the Eucharist he commented on the invocation, and said at the taking of the bread and wine, "When we have sanctified ourselves with these spiritual hymns, we beseech the loving God to send forth his Holy Spirit upon the gifts lying before us, that He may make the bread the body of Christ, and the wine the blood of Christ. For whatsoever the Holy Spirit touches is sanctified and changed."[80] Here there is an unequivocal prayer for the Holy Spirit to bring about a transformation or conversion of the elements. Cyril's teaching led on to both the Eastern and Western churches developing the idea of a moment of consecration which ultimately led on to the classic metaphysical explanation of transubstantiation. Dix pointed out that from Cyril's time forward Christ began to assume only a passive part in the Eucharist. He became "the divine victim", whose body and blood were "made" by the action of the Holy Spirit, that the earthly Church might offer him to the Father as a propitiation for sin.[81] Certainly this teaching

---

[79] Dix, *The Shape of the Liturgy*, p. 163.
[80] Cyril, *Catechetical Lectures* 23.7.
[81] Dix, *The Shape of the Liturgy*, p. 278.

was clearly visible in the *Liturgy of James* and echoed in the writings of Athanasius, the Cappadocian Fathers, Ambrose and Chrysostom.[82]

Clearly, by the end of the fourth century, major changes had taken place in the theology and practice of the Lord's Supper. Congregations for the most part became spectators who looked on while priests clad in ornate vestments presided over a lengthy ritual which focused on changing bread and wine into the body and blood of Christ which could then be offered up for the sins of the people. The Eucharist which Theodore (*c*.350–428), Bishop of Mopsuestia, described in his *Catechetical Lectures* was marked by advanced ritual splendour, and at Antioch John Chrysostom's church possessed finely wrought chalices, candelabra, silk veils, white vestments, and sometimes silver work decorating the altar itself.[83]

Organization

The most obvious and significant change in the life of the Church was that it became a state Church. Far from being hostile to the very existence of the Church, the Emperors had become its patrons and rulers. Emperors such as Constantine and Theodosius the Great now convened Church Councils, appointed bishops and made doctrinal statements. For their part, bishops had become ministers of state and often proved to be the Emperor's administrators. Theodosius, in the words of Sozomen, had "contributed to the aggrandisement of the church".[84]

In the early days, Christianity was largely an urban religion with most bishops' pastoral care being confined to congregations in or near to the town or city where they lived and pastored their own main church. The area over which the early bishops presided became known as the diocese. This was simply the existing pre-Christian unit of administration within each Roman province. As Christianity spread across the Empire new dioceses were formed and some bishops were invested by the 4th Canon of the Council of Nicaea in 325 with authority over more than one See. Such honour was given to the bishops of Nicomedia and Constantinople

---

[82] N. A. D. Scotland, *Eucharistic Consecration in the First Four Centuries* (Oxford: Latimer House, 1989), pp. 33–42.

[83] Chadwick, *The Early Church*, pp. 267–8.

[84] Sozomen, *Ecclesiastical History* VII.6–8.

which was also declared the second most important See in the Catholic Church.[85] The Council of Sardica, which was held about the year 343 at the behest of the Emperors Constans and Constantius, marked the very early beginnings of what would later be the complete separation of the Eastern and Western Churches. The Eastern bishops withdrew because they could not accept the orthodoxy of Athanasius.[86]

Denouement

By the mid-fifth century, the Church and its life and worship had therefore become much more structured with a focus on festivals which celebrated the important salvation doctrines at set times in the year. Keeping Holy Week and Easter began at a very early point; Irenaeus mentioning Easter as being kept in 119. It seems likely that the name Easter was derived from Eostre, the spring goddess, whose festival in many places the Christian churches came to replace. The earliest mention of Christmas is in 336. Pentecost is referred to in the Canons of Nicaea as is the 40 days of Lent. Public worship became more structured with confession, absolution, creeds and music. Greek was the universal language of the Roman Empire, but by the beginning of the third century some of the Western churches began to worship in Latin. This trend became more widespread after 384 in which year Jerome completed a Latin Bible known as the Vulgate, the word coming from the Latin meaning "common tongue". Music and singing were a continuing feature of church worship. In the second century, Clement of Alexandria expressed his concern that hymns were being sung to local dance music, but for the most part Christian worship became progressively dignified. Basil the Great (*c*.330–379), Bishop of Caesarea, wrote the great hymn "Hail, gladdening light". Hymns were sung in Ambrose's diocese of Milan and antiphonal singing became popular in Augustine's time.

By the later years of the second century, art was beginning to feature in places of Christian worship. Tertullian mentions cups on which there

---

[85] Socrates, *Ecclesiastical History* I.13.
[86] Sozomen, *Ecclesiastical History* III.13.

were representations of the Good Shepherd carrying sheep.[87] There were pictures on the wall of the private house church at Dura Europos which was in use in 232. There were also many murals on the walls of the catacombs in Rome. The catacomb of Callixtus has early-third-century murals of the Baptism of Jesus, Jesus the Good Shepherd carrying a lamb on his shoulders, and the feeding of the five thousand. Epiphanius (c.310–403), Bishop of Salamis, did his best to prevent pictures in churches but to little effect. Henry Chadwick wrote: "By 403, when he died, portrayals of Christ and the saints were widespread."[88]

We catch glimpses of penance in the writings of Hermas, Tertullian and other church leaders. Penance was the idea that Christians should know what works they should do in order to demonstrate that they had truly repented of their sins. Among other penitential practices Hermas commended public confession of sins, fasting and almsgiving.[89] Tertullian, who wrote *Concerning Penance,* took a hard line against serious sins committed after baptism,[90] whereas Dionysius, Bishop of Corinth, writing about 170, had earlier asserted "that all who repent of some fall, error or even a heresy . . . are received again".[91]

The question which was beginning to arise, and would continue to be asked down through the centuries, was did the Church still bear the outward image and the truth taught and envisioned by its founder? To put it another way would be: "Did the fifth-century tree into which the Church had grown bear a sufficient likeness to the apostolic Church?" Whilst it is the case that some of the simplicity and straightforwardness of first-century Christianity had been lost, the core doctrines of the Virgin birth, the incarnation, the atonement, the death, resurrection and ascension of Jesus were all still upheld, proclaimed and lived out in public life. In this sense the early Christians had proved to be "more than conquerors". The Catholic Church which they had founded was continuing to preserve the apostolic teaching and gospel message. There

---

[87] Chadwick, *The Early Church*, p. 277.
[88] Chadwick, *The Early Church*, p. 281.
[89] Jedin, *From the Apostolic Community to Constantine*, p. 323.
[90] Foakes-Jackson, *The History of the Christian Church to* AD *461*, p. 237.
[91] Jedin, *From the Apostolic Community to Constantine*, p. 324.

were still countless vibrant churches and expressions of the Christian faith in many parts of the Roman Empire at the close of the fifth century. A pattern of leadership which focused on preaching, teaching and pastoral care remained widespread and effective. The Church had established an organization which was in step with the Empire's pre-Christian structure of diocese and parish. The production of three historic creeds and other statements of faith and apologetic writing had strengthened and articulated the basic first order core articles of the Christian faith.

These and many other accomplishments, as has been seen in the foregoing chapters, were born of hard-fought debate and sometimes conflict. Such was particularly the case in the early centuries during periods of Empire-wide persecution. Christian men and women had boldly stood firm in their faith, many thousands paying with their lives to declare "Jesus, not Caesar, is Lord". By the middle of the fifth century, the apostolic good news was still impacting the life, worship and values of both the Eastern and Western sides of the Empire. Indeed, the Roman Empire had become a Christendom. What was now needed was Augustine's vision that it might begin to reflect the City of God.

Bibliography

Early Christian texts

Selections of early Christian texts on the subjects discussed in this book can be found in:

Ayer, Joseph Cullen, *A Source Book for Ancient Church History: From the Apostolic Age to the Close of the Conciliar Period* (New York: Charles Scribner's Sons, 1913).
Bettenson, Henry (ed.), *Documents of the Christian Church*, 2nd edn (Oxford: Oxford University Press, 1967).
James, Montague Rhodes (tr.), *The Apocryphal New Testament* (Oxford: Clarendon Press, 1966).
Lee, A. Douglas, *Pagans and Christians in Late Antiquity: A Sourcebook* (New York: Routledge, 2016).
Richardson, Cyril (ed.), *Early Christian Fathers* (London: SCM Press, 1953).
Roberts, Alexander and Donaldson, James, *The Ante-Nicene Fathers* (Grand Rapids, MI: W. B. Eerdmans, 1978).
Russell, Norman (tr.), *The Lives of the Desert Fathers* (London: Mowbray, Cistercian Publications, 1981).
Stevenson, J. (ed.), *A New Eusebius: Documents illustrating the history of the Church to AD 337* (London: SPCK, 1986).
Stevenson, James (ed.), *Creeds, Councils and Controversies: Documents illustrating the history of the Church, AD 337–461* (London: SPCK, 1989).
Ward, Benedicta, *The Desert Fathers: Sayings of the Early Christian Monks* (London: Penguin Books, 2003).

Modern sources

Barclay, William, *The Letter to Jude* (Edinburgh: St Andrew Press, 1965).
Baus, Karl, *History of the Church from the Apostolic Community to Constantine* (London: Burns & Oates, 1980).
Bethune-Baker, James, *An Introduction to the Early History of Christian Doctrine* (London: Methuen & Co., 1903).
Bradshaw, Paul E., *Eucharistic Origins* (London: SPCK, 2004).
Brown, Peter, *The Body and Society* (New York: Columbia University Press, 1988).
Browne, Gordon and Swallow, James, *Select Orations of Saint Gregory Nazianzen* (Buffalo, New York: Christian Literature Publishing Co., 1894).
Brox, Norbert, *A History of the Early Church* (London: SCM Press, 1994).
Bruce, Frederick F., *The Spreading Flame* (Carlisle: The Paternoster Press, 1992).
Byrne, Lavinia, *The Life and Wisdom of Benedict* (London: Hodder & Stoughton, 1998).
Campenhausen, Hans von, *The Fathers of the Latin Church* (London: Adam & Charles Black, 1964).
Carnelley, Elizabeth, "Tertullian and Feminism", *Theology 92*:745 (1989), 31–5.
Chadwick, Henry, *The Early Church* (Harmondsworth: Penguin Books, 1993).
Cross, Frank L. and Livingstone, Elizabeth A. (eds), *The Oxford Dictionary of The Christian Church*, 2nd edn (Oxford: Oxford University Press, 1998).
Cullmann, Oscar, *The Early Church* (London: SCM Press, 1956).
Davies, John G. G., *The Early Christian Church* (New York: Anchor, 1967).
Dix, Gregory, *The Shape of the Liturgy* (London: Dacre, 1943).
Donaldson, Christopher, *Martin of Tours: Parish Priest, Mystic and Exorcist* (London: Kegan Paul, 1985).

Farrar, Frederick W., *Lives of the Fathers: Sketches of Church History in Biography* (London: Adam & Charles Black, 1907).
Filson, Floyd V., *A New Testament History* (London: SCM Press, 1964).
Foakes-Jackson, Frederick J., *The History of the Christian Church to AD 461* (London: George Allen & Unwin Ltd, 1909).
Freeman, Charles, *A New History of Early Christianity* (Yale: Yale University Press, 2009).
Frend, William H. C., *The Donatist Church* (Oxford: Oxford University Press, 1942).
Frend, William H. C., *The Rise of Christianity* (London: Darton, Longman & Todd Ltd, 1984).
Frend, William H. C., *The Early Church* (London: SCM Press, 1991).
Frend, William H. C., *Martyrdom and Persecution in the Early Church* (Cambridge: James Clarke & Co Ltd, 2008).
Gilbert, Carlos, *The Teachings of the Mandaean John the Baptist* (Fairfield, NSW: Living Water Books, 2017).
Green, Michael, *Evangelism in the Early Church* (Grand Rapids, MI: William B. Eerdmans, 1970).
Guistozzi, N., *The Colosseum* (Venice: Mandori Printing Spa, 2002).
Hardinge, Leslie, *The Celtic Church in Britain* (London: SPCK, 1968).
Hogg, Sally, *Invisible Women: A History of Women in the Church* (lulu.com, 2011).
Hood, Alan B., *St Patrick: His Writings and Muirchu's Life* (London: Phillimore, 1978).
Hueck Doherty, Catherine de, *Poustinia: Christian Spirituality of the East for Western Man* (Notre Dame, IN: Ave Maria Press, 1983).
Hultgren, Arland J. and Haggmark, Steven A., *The Earliest Christian Heretics* (Minneapolis, MN: Fortress Press, 1996).
Jones, Arnold, *Constantine and the Conversion of Europe* (London: Macmillan, 1948).
Kelly, J. N. D., *Early Christian Doctrines* (London: Adam & Charles Black, 1980).
Lietzmann, Hans, *The Founding of the Church Universal* (London: Lutterworth Press, 1953).
Lowther-Clarke, Henry, *St Basil the Great: A Study in Monasticism* (Cambridge: Cambridge University Press, 1913).

Martin, Ralph P., *Worship in the Early Church* (London: Marshall, Morgan & Scott, 1964).

Maxwell, William D., *An Outline of Christian Worship* (Oxford: Oxford University Press, 1936).

McGrath, Alister, *Historical Theology: An Introduction to the History of Christian Thought* (Oxford: Blackwell, 1998).

McGrath, Alister, *Christian Theology: An Introduction* (Oxford: Blackwell, 2011).

McGuckin, John A., *Saint Gregory of Nazianzus: An Intellectual Biography* (Crestwood, NY: St Vladimir's Seminary Press, 2001).

Reardon, Bernard M. G., *Religious Thought in the Reformation* (London: Longman, 1981).

Rosen, Ceil and Moishe, *Christ in the Passover* (Chicago, IL: Moody Press, 1978).

Schillebeeckx, Edward, *The Church with a Human Face* (London: SCM Press, 1985).

Scotland, Nigel A. D., *Eucharistic Consecration in the First Four Centuries* (Oxford: Latimer House, 1989).

Scotland, Nigel A. D., *A Pocket Guide to Sects and New Religions* (Oxford: Lion Hudson, 2005).

Scotland, Nigel, *Christianity Outside the Box* (Eugene, OR: Wipf & Stock, 2012).

Scotland, Nigel A. D., *The New Passover* (Eugene, OR: Wipf & Stock, 2016).

Steven, James, *Ambrose of Milan on Baptism: A Study of De Sacramentis and De Mysteriis*, *Joint Liturgical Studies* 84 (2017).

Swete, Henry B., "Penitential Discipline in the First Three Centuries", *The Journal of Theological Studies* 4 (April 1908).

Todd, Malcolm, *Research in Roman Britain*, Britannia Monograph Series 11 (Gloucester: Alan Sutton Publishing Ltd, 1989).

Wagner, Monica, *Saint Basil Ascetical Works Translated from the Greek* (Washington D.C.: The Catholic University America Press, 1950).

Walker, Benjamin, *Gnosticism: Its History and Influence* (Wellingborough: The Aquarian Press, 1989).

Walsh, Catherine, *The Cult of St Catherine of Alexandria in Medieval Europe* (Aldershot: Ashgate, 2007).

Watson, F. W., "Christianity in the Roman army" in R. C. P. Hanson (ed.), *Christianity in Britain 300–700* (Leicester: Leicester University Press, 1968).

Westcott, Brooke F., *A General Survey of the History of the Canon of the New Testament* (Edinburgh: T&T Clark, 1881).

Whitworth, Patrick, *Three Wise Men from the East* (Durham: Sacristy Press, 2015).

Timelines

Emperors

Tiberius 14–37
Nero 37–68
Domitian 81–96
Trajan 98–117
Marcus Aurelius 161–80
Septimus Severus 193–211
Decius 249–51
Valerian 253–60
Diocletian 284–305
Constantine 312–37
Constantius 337–61}
Constantine II 337–40} shared rule
Constans 337–50}
Julian 361–3
Theodosius I 379–95
Honorius 393–423 (Western Empire)
Theodosius II 408–450 (Eastern Empire)

Theologians

Paul d.c.62–5
John c.8–c.100
Papias of Hierapolis c.60–c.130
Irenaeus 130–c.202
Clement of Alexandria c.150–c.215
Hippolytus c.170–c.235

Tertullian   c.160–240
Cyprian   c.200–258
Athanasius   295–373
Basil of Caesarea   330–78
Gregory of Nyssa   c.335–c.394
Gregory of Nazianzus   c.329–c.390
Ambrose of Milan   c.339–97
John Chrysostom   347–407
Epiphanius of Salamis   310–403
Cyril of Alexandria   c.376–444
Augustine of Hippo   354–430

Controversies

Judaizers   c.35–50
Gnosticism   c.120–200
Marcionism   c.140
Montanism   c.130–80
Monarchianism   c.190–c.230
Novatianism   c.251–c.500
Arianism   c.315–81
Donatism   c.312–430
Apollinarism   c.352
Pelagianism   390–418
Nestorianism   c.420–30
Eutychianism   c.450

Church Councils

Council of Jerusalem   c.48–50
Synod of Arles   314
Council of Nicaea   325
Council of Rimini   359
Council of Constantinople   381

Council of Carthage   397
Council of Carthage   411
Council of Ephesus   431
Council of Chalcedon   451

Significant events

Council of Jerusalem   c.48–50
Fire in Rome   64
Death of Paul   65
First Jewish War   66–74
Destruction of Second Temple   70
Martyrdom of Ignatius   c.107
Martyrdom of Polycarp   155
Death of Justin Martyr   c.165
Martyrdom of Blandina   c.203
Persecution of Decius   250
Anthony's Community at Comas   c.270
Diocletian persecution   303
Battle of Milvian Bridge   312
Edict of Milan   313
Edict of Toleration   321
Death of Licinius   328
Constantinople completed   334
Death of Constantine   337
Pachomius at Tabenna   c.340
Athanasius' festal address   367
Theodosius established Christianity   381
Vulgate published   404
Rome captured by Alaric   410
Death of Augustine   430
Death of Leo the Great   461

Index

Aidan (*d*.651)   231
Alban (*d*.304)   32, 217
Alexander, Bishop of Jerusalem (*d*.215)   42,164,165
Alexandria   20, 41, 116, 131,139, 160, 171
Ambrose (*c*.339-97) Bishop of Milan   235, 240 251, 252
Anthony (251-356)   202, 203
Antioch   18
Apocryphal books   98, 99
Apollinarius (*c*.310-*c*.390)   190-4
Apologies   47-50
Apostles   v, 5, 89, 91, 142
Apostolic writings   86, 137, 138, 156
Arcadius ((*d*.408)), emperor   6
Areopagus   4
Aristides (*d*.134)   21, 47-50
Arius (250-336)   160-3, 165, 166, 168-70, 172, 190, 207
Athanasius (*c*.296-373), Bishop of Alexandria   99, 138, 166, 168, 170-2, 190, 204
Athenagoras (133-90)   47, 48, 50
Athens   18, 24
Augustine (354-430), Bishop of Hippo   27, 62, 65-8, 209, 228, 229, 230, 254
Augustus, emperor (27-14 BC)   21

baptism   11-13, 28, 60, 62, 121, 123, 126, 128, 129, 144, 154, 222, 242-6
Basil, Bishop of Caesarea (*c*.329-79)   174-5, 177-84, 187, 190, 206, 210, 252
Basilides (85-145)   75, 76, 84, 85, 241
Bede (*d*.735)   217, 231
Benedict (*c*.480-547)   210, 211, 214
Butrint   21
Byzantium   104

Caecilian (*d. c*.343), Bishop of Carthage   59, 60, 153
Callistus (*d*.222), Bishop of Rome   200
canon   86, 87, 90, 96, 99-101, 238
Cappadocia   2, 38, 131
Cappadocian Fathers   174, 176, 178-81, 184-6, 188, 206
Caracalla (188-217), emperor   139
Carpocrates (78-138)   83
Carthage   2, 52
  First Council of (411)   230
  Second Council of (418)   230
  Third Council of (397)   92, 100, 248
Catechetical School   26
Celsus   140, 143
Celts   159, 218-26
Cerinthus (*c*.100)   76, 83
Chalcedon (451), Council of   190, 197, 199, 213, 237
Christmas   252
Chrysostom (*c*.347-407), Bishop of Constantinople   212-39, 241, 245, 251
church buildings   233, 247
Circumcellions   64, 67
Clement of Rome, (*c*.150-*c*.125)   93, 200, 237
Clement of Alexandria (*c*.130-*c*.200)   20, 41, 83, 85, 116, 131-9, 252
Constans (*c*.323-50), emperor   65
Constantine the Great (*c*.272-337), emperor   v, vi, 4, 22, 56, 62, 65, 148-62, 165, 167, 169, 200, 201, 217, 233, 234, 247
Constantinople (381), Council of   167, 190, 193
Constantius (317-61), emperor   169-70

263

Constantius Chlorus (*c*.250–306)   44
Corinium (Cirencester)   217
Corinth   8, 15, 25, 28, 83, 84, 91, 246
Creeds   235, 254
  Apostles' Creed   235
  Athanasian Creed   235
Cyprian (*d*.258), Bishop of Carthage   45, 52–4, 60, 62, 116, 125–30, 238, 241, 242, 245
Cyril (*c*.313–86), Bishop of Jerusalem   250
Cyril (*d*.444), Bishop of Alexandria   195

Damasus, Bishop of Rome (*c*.304–84)   207
Decius (*c*.201–51), emperor   38, 42, 44, 51, 202
Diatessaron   26
Didache   25, 243, 248
Diocletian (*c*.242–305), emperor   43, 44, 202
Dionysius (*d*.171), Bishop of Corinth   29
Domitian (51–96), emperor   35
Donatists   58, 61–9, 126, 127, 165
Donatus (*d*.355), Arian Bishop of Casae Nigrae   51, 58, 65, 66
Dura Europos   233, 253

Easter   244, 245, 252
Elvira, Council of (306)   243
Ephesus   15, 18
Epiphanius (*c*.310–403), Bishop of Salamis   108, 109, 146, 252
Ethiopia   24
eucharist   5–7, 9, 10, 27, 36, 52, 54, 57, 60, 130, 138, 144, 222, 238, 242, 244, 246–50
Eunomius (*d*.394), Arian Bishop of Cyzicus   183, 184
Eudoxius (*d*.370), Arian Bishop of Antioch   169–70
Eusebius (*d. c*.342), Bishop of Nicomedia   163, 168, 169
Eusebius (*c*.260–339), Bishop of Caesarea   19, 25, 26, 39, 42–44, 51, 58, 85, 97, 105, 139, 149, 150, 155, 156, 165, 168

Eutyches (378–454)   196, 197

gladiators   84
God, doctrine of   136, 141–2
Gnosticism   70–3, 75, 78–88, 119, 124, 133, 134
Gregory of Nazianzus (*c*.329–89)   174, 176, 177, 182, 184–6, 188, 192, 206
Gregory of Nyssa (*c*.335–95)   174, 178–184, 187–9, 206

Hadrian (117–38), emperor   41
Hegessippus (110–80)   3
Hermas (second century)   94, 99
Hexapla   140
Hilary (*c*.315–*c*.367), Bishop of Poitiers   208
Hinton St Mary   217
Hippolytus (*c*.170–*c*.234)   77, 79, 82, 105, 107–9, 111, 112, 234, 249
Holy Spirit   2, 13, 14, 27, 88, 90, 91, 108–10, 130, 138, 143, 154, 175–177, 179, 182, 185, 186, 222, 235, 245, 250
Honorius (384–423), emperor   67, 68

Ignatius (*c*.35–*c*.107), Bishop of Antioch   40, 45, 94
Ireland   218, 219
Irenaeus (*c*.130 – *c*.200), Bishop of Lyons   21, 79, 83, 84, 89, 95, 96

Jerome (347–420)   154, 170, 202, 207, 208
Jerusalem   6, 17, 160
Jesus   22, 29, 34, 35, 76, 79, 80, 82, 86, 89, 93, 95, 111, 120, 157, 162, 191, 197, 201
Jews   3, 9, 12, 22, 28, 88, 160
John the Baptist   12, 73, 75
Jovian (*c*.332–64), emperor   192
Julian (331–63), emperor   30, 171
Justin Martyr (100–65), Bishop of Lyons   26, 41, 79, 85, 95, 237, 244, 246, 248

Kiddush   7

Lactantius (*c*.250–*c*.325) 51, 149, 150
lapsed Christians 53, 126
Leo the Great (*d*.461), Bishop of Rome 198
Lent 245, 252
Licinius (263–325), emperor 150, 157, 165
love feast 247
Lullingstone 217
Lyons 36, 41

Macarius the Great (*c*.300–90) 82, 214
Macrina (*c*.330–79) 189
Mandaeans 75
Mandela, Nelson (1918–2013) 2
Marcellus (*d. c*.374), Bishop of Ancyra 168
Marcian (392–457), emperor 197
Marcion (*c*.85–165) 73, 77–9, 81, 86, 88, 97
Marcus Aurelius (121–80), emperor 36, 41, 46
marriage 50, 122
Martin (316–97), Bishop of Tours 208, 209, 219, 220
Maxentius (*c*.283–312), emperor 148
Melito (*d. c*.190), Bishop of Sardis 25
Mensurius (*d. c*.311), Bishop of Carthage 59
Milan, Edict of 44, 150, 151
Milvian Bridge 39, 44, 148
Mishnah 7, 8, 10
missionary journeys 17–18
Monarchianism 102, 104, 109, 110, 113–17, 124, 167, 168
monasticism 186, 188, 202–7, 212, 214, 227, 228
Montanism 88, 121, 123, 124, 234, 236
Muratorian Canon 99

Nero (37–68), emperor 19, 37, 39
Nestorius (386–451), Archbishop of Constantinople 193–6
Nicaea, Council of (325) 55, 158, 159, 163–5, 168, 170, 172, 175, 188, 251
Ninian (*c*.360–*c*.432) 220

Noetus (second century) 220
Novatian (200–58) 51–8, 69, 126, 128
Numidia 20, 153

Old Testament 22, 49, 71, 77, 80, 87, 88, 100, 133, 139, 160, 201
Optatus (*d. c*.390), Bishop of Milevis 61
Optatus (*d. c*.398), Donatist Bishop of Thamagadi 61
Origen (185–*c*.254) 20, 26, 42, 47, 49, 97, 99, 116, 138, 142, 143, 145, 202, 238

Pachomius (292–346) 205, 206, 210
Pantaenaus (*d. c*.200) 20, 27, 131
Pantheon 34, 35
Papias (*c*.60–130), Bishop of Hierapolis 89, 92
Parmenian (*d. c*.392,), Donatist Bishop of Carthage 66
Passover 1, 3, 7–11, 27
Patrick (*c*.389–461) 218–22, 224, 226
Paul (*c*.5–*c*.65), Apostle 16, 17, 22, 24, 28, 29, 32, 34, 78, 81, 83, 84, 88, 91, 94
Paul of Samosata (*c*.200–*c*.275), Bishop of Antioch 102
Pelagius (355–420) 228, 229–31
penance 123
Pentateuch 88
Pentecost 1, 12, 23, 24, 51, 91, 242, 244
persecution 34–46
Peter, Apostle 1, 12, 51, 92–4, 129
Philip, Apostle 24
Philo (*c*.20 BC–50) 19
Plato (*c*.427–348 BC) 72, 202
Pliny the Younger (*c*.61–*c*.113) 11, 40
Polycarp (*c*.69–155) 45, 89, 95
Pontus 2, 77, 187, 189
Praxeas (late third century) 103, 106, 110, 113
presidents of churches 121
priests 3, 129, 138, 153, 154, 238, 239
prophets 225, 236
Pulcheria (399–453) 211, 212

Rimini, Council of (359)   167, 170
Roman Empire   16, 17, 21, 52, 59, 63, 102, 147, 152, 189, 216, 236, 254
Rome   18, 19, 20, 51, 52, 88, 108, 110, 128, 156
  Council of (382)   100

Sabellius (active c.250)   108, 109
sacraments   54, 55, 61, see also baptism and eucharist
Septimus Severus (145–211), Emperor   41, 131
Shenoute (c.348–466)   204, 205
Silchester   217
Simon Magus   73, 76
Simon Stylites (390–460)   207
Socrates (c.380–450), church historian   56, 205
Sozomen (c.400–c.450), church historian   55, 57, 155, 159, 166, 191, 203, 211
Sundays   8
synagogues   2–4, 16, 19, 22, 236

Tacitus (56–120), Roman historian   22, 37
Tatian (120–80)   26, 31
temple   2, 14
Tertullian (c.160–c.220)   11, 29, 32, 38, 47, 50, 77, 80, 81, 97, 102, 107, 110–16, 118, 123–5, 133, 167, 244, 246, 252
Thalia   162, 165
Theodore (c.350–428), Bishop of Mopsuestia   251
Theodoret (c.393–458), Bishop of Cyrrhus   148, 168, 191, 193, 207
Theodosius I, the Great (347–95)   172, 193, 196, 197, 218
Thessalonica   15, 18
Thomas, Gospel of   72, 90
Timothy   16
Titus (39–81), emperor   4
tongues, speaking in   1
Trajan (45–117), emperor   11, 40, 45, 48
Trent, Council of (1545–63)   90

Trinity, doctrine of   12, 53, 60–61, 102, 112–14, 143, 144, 146, 167, 172, 180–4, 185, 189, 214, 221, 222, 243

Valens (328–78), emperor   72, 187
Valens (b. c.300), Bishop of Mursa   169
Valentinus (110–75)   197, 241
Valerian, emperor (253–60) 42, 43, 51, 56, 128, 197, 241
Victor (d. c.199), Bishop of Rome   105
Vienne   36, 41

Water Newton   216
worship   5, 8, 14, 16, 234

Zephyrinus (d.217), Bishop of Rome   111

EU GPSR Authorized Representative:

LOGOS EUROPE, 9 rue Nicolas Poussin, 17000 La Rochelle, France

contact@logoseurope.eu

www.ingramcontent.com/pod-product-compliance
Lightning Source LLC
Chambersburg PA
CBHW071425150426
43191CB00008B/1051